13½
INCREDIBLE THINGS
YOU NEED TO KNOW ABOUT EVERYTHING

Senior art editor Stefan Podhorodecki
Senior editor Jenny Sich
US Senior editor Shannon Beatty·
Designers Sheila Collins, Jemma Westing
Editors Carron Brown, Anna Fischel
US Editor Jill Hamilton
Design assistant Kit Lane
Assistant editor Vicky Richards

Picture research Liz Moore
Creative retouching Steve Crozier
Jacket design Stefan Podhorodecki, Simon Mumford
Jacket editor Claire Gell
Jacket design development manager
Sophia M Tampakopoulos Turner
Producer (pre-production) Jacqueline Street
Senior producer Gary Batchelor

Managing editor Francesca Baines
Managing art editor Philip Letsu
Publisher Andrew Macintyre
Art director Karen Self
Associate publishing director Liz Wheeler
Publishing director Jonathan Metcalf

Illustrators
Peter Bull, Jason Harding, Stuart Jackson-Carter,
Jon @KJA, Arran Lewis, Peter Minister, Simon Mumford

Contributors
Laura Buller, Stella Caldwell, Derek Harvey,
Susan Kennedy, Polly Goodman, Andrea Mills,
Sarah Tomley, Victoria Pyke

Consultants
Dr. Sarah Brewer, Jack Challoner, Hilary Davidson,
Clive Gifford, Derek Harvey, Jacqueline Mitton,
Darren Naish, Philip Parker, John Woodward

First American Edition, 2017
Published in the United States by DK Publishing
345 Hudson Street, New York, New York 10014

Copyright © 2017 Dorling Kindersley Limited
DK, a Division of Penguin Random House LLC
17 18 19 20 21 10 9 8 7 6 5 4 3 2 1
001-288640-Sept/2017

Published in Great Britain by Dorling Kindersley Limited.

A catalog record for this book is available from the Library of Congress.
ISBN 978-1-4654-6112-4

DK books are available at special discounts when purchased in bulk for
sales promotions, premiums, fund-raising, or educational use. For details,
contact: DK Publishing SpecialMarkets, 345 Hudson Street, New York,
New York 10014 SpecialSales@dk.com

Printed and bound in China

A WORLD OF IDEAS
SEE ALL THERE IS TO KNOW
www.dk.com

13½ INCREDIBLE THINGS

YOU NEED TO KNOW ABOUT EVERYTHING

LOOK INSIDE!

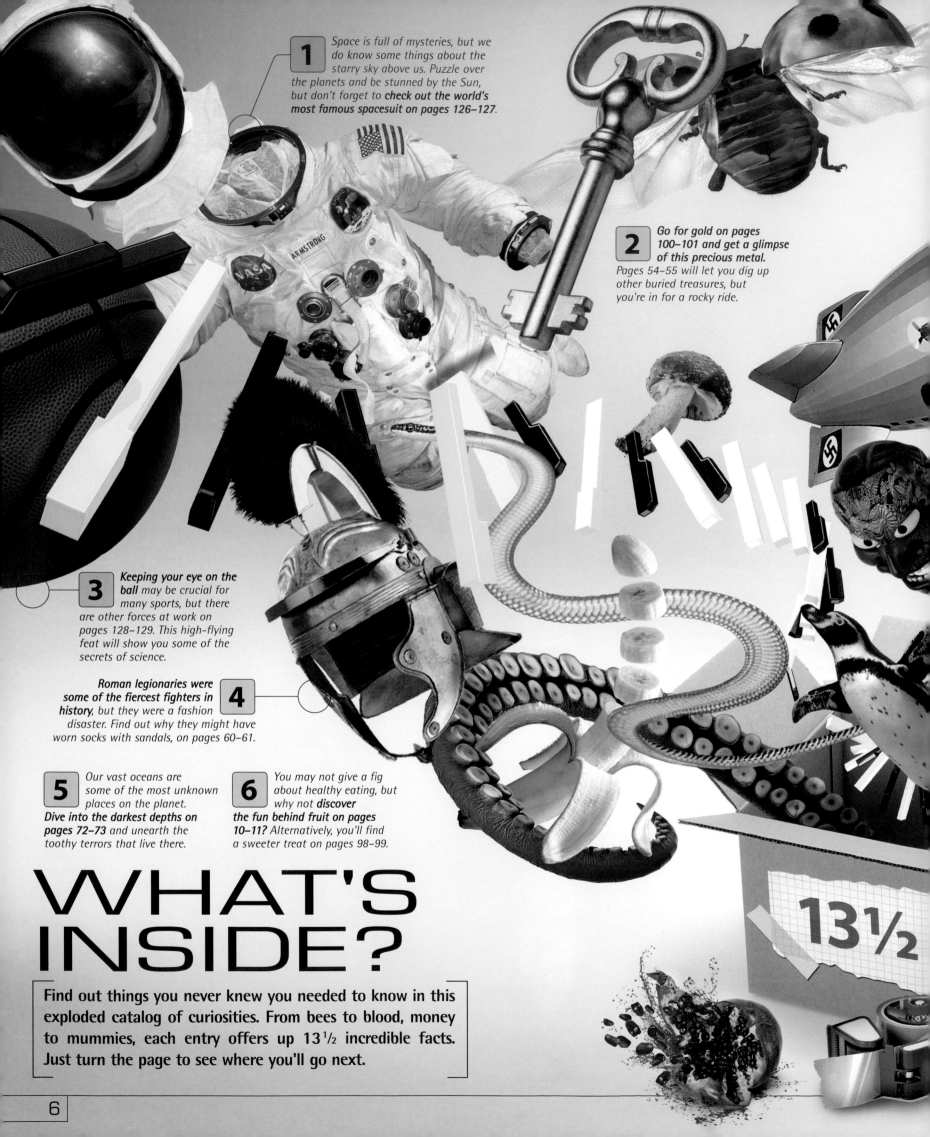

1 Space is full of mysteries, but we do know some things about the starry sky above us. Puzzle over the planets and be stunned by the Sun, but don't forget to **check out the world's most famous spacesuit on pages 126–127.**

2 Go for gold on pages 100–101 and get a glimpse of this precious metal. Pages 54–55 will let you dig up other buried treasures, but you're in for a rocky ride.

3 Keeping your eye on the **ball** may be crucial for many sports, but there are other forces at work on pages 128–129. This high-flying feat will show you some of the secrets of science.

4 *Roman legionaries were* **some of the fiercest fighters in history**, *but they were a fashion disaster. Find out why they might have worn socks with sandals, on pages 60–61.*

5 Our vast oceans are some of the most unknown places on the planet. **Dive into the darkest depths on pages 72–73** and unearth the toothy terrors that live there.

6 You may not give a fig about healthy eating, but why not **discover the fun behind fruit on pages 10–11?** Alternatively, you'll find a sweeter treat on pages 98–99.

WHAT'S INSIDE?

Find out things you never knew you needed to know in this exploded catalog of curiosities. From bees to blood, money to mummies, each entry offers up 13½ incredible facts. Just turn the page to see where you'll go next.

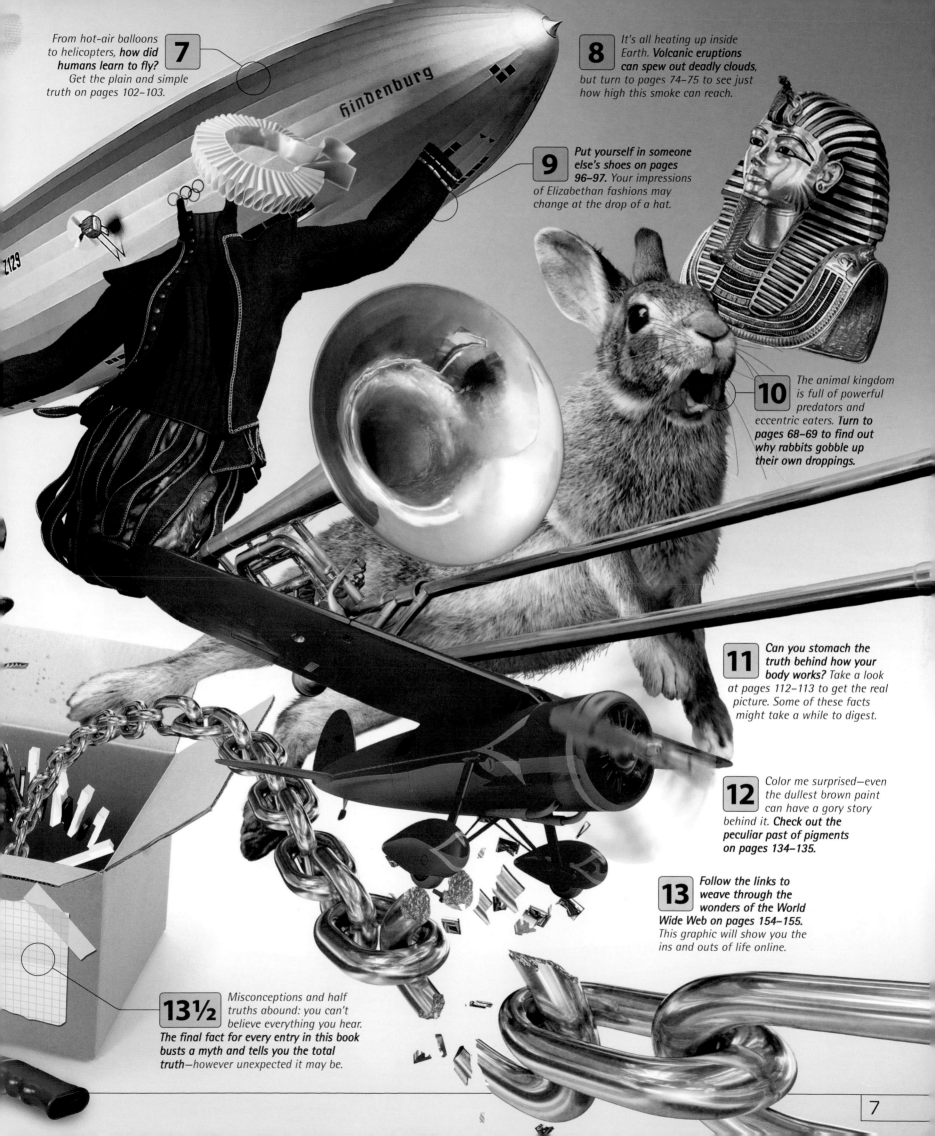

7 From hot-air balloons to helicopters, **how did humans learn to fly?** Get the plain and simple truth on pages 102–103.

8 It's all heating up inside Earth. **Volcanic eruptions can spew out deadly clouds,** but turn to pages 74–75 to see just how high this smoke can reach.

9 **Put yourself in someone else's shoes on pages 96–97.** Your impressions of Elizabethan fashions may change at the drop of a hat.

10 The animal kingdom is full of powerful predators and eccentric eaters. **Turn to pages 68–69 to find out why rabbits gobble up their own droppings.**

11 **Can you stomach the truth behind how your body works?** Take a look at pages 112–113 to get the real picture. Some of these facts might take a while to digest.

12 Color me surprised—even the dullest brown paint can have a gory story behind it. **Check out the peculiar past of pigments on pages 134–135.**

13 **Follow the links to weave through the wonders of the World Wide Web on pages 154–155.** This graphic will show you the ins and outs of life online.

13½ Misconceptions and half truths abound: you can't believe everything you hear. **The final fact for every entry in this book busts a myth and tells you the total truth**—however unexpected it may be.

EXPLODED EARTH

Earth came into being about 4.6 billion years ago. This huge spinning ball of rock and metal is not as rigid as it seems. The surface of our planet is constantly changing as continents collide, mountains rise up, and oceans widen.

1 The ground may feel firm beneath your feet, but **Earth's rigid outer layer, the crust, is only a few miles thick in places**. This rocky surface makes up just 1 percent of Earth's total volume.

2 *The crust is broken into pieces called tectonic plates, which fit together like a giant jigsaw puzzle. However, unlike puzzle pieces, these plates are constantly on the move—shifting around and crashing into each other.*

3 *Earth's largest layer, the mantle, is about 1,800 miles (2,900 km) thick. The tectonic plates float on the mantle, which is made of solid rock but flows very slowly due to the extreme temperature and pressure.*

4 *Wrapped around the center of our planet, the outer core is a liquid layer of iron and nickel. These swirling metals create Earth's magnetic field.*

5 *Tectonic plates all move at different rates, and the Nazca plate (the plate to the west of South America) is the fastest. Every year it moves approximately 6 in (16 cm)— about as fast as hair grows.*

6 *Earthquakes and volcanoes often happen along plate boundaries. One such hot spot is the East African Rift—where the African plate is slowly splitting in two. Eventually, a new ocean will fill the ever-widening gap.*

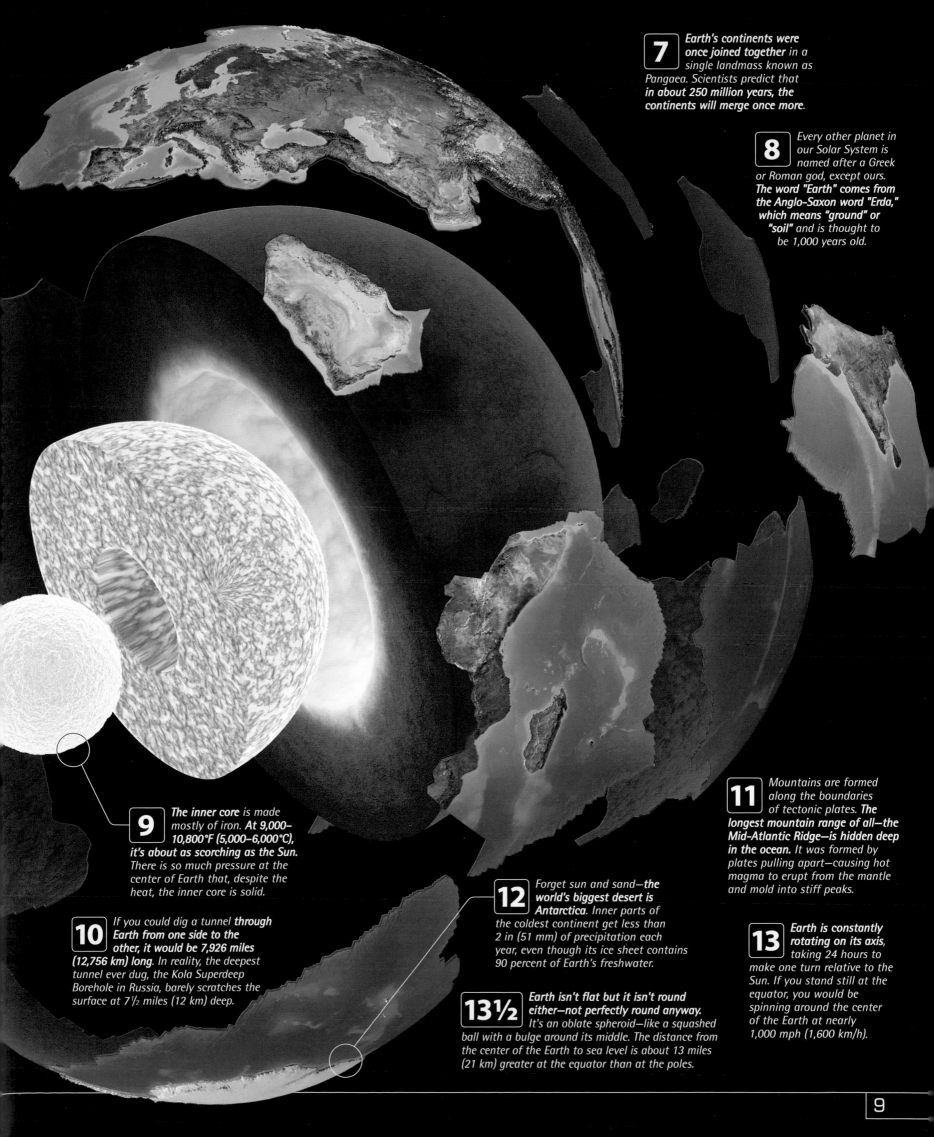

7 *Earth's continents were once joined together* in a single landmass known as Pangaea. Scientists predict that *in about 250 million years, the continents will merge once more.*

8 *Every other planet in our Solar System is named after a Greek or Roman god, except ours. **The word "Earth" comes from the Anglo-Saxon word "Erda," which means "ground" or "soil"** and is thought to be 1,000 years old.*

9 ***The inner core** is made mostly of iron. **At 9,000–10,800°F (5,000–6,000°C), it's about as scorching as the Sun.*** There is so much pressure at the center of Earth that, despite the heat, the inner core is solid.

10 *If you could dig a tunnel **through Earth from one side to the other, it would be 7,926 miles (12,756 km) long.*** In reality, the deepest tunnel ever dug, the Kola Superdeep Borehole in Russia, barely scratches the surface at 7¹/₂ miles (12 km) deep.

12 *Forget sun and sand—**the world's biggest desert is Antarctica**. Inner parts of the coldest continent get less than 2 in (51 mm) of precipitation each year, even though its ice sheet contains 90 percent of Earth's freshwater.*

13¹/₂ ***Earth isn't flat but it isn't round either—not perfectly round anyway.*** It's an oblate spheroid—like a squashed ball with a bulge around its middle. The distance from the center of the Earth to sea level is about 13 miles (21 km) greater at the equator than at the poles.

11 *Mountains are formed along the boundaries of tectonic plates. **The longest mountain range of all—the Mid-Atlantic Ridge—is hidden deep in the ocean.*** It was formed by plates pulling apart—causing hot magma to erupt from the mantle and mold into stiff peaks.

13 ***Earth is constantly rotating on its axis,*** taking 24 hours to make one turn relative to the Sun. If you stand still at the equator, you would be spinning around the center of the Earth at nearly 1,000 mph (1,600 km/h).

FABULOUS FRUIT

Many fruits have tasty flesh, to tempt animals to eat them and so spread the seeds inside. But not all fruits are sweet and some aren't even fleshy. Fruit is the seed-bearing part of a flowering plant and forms from the flower's ovary.

1 *Raspberries are not berries at all but aggregate fruits*—lots of fruitlets grown from a flower with multiple ovaries. True berries form from a single ovary, and include cucumbers, bananas, tomatoes, oranges, and grapes.

2 *Watermelons were first farmed in Africa 5,000 years ago*. Prized for their high water content, they appear in ancient Egyptian hieroglyphs, and *seeds were even found in the tomb of King Tutankhamun*.

3 *Many nuts are actually a type of fruit.* Instead of soft flesh, walnuts have a hard casing with a large, edible seed inside.

Blueberry

4 *The durian is renowned as the world's smelliest fruit.* Its powerful pong is often described as smelling like onions, cheese, or stinky socks.

5 Also known as pitaya, *the dragon fruit has a striking appearance but a bland taste.* It's the fruit of a night-blooming cactus grown across Asia and Central America.

6 *Apples and pears are false fruits*—the flesh develops from the flower's base not its ovary. The true "fruit" is the core that surrounds the seeds, which most people throw away.

Passion fruit

7 Wild bananas are full of bitter, inedible seeds. The bright yellow variety familiar from supermarket shelves has been **cultivated to remove the seeds**. Each fruit is a seedless clone genetically identical to all the others.

8 A pineapple plant produces just one fruit every 2–3 years. Pineapples are multiple fruits that form from up to 200 scalelike flowers fusing together.

Strawberry

Tomatoes were once believed to be poisonous, possibly because they are related to deadly nightshade. Today more than 100 million tons of tomatoes are produced every year as food. **9**

10 A coconut is a fruit but its white flesh is part of the seed. It is sometimes reported that **falling coconuts account for 150 deaths every year.** This figure hasn't been proven but many tropical beaches have been cleared of coconut palms, just in case.

Native to Australia, the **hala fruit is formed of fibrous sections called keys.** The top, seed-bearing part of each key is hard and woody but the fleshy bottom part can be eaten raw or cooked. **11**

Not all fruits are sweet. **Cucumbers,** eggplants, zucchini, peppers, pumpkins, peas, and beans are all **fruits that we usually think of as vegetables.** **12**

13 Pomegranates may have antiaging properties. They release a substance called urolithin-A that helps cells regenerate. In studies, **worms fed this molecule lived almost twice as long as other worms.**

13½ Is eating apple cores bad for you? It's true that **apple seeds contain amygdalin, a chemical that releases the deadly poison cyanide.** But you'd need to eat hundreds of pips, finely ground, to reach a dangerous dose.

Blackberry

❯❯ How fruit forms

Fruit grows as part of the lifecycle of a flowering plant. When pollen from the male parts of a flower lands on the female parts of another flower, the flower is fertilized and a seed is produced inside the ovary (the part of the flower that produces female egg cells). The ovary wall swells up to protect the fertilized seed, forming the fruit. In a simple fleshy fruit, such as this peach, the skin, flesh, and seed case all form from the swollen ovary wall.

Carpel (female part)

Stamen (male part)

Seed forms inside ovary

Flower

Outer skin

Flesh

Woody seed casing

Seed

Fruit

COOL CARS

The invention of the motor car changed the world. Today's cars have a come a long way from the first horseless carriages created over 130 years ago. Faster than ever, these sleek, ultrasophisticated machines will soon be driving themselves.

1 There are more than **one billion cars in the world—one for every seven people.** Around 165,000 new cars are produced every day—that's **60 million a year.**

2 In the 1700s, **several inventors tried to create steam-powered cars.** These vehicles were not a success. They contained **enormous boilers** and had to carry large amounts of coal and water—making them bulky and slow.

3 Invented in the second half of the 19th century, the internal combustion engine paved the way for the modern car. It is fueled by gasoline or diesel, which produce around 100 tiny explosions every second inside metal cylinders. These power pistons pass the force onto the wheels.

4 The **first modern car to be sold to the public was built by German engineer Karl Benz** in 1885. The lightweight Motorwagen **had three wheels, no roof, and a top speed of 10 mph (16 km/h).** It could have been overtaken by a trotting horse.

5 There are over 200 materials in a typical tire. **The natural color of rubber is in fact white**, but an added carbon filler, designed to increase strength and durability, gives tires their distinctive color.

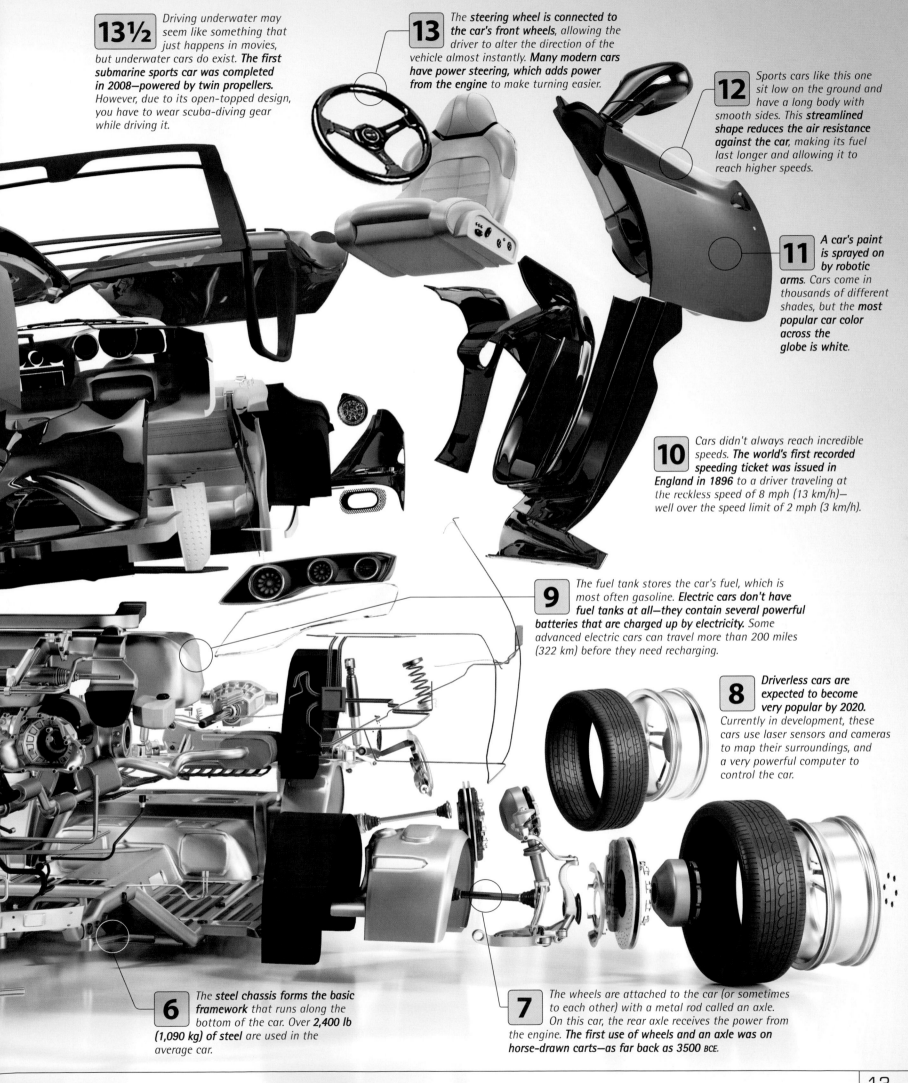

13½ *Driving underwater may seem like something that just happens in movies, but underwater cars do exist.* **The first submarine sports car was completed in 2008—powered by twin propellers.** *However, due to its open-topped design, you have to wear scuba-diving gear while driving it.*

13 *The* **steering wheel is connected to the car's front wheels,** *allowing the driver to alter the direction of the vehicle almost instantly. Many modern cars have power steering, which adds power from the engine to make turning easier.*

12 *Sports cars like this one sit low on the ground and have a long body with smooth sides. This* **streamlined shape reduces the air resistance against the car,** *making its fuel last longer and allowing it to reach higher speeds.*

11 *A car's paint is sprayed on by robotic arms. Cars come in thousands of different shades, but the* **most popular car color across the globe is white.**

10 *Cars didn't always reach incredible speeds.* **The world's first recorded speeding ticket was issued in England in 1896** *to a driver traveling at the reckless speed of 8 mph (13 km/h)— well over the speed limit of 2 mph (3 km/h).*

9 *The fuel tank stores the car's fuel, which is most often gasoline.* **Electric cars don't have fuel tanks at all—they contain several powerful batteries that are charged up by electricity.** *Some advanced electric cars can travel more than 200 miles (322 km) before they need recharging.*

8 *Driverless cars are expected to become very popular by 2020. Currently in development, these cars use laser sensors and cameras to map their surroundings, and a very powerful computer to control the car.*

6 *The* **steel chassis forms the basic framework** *that runs along the bottom of the car. Over* **2,400 lb (1,090 kg) of steel** *are used in the average car.*

7 *The wheels are attached to the car (or sometimes to each other) with a metal rod called an axle. On this car, the rear axle receives the power from the engine.* **The first use of wheels and an axle was on horse-drawn carts—as far back as 3500 BCE.**

TOP CAT

The biggest of all the cats, this solitary hunter feeds only on meat and needs to eat large quantities to survive. The tiger stalks large prey, using its incredible strength to pull the victim to the ground, then killing it with a suffocating bite.

1 There are six subspecies of tigers. The **Bengal tiger, shown here, is the most common,** and lives in the forests and mangroves of India and Bangladesh. Only around **4,000 tigers remain in the wild today,** of which about 2,500 are Bengals.

2 Most cats avoid water but **tigers can swim well** and will visit pools and streams to take a dip.

3 A tiger's stripes are on its skin, not just its fur. **If you shaved a tiger it would still be striped.** The stripes are like human fingerprints in that no two tigers have the same pattern.

4 **The name tiger comes from a Persian word meaning "arrow,"** in reference to the animal's great speed. Tigers can run at up to 40 mph (65 km/h) in short bursts.

5 The tiger dwarfs most of its cat relatives, **weighing up to 660 lb (300 kg).** That's as much as four grown men. Lions are almost as big, but less muscular.

6 A tiger hunts by creeping up on its prey then jumping on it from behind. **Extending its muscular front legs, the tiger uses its claws to pull down the prey animal.** Tigers are strong enough to tackle animals up to six times their weight, but nimble enough **to leap up to 33 ft (10 m) in a single bound.**

7 Soft, padded paws allow a tiger to silently stalk its prey. A tiger's paw can deal a knock-out blow, smashing a victim's skull with a single strike.

⌄⌄ Feline family

The cat family is divided into two groups—the pantherines and nonpantherines. Tigers and most of the other big cats, including the lion, jaguar, and leopard, belong to the pantherines. All other cats, from the domestic cat to the cheetah, are nonpantherines. All cats have similar-shaped skulls, which are short and rounded, designed to focus power in the jaw. The lower jaw can only move up and down, not sideways. Pantherines have fleshier vocal folds that allow them to roar, while the nonpantherines cannot.

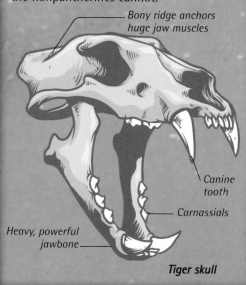

Bony ridge anchors huge jaw muscles

Canine tooth

Carnassials

Heavy, powerful jawbone

Tiger skull

9 The tiger's **orange fur and dark stripes provide camouflage** in long grass. White tigers are sometimes seen in zoos, but they are very rare.

10 The **eyes are a distinctive yellow-amber color** and have a special reflective layer at the back to enhance sight in low light. *A tiger's night vision is six times better than a human's.*

11 People working in tiger territory sometimes **wear face masks on the backs of their heads.** This is thought to deter tiger attack, because tigers hunt by stealth and **won't stalk a person they think can see them.**

12 Super-sensitive whiskers help the animal navigate and sense prey in the dark. The whiskers can even help the tiger decide where to bite and sense whether the victim's pulse has stopped afterward.

13 A tiger's **claws are made of the same substance as human fingernails—** keratin. Like all cats except the cheetah, the tiger fully retracts its claws into sheaths in its paws to keep them razor sharp.

8 Up to 3 in (7.5 cm) in length, **a tiger's huge canine teeth are the largest of any cat's,** and deliver a killer bite. Carnassial teeth cut through bone and sinew, while **the barbed tongue can rasp meat off the bone.**

13½ A liger sounds like a madeup animal, but this cross between a male lion and a female tiger does exist. Big cats in captivity do sometimes interbreed, but ligers are unhealthy and unable to breed, and do not exist in the wild.

FANTASTIC FUNGI

Without fungi, there would be no life on Earth. Totaling around 100,000 species, these organisms play a vital role in recycling animal and plant matter, but can also be deadly parasites. Their spores are found practically everywhere.

2 Networks of fungal threads can spread to gargantuan proportions. One **humongous honey fungus** in Oregon, **stretches underground over 3³/₄ sq miles (9.7 sq km)**—making it the largest living organism.

1 Most fungi are **microscopic tangles of threads that spread through wood and soil** with no distinct shape. Just one gram of soil can contain 328 ft (100 m) of these minuscule threads. **Mushrooms are the "fruiting bodies" of a fungus**—they release spores so the fungus can reproduce.

3 Some mushrooms can spread their own spores, but others need a little help. The **foul smell of the devil's fingers fungus entices flies** that unwittingly scatter its spores to new locations.

4 When Scottish scientist Alexander Fleming accidentally let fungus grow on a dish of bacteria in 1929, he made one of the greatest discoveries of all time. **The fungus produced penicillin, which became the first lifesaving antibiotic drug.**

5 **Truffles** are one of several fungi considered a delicacy. Found underground, pigs' and dogs' sensitive noses can sniff them out. **White truffles are the most expensive, selling for up to $6,600 per pound.**

6 **Fungi feed in an unusual way—by living inside their food.** Their threads pass through animal and plant matter, where they release chemicals to break the food down, so the fungus can absorb the nutrients.

Cep

7 One of the most widely recognized fungi, **the fly agaric's bright red-and-white cap warns of its poisonous nature.** In folklore, this mushroom was often associated with fairies.

8 You may think a cheetah is a speedy sprinter, but **the tiny hat-thrower fungus can accelerate faster.** To release its spores, it throws a "hat" (a spore capsule), which accelerates **more than twice as fast as a speeding bullet.**

The **green elfcup fungus** has one of the most vivid pigments of any mushroom. *Its shocking bright blue-green color also stains the wood of the trees it lives in.* The colorful wood is sometimes used to make furniture.

9

Mushroom lifecycle

When a mushroom is ready to reproduce, it produces spores in a tissue below its cap, which are released into the air. Spores must land in a suitable place, such as on soil or a plant, before they are able to germinate. They then begin to grow, producing a network of underground threads called mycelium. These threads eventually spread toward the surface and form a new mushroom, and the cycle begins again.

Mushroom cap

Mushroom stem

Spores released into the air

Budding mushrooms

Adult mushroom's mycelium

New mycelium

10 Fungi are not just found outdoors, but are everywhere in our homes. *The pillow you lay your head on at night may host over 1 million fungal spores.*

11 Most fungal spores cannot be seen by the naked eye. However, the **Giant Puffball**—a mushroom that can grow up to the size of a soccer ball—**throws up 7 trillion spores into the air in clearly visible clouds.**

12 The yeast that gives bread its light, fluffy texture is a type of fungus. As yeast makes its food, it releases carbon dioxide, causing the bread to bubble up and rise when baked.

Morel

13 The fuzzy growth on a moldy piece of fruit is a type of fungus— although not the kind you'd want to eat. Some are edible— the blue veinlike patterns in some cheeses are fungi related to those that make penicillin.

Yellow brain fungus

13½ Lots of people think that mushrooms are a vegetable. They may be found near the carrots in the supermarket, but they belong to their own separate kingdom of life. What's more, fungi are **biologically closer to animals than they are to plants.**

Chanterelle

BANG GOES THE THEORY

The science of physics asks questions about the way things work, here on Earth and in the Universe beyond. Physicists have discovered some extraordinary answers, and come up with some theories and ideas that are out of this world.

1 One of the first real scientists was an Italian called Galileo. However, some of his new ideas about the Universe did not go down well, particularly with the Church. The theory at the time was that the Sun went around the Earth. **When he wrote in 1632 that in fact Earth orbited the Sun, he was imprisoned.**

2 Born in 1642, English genius **Isaac Newton realized that there were invisible forces at work in the Universe, pushing and pulling and making things move.** He was the first to describe how forces work in his book about the laws of motion. Newton discovered and invented many other important things, including the cat flap!

3 Everything is made up of atoms. **You are made up of countless trillions of atoms, of many different types.** They are very small. Half a million lined up in a row could hide behind a hair. For centuries, scientists thought atoms were indivisible and the smallest things possible.

4 We now know that **atoms are made up of tiny particles called protons, neutrons, and electrons.** Protons and neutrons clump together at the centre of the atom to make the nucleus, and the electrons whizz around it. Most of an atom is empty space. **An atom the size of Earth would have a nucleus the size of a football stadium.**

5 The **protons and neutrons inside the nucleus are made of even tinier particles, known as quarks.** A quark is super small and comes in six different types, called flavours: up, down, top, bottom, strange, and charm. **The science of the smallest things in the Universe is called Quantum Physics.**

6 German physicist **Max Planck pushed the super-small to the limit.** He was looking for a length of measurement so small it couldn't be divided any further. When he found it he called it Planck length. He then worked out **Planck time, splitting the second until it could go no smaller.**

7 British physicist Peter Higgs **has a particle named after him.** Along with other scientists, he felt sure there was an unknown particle out there giving other particles their mass. In 2012, experiments in a particle-smashing machine called the Large Hadron Collider revealed **a new particle, now known as the Higgs boson.**

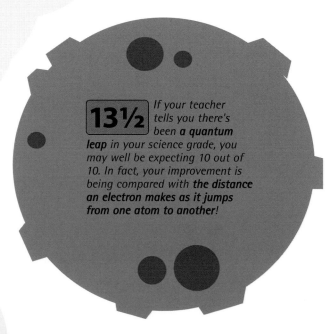
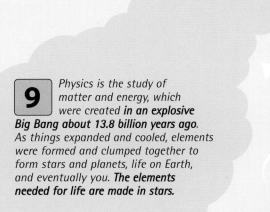
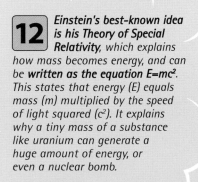

8 Light is another mystery of physics. **It's the fastest thing in the Universe, and weighs nothing.** We see it all the time but can't see what it's made of. And it doesn't always behave in the same way. **Sometimes it ripples like a wave. Other times it acts like particles.** Even the biggest physics brains are still baffled.

9 Physics is the study of matter and energy, which were created **in an explosive Big Bang about 13.8 billion years ago.** As things expanded and cooled, elements were formed and clumped together to form stars and planets, life on Earth, and eventually you. **The elements needed for life are made in stars.**

10 Study of the Universe has revealed something odd going on. Scientists think there is a large amount of unknown stuff in the space between the stars—perhaps as much as **95 percent of the Universe is made of this dark matter and dark energy.** Now they just have to find it.

11 Super-genius Albert Einstein (1879–1955) had ideas that were mind-boggling—for example, that **time can slow down, space-time is curved, gravity is a distortion of space and time, and nothing is fixed except the speed of light.** Ideas like these are called Theoretical Physics. When he wasn't working, Einstein liked to play the violin.

12 Einstein's best-known idea is his Theory of Special Relativity, which explains how mass becomes energy, and can be **written as the equation $E=mc^2$.** This states that energy (E) equals mass (m) multiplied by the speed of light squared (c^2). It explains why a tiny mass of a substance like uranium can generate a huge amount of energy, or even a nuclear bomb.

13 When theories of physics are put into action, they are often easier to grasp. In 1961, for example, Russian astronaut **Yuri Gagarin became the first human to escape the force of Earth's gravity and travel into space.** At speeds in excess of 17,000 mph (27,000 km/h) he orbited Earth for 108 minutes. Gagarin hadn't told his mother where he was going—she found out on the TV news.

13½ If your teacher tells you there's been **a quantum leap** in your science grade, you may well be expecting 10 out of 10. In fact, your improvement is being compared with **the distance an electron makes as it jumps from one atom to another!**

1 Diamonds form deep in the Earth—124 miles (200 km) down in the mantle, where carbon crystallizes under the intense heat and pressure. Volcanic activity brings the resulting diamonds closer to the surface. **Most diamonds are thought to have formed between one and three billion years ago.**

2 Most diamonds are found in the **volcanic rock kimberlite,** named after the mining town Kimberley, in South Africa. Every year, around **57,000 lb (26,000 kg) of diamonds are mined around the world—** enough to fill more than nine trucks.

3 Diamonds are rough chunks when mined, only taking on their characteristic sparkle when they are cut and polished into gems. **The most common shape of a rough, gem-quality diamond is an octohedron** (with eight faces), which looks like two square-based pyramids back-to-back.

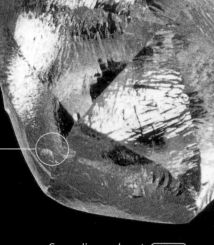

4 Some diamonds get knocked out of rock naturally and are **bashed into rough shapes by water** and erosion. These "alluvial" diamonds can be found on shorelines. **A stretch of the west coast of Africa is known as the Diamond Coast** because of the many gems washed up on its beaches.

DAZZLING DIAMONDS

Named after the Greek word *adamas*—"indestructible"— diamond is the hardest-known mineral. Made from pure carbon, its supreme strength is matched by a dazzling sparkle, making it the most desirable gem on the planet.

5 Around 50 light-years away from us in the constellation of Centaurus is a diamond bigger than anything on Earth. The **dying star BPM 37093, made from crystallized carbon, is an Earth-sized diamond** of around 10 billion trillion trillion carats.

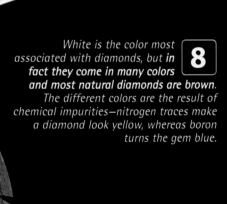

6 Only 20 percent of mined diamonds are gem quality. The majority are put to a much more practical use—lining the edge of powerful industrial tools like drills, metal cutters, and grinding wheels.

7 In 2016, the Oppenheimer Blue became **the most expensive diamond ever sold at auction,** fetching a price of more than $50 million (£40 million).

8 White is the color most associated with diamonds, but **in fact they come in many colors and most natural diamonds are brown.** The different colors are the result of chemical impurities—nitrogen traces make a diamond look yellow, whereas boron turns the gem blue.

9 A diamond's **distinctive sparkle** is caused by light passing through the gem, bouncing off its numerous flat faces, and being **split into all colors of the rainbow** by the very dense structure of the diamond crystal.

The **first diamond engagement ring dates back to 1477,** when Archduke Maximilian of Austria gave one to his fiancée, Mary of Burgundy. The tradition really took off in 1947 when **the De Beers company came up with the advertising slogan "a diamond is forever."** **10**

The brilliant blue **Hope Diamond is famous for its alleged curse.** Legend has it that the walnut-sized diamond was stolen from a religious statue in India, **leading its future owners to meet unfortunate fates—ranging from execution to bankruptcy.** **11**

What took nature billions of years can now be achieved in a laboratory in a matter of days. Using high temperatures and extreme pressure, **scientists can create synthetic diamonds that are almost indistinguishable from the real thing.** **12**

The Cullinan Diamond was the largest gem-quality diamond ever found. At 4 in (10 cm) long, it was as big as a potato and was cut into nine large pieces and more than 100 smaller ones. The two largest are today part of the British Crown Jewels. **13**

⊻ Carbon molecules

Diamond is the hardest of all known minerals, but it's made from the same substance as one of the softest. The carbon atoms that make diamond can also form graphite (the lead in a pencil). The properties of the two materials are so different because of the way the atoms are arranged.

In diamond, each carbon atom is joined to four other carbon atoms, all arranged in a strong network of pyramids.

In graphite, the carbon atoms are joined to only three others and form layers that slide over each other.

13½ You might think that diamonds are rare, since they are so expensive. In fact, **they are the most common gemstone.** Big diamond companies limit the market supply, making the gem seem scarce and pushing up the value.

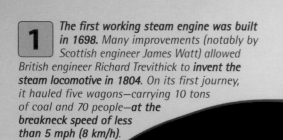

1 The first working steam engine was built in 1698. Many improvements (notably by Scottish engineer James Watt) allowed British engineer Richard Trevithick to **invent the steam locomotive in 1804**. On its first journey, it hauled five wagons—carrying 10 tons of coal and 70 people—at the breakneck speed of less than 5 mph (8 km/h).

2 It could take six hours to get a locomotive started from cold: to fill the boiler with water, get the fire burning, heat the water, and create the steam to pump the pistons and, finally, turn the wheels.

STEAM POWER

Harnessing steam power was revolutionary. Not only did steam engines drive factory machinery, so that goods could be mass produced, they turned the wheels in locomotives that could transport people and goods faster than ever before.

⌄ Steam engineering

Moving a train that weighs thousands of tons starts by burning fuel in the firebox. Hot air from inside the firebox travels down metal tubes into the boiler. These hot tubes turn water inside the boiler into steam, which passes along a cylinder at the front of the engine. The pressure of the steam pushes a piston inside the cylinder back and forth. The piston is connected to rods attached to the wheels, so when the piston moves the rods, the wheels turn.

1 Burning fuel creates heat inside firebox

2 Heated tubes turn water in the boiler into steam

3 Steam travels down to cylinder and pushes piston to turn wheels

4 Steam and smoke escape through chimney

13 Trains were not the only steam vehicles. **Steam cars first appeared in 1769**, but were driven out by gasoline engines; and while **the first powered aircraft was a steam-driven airship** in 1852, steam flight never really took off!

13½ With modern gasoline and electric power, you might think the age of steam is over. However, power plants still steam. Heat from burning coal or from nuclear reactions creates steam that turns turbines to generate electricity.

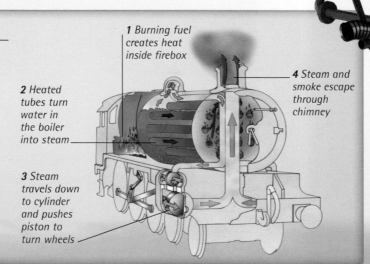

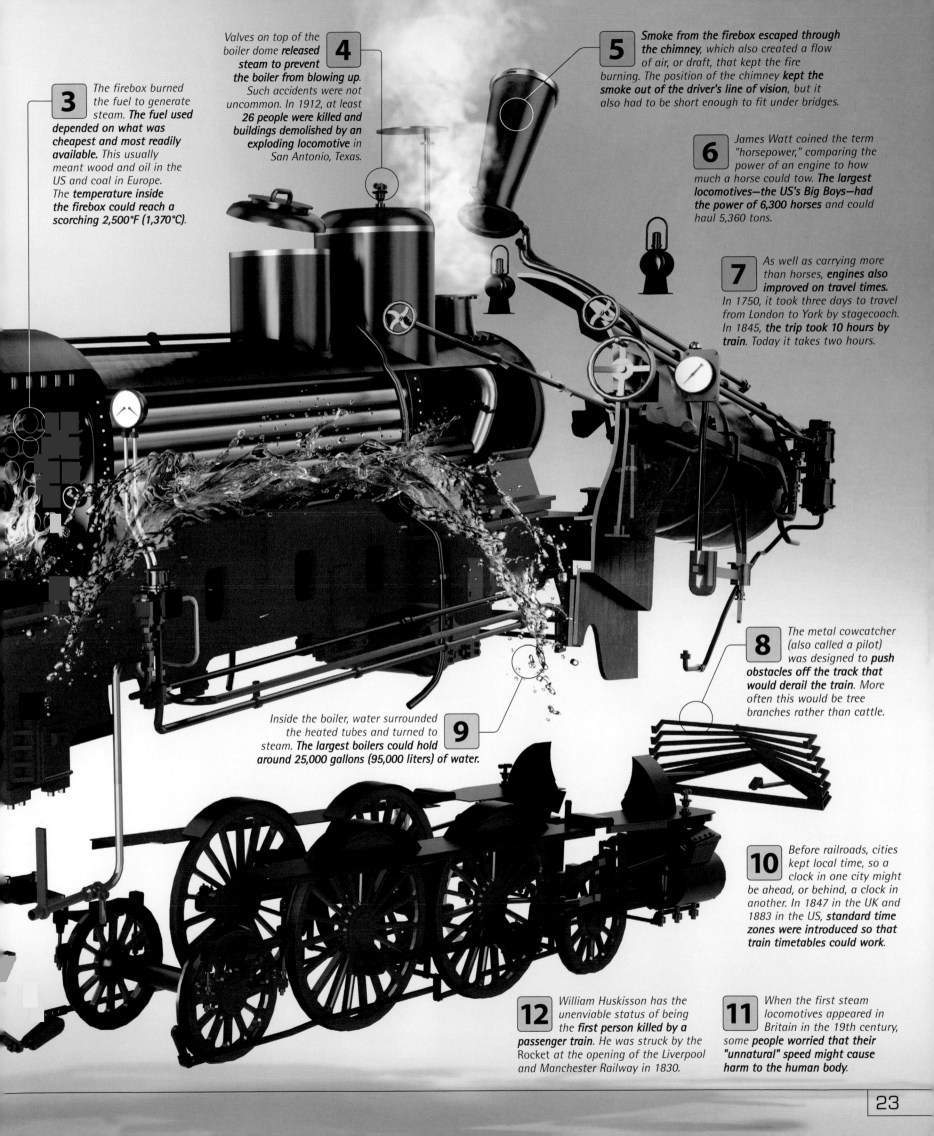

3 The firebox burned the fuel to generate steam. **The fuel used depended on what was cheapest and most readily available.** This usually meant wood and oil in the US and coal in Europe. **The temperature inside the firebox could reach a scorching 2,500°F (1,370°C).**

4 Valves on top of the boiler dome **released steam to prevent the boiler from blowing up.** Such accidents were not uncommon. In 1912, at least **26 people were killed and buildings demolished by an exploding locomotive** in San Antonio, Texas.

5 **Smoke from the firebox escaped through the chimney,** which also created a flow of air, or draft, that kept the fire burning. The position of the chimney **kept the smoke out of the driver's line of vision,** but it also had to be short enough to fit under bridges.

6 James Watt coined the term "horsepower," comparing the power of an engine to how much a horse could tow. **The largest locomotives—the US's Big Boys—had the power of 6,300 horses** and could haul 5,360 tons.

7 As well as carrying more than horses, **engines also improved on travel times.** In 1750, it took three days to travel from London to York by stagecoach. In 1845, **the trip took 10 hours by train.** Today it takes two hours.

8 The metal cowcatcher (also called a pilot) was designed to **push obstacles off the track that would derail the train.** More often this would be tree branches rather than cattle.

9 Inside the boiler, water surrounded the heated tubes and turned to steam. **The largest boilers could hold around 25,000 gallons (95,000 liters) of water.**

10 Before railroads, cities kept local time, so a clock in one city might be ahead, or behind, a clock in another. In 1847 in the UK and 1883 in the US, **standard time zones were introduced so that train timetables could work.**

11 When the first steam locomotives appeared in Britain in the 19th century, some **people worried that their "unnatural" speed might cause harm to the human body.**

12 William Huskisson has the unenviable status of being the **first person killed by a passenger train.** He was struck by the Rocket at the opening of the Liverpool and Manchester Railway in 1830.

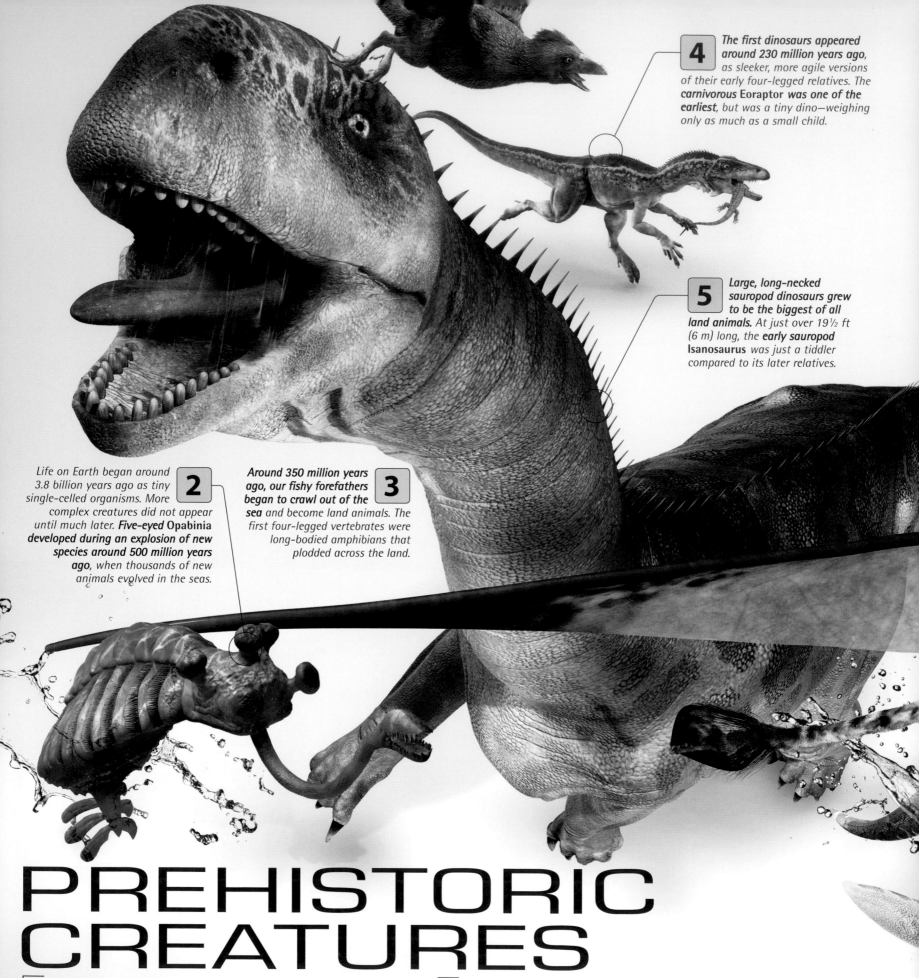

4 *The first dinosaurs appeared around 230 million years ago, as sleeker, more agile versions of their early four-legged relatives. The* **carnivorous Eoraptor** *was one of the earliest, but was a tiny dino—weighing only as much as a small child.*

5 *Large, long-necked sauropod dinosaurs grew to be the biggest of all land animals. At just over 19½ ft (6 m) long, the* **early sauropod Isanosaurus** *was just a tiddler compared to its later relatives.*

Life on Earth began around 3.8 billion years ago as tiny single-celled organisms. More complex creatures did not appear until much later. **Five-eyed Opabinia** *developed during an explosion of new species around 500 million years ago, when thousands of new animals evolved in the seas.*

2

3 *Around 350 million years ago, our fishy forefathers began to crawl out of the* **sea** *and become land animals. The first four-legged vertebrates were long-bodied amphibians that plodded across the land.*

PREHISTORIC CREATURES

Animals have lived on Earth for hundreds of millions of years. The first creatures were tiny microbes in ancient oceans that over millions of years evolved into giants—huge dinosaurs, mighty ocean predators, and powerful flying reptiles.

1 *Earth's inhabitants are changing all the time, with new species emerging and others dying out. We will never know most of the creatures that occupied the planet—more than 99 percent of all the species that have ever existed are now extinct.*

9 Thrush-sized **Confuciusornis was one of the very first birds.** It had the toothless beak and long wings of a modern bird, as well as some added extras—clawed fingers on each of its wings.

10 The dinosaurs roamed on Earth for almost 150 million years, until an asteroid strike caused a mass extinction 66 million years ago. **We have discovered fossils for around 700 species so far,** but there were likely many more.

11 Some creatures alive today are considered "living fossils" because they are so similar to their ancient ancestors. **Flat-bodied horseshoe crabs have remained almost unchanged for around 450 million years.**

12 For millions of years most **mammals were tiny, living in the shadow of the dinosaurs.** When the giant dinosaurs died out, these small, rodentlike creatures evolved and grew into new and bigger species.

6 In the prehistoric world **land invertebrates reached monstrous sizes—**including millipedes the length of buses and dragonflies the size of ravens.

7 Some dinosaur relatives **took to the skies, becoming pterosaurs—**the first backboned flying animals. Long-tailed Rhamphorhynchus had needlelike teeth for spearing fish.

8 While dinosaurs ruled the prehistoric land, **the masters of the sea were huge reptiles like** Liopleurodon. As long as the great white sharks of today, Liopleurodon had enormous jaws and four powerful flippers.

13½ Don't be fooled by movies that depict people living alongside dinosaurs. **All the giant dinosaurs had been extinct for 66 million years** when modern humans appeared 200,000 years ago.

13 After the dinosaurs, mammals dominated the Earth. This **saber-toothed Thylacosmilus** lived 3 million years ago. It looks like a cat, but is actually a relative of modern marsupials.

EYE OPENER

Our eyes are our windows onto the world, sending images of everything we see to the brain with split-second timing. An eyeball contains some of the most delicate, intricate, and fast-moving parts of the body.

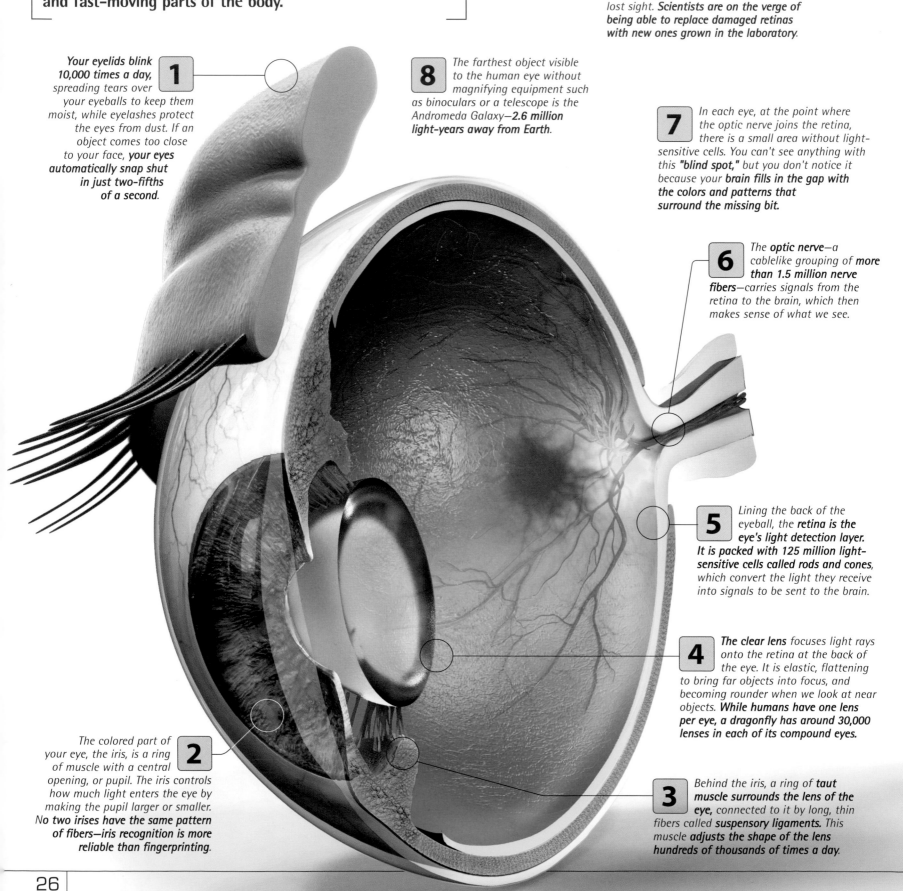

1 Your eyelids blink **10,000 times a day,** spreading tears over your eyeballs to keep them moist, while eyelashes protect the eyes from dust. If an object comes too close to your face, **your eyes automatically snap shut in just two-fifths of a second.**

8 The farthest object visible to the human eye without magnifying equipment such as binoculars or a telescope is the Andromeda Galaxy—**2.6 million light-years away from Earth.**

9 The world's first **"bionic eye" operation was performed in the UK in 2015.** Surgeons implanted a small electrode in a man's retina that, combined with a tiny video camera, partly restored his lost sight. **Scientists are on the verge of being able to replace damaged retinas with new ones grown in the laboratory.**

7 In each eye, at the point where the optic nerve joins the retina, there is a small area without light-sensitive cells. You can't see anything with this **"blind spot,"** but you don't notice it because your **brain fills in the gap with the colors and patterns that surround the missing bit.**

6 The **optic nerve**—a cablelike grouping of **more than 1.5 million nerve fibers**—carries signals from the retina to the brain, which then makes sense of what we see.

5 Lining the back of the eyeball, the **retina is the eye's light detection layer. It is packed with 125 million light-sensitive cells called rods and cones,** which convert the light they receive into signals to be sent to the brain.

4 **The clear lens** focuses light rays onto the retina at the back of the eye. It is elastic, flattening to bring far objects into focus, and becoming rounder when we look at near objects. **While humans have one lens per eye, a dragonfly has around 30,000 lenses in each of its compound eyes.**

2 The colored part of your eye, the iris, is a ring of muscle with a central opening, or pupil. The iris controls how much light enters the eye by making the pupil larger or smaller. *No two irises have the same pattern of fibers—iris recognition is more reliable than fingerprinting.*

3 Behind the iris, a ring of **taut muscle surrounds the lens of the eye,** connected to it by long, thin fibers called **suspensory ligaments.** This muscle **adjusts the shape of the lens hundreds of thousands of times a day.**

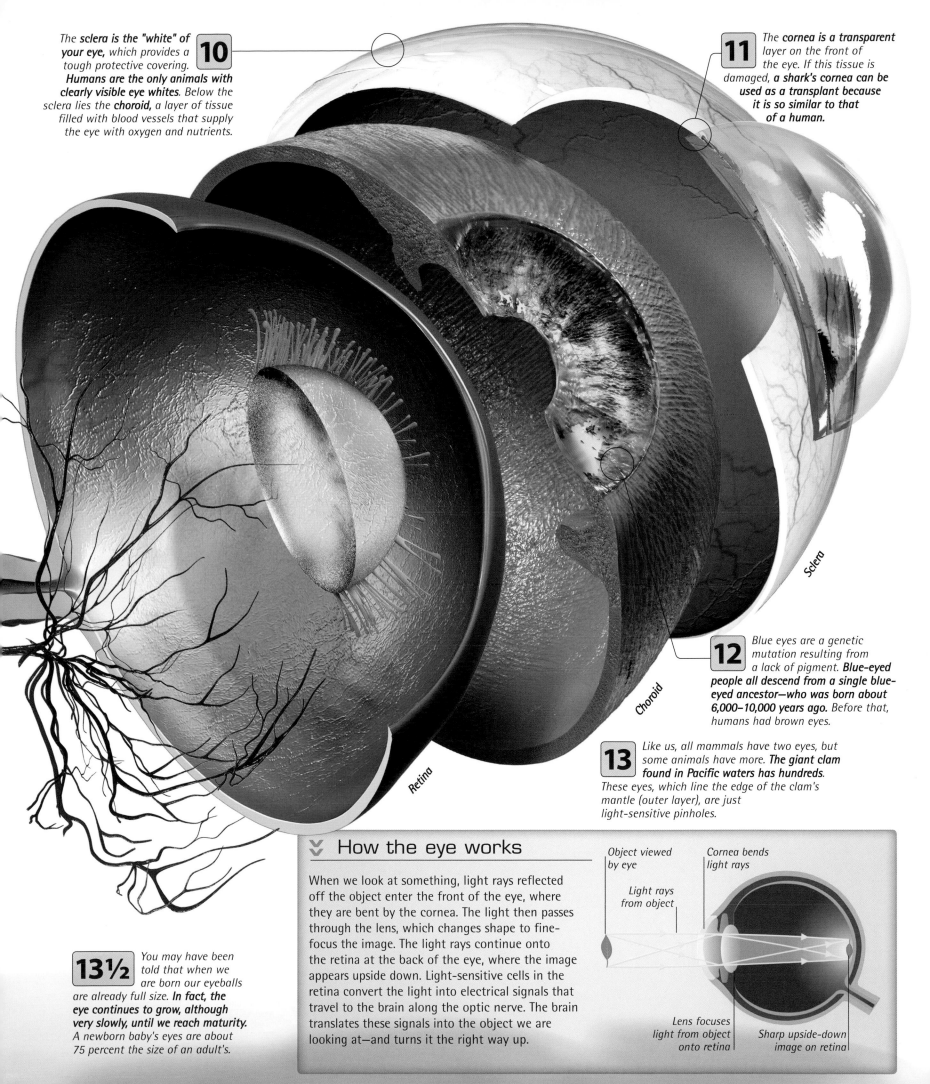

The **sclera is the "white" of your eye**, which provides a tough protective covering. *Humans are the only animals with clearly visible eye whites. Below the sclera lies the choroid, a layer of tissue filled with blood vessels that supply the eye with oxygen and nutrients.*

10

11

The **cornea is a transparent layer on the front of the eye.** If this tissue is damaged, *a shark's cornea can be used as a transplant because it is so similar to that of a human.*

Sclera

Choroid

Retina

12 Blue eyes are a genetic mutation resulting from a lack of pigment. **Blue-eyed people all descend from a single blue-eyed ancestor—who was born about 6,000–10,000 years ago.** *Before that, humans had brown eyes.*

13 *Like us, all mammals have two eyes, but some animals have more.* **The giant clam found in Pacific waters has hundreds.** *These eyes, which line the edge of the clam's mantle (outer layer), are just light-sensitive pinholes.*

13½ *You may have been told that when we are born our eyeballs are already full size.* **In fact, the eye continues to grow, although very slowly, until we reach maturity.** *A newborn baby's eyes are about 75 percent the size of an adult's.*

⌄ How the eye works

When we look at something, light rays reflected off the object enter the front of the eye, where they are bent by the cornea. The light then passes through the lens, which changes shape to fine-focus the image. The light rays continue onto the retina at the back of the eye, where the image appears upside down. Light-sensitive cells in the retina convert the light into electrical signals that travel to the brain along the optic nerve. The brain translates these signals into the object we are looking at—and turns it the right way up.

Object viewed by eye

Cornea bends light rays

Light rays from object

Lens focuses light from object onto retina

Sharp upside-down image on retina

PLANET PARADE

We know of eight major planets in the Solar System. Mercury, Venus, Mars, and Earth are the rocky planets, made of a mixture of rock and metal. Jupiter, Saturn, Uranus, and Neptune are the giants, made mostly of gas and liquid.

1 Pluto used to be the Solar System's ninth planet, but in 2006 *it was downgraded to dwarf planet status* after other objects of similar size were discovered in its orbit. It is so small, two Plutos could sit side-by-side across the US.

2 There may be a **ninth planet in an orbit around the Sun, way beyond Neptune**. There is evidence of a "Planet Nine" having an effect on other bodies' orbits, but the planet itself hasn't been found yet.

3 *Mercury is the smallest planet.* Sunlight here is seven times brighter than on Earth, and the planet also has the biggest range of temperatures: from **800°F (430°C) in the day** down to **–290°F (–180°C) at night**.

4 Although it's only second-nearest to the Sun, **Venus is the hottest planet**, with a **surface temperature of 464°C (867°F)**. It is surrounded by **thick clouds containing deadly sulfuric acid**.

5 *Earth is the only planet known to support life and have liquid water*: two-thirds of the surface is ocean. Much farther from the Sun, the water would turn to ice; nearer the Sun, it would evaporate.

6 Mars is the "Red Planet," covered in iron-rich red dust. Evidence suggests that the planet was **warm and wet 3 billion years ago, but it is cold and dry now**. Mars is experiencing an ice age and the water is frozen into the ground.

7 The biggest planet in the Solar System, **Jupiter is two and a half times the mass of all the other planets** put together. However, it is still much smaller than the Sun: **10 Jupiters could line up across the Sun**.

⌄ Planetary orbits

Each planet in the Solar System follows a path, or orbit, around the Sun. These orbits are almost circular, pulled into shape by gravity. The point at which the planet is nearest the Sun is called the perihelion; the aphelion is the point when the planet is farthest away. The time it takes to make one complete orbit forms a "year" on that planet. Mercury has the shortest year, just 88 Earth-days long; and Neptune has the longest (165 Earth-years).

8 So far, **172 moons have been discovered in orbit around six of the planets**. Jupiter has the most, with 67. Saturn has 62, Uranus 27, Neptune 13, Mars two, and Earth one. Venus and Mercury have none.

9 The **giant planet Saturn is made mostly of helium and hydrogen**. Although it has a solid core, on average **the planet is less dense than water, so in theory it could float**—if you could find a bucket big enough!

10 All the planets spin on their axis. While the other planets spin almost upright, **Uranus is tilted and spins on its side**. It takes **17 hours and 14 minutes for Uranus to rotate once**. Earth takes 23 hours and 56 minutes, but Venus takes a whopping 5,832 hours.

11 Asteroids are rocky bodies made from material left over when the planets formed. **Billions of asteroids orbit the Sun** between Mars and Jupiter, but the **total mass of all of them is less than the mass of the Moon**.

12 Farthest from the Sun, **Neptune is the coldest planet** and also the windiest with gusts up to 1,340 mph (2,160 km/h). It's the smallest giant, but still **four times the size of Earth**.

13 Thousands of icy objects the size of cities orbit the Sun beyond Neptune. When one is diverted nearer the Sun, it grows a **huge tails of gas and dust thousands of miles long to become a comet**.

13½ Meteorites—space rocks that fall through Earth's atmosphere and hit the ground—are not as rare as you might think. On average, **people see only about 10 come down each year, but hundreds more are thought to fall undetected** and many other space rocks burn up in the air.

SHARK ATTACK

The great white shark is one of the ocean's top predators, equipped with super senses, bone-crushing jaws, and a fearsome reputation. There are around 526 different species of sharks, which roam across every ocean in the world.

1 Great white sharks can grow up to 24 ft (7.2 m) in length—around four times the height of an adult man—and can weigh up to 2 tons. This powerful predator *targets seals, dolphins, turtles, and fish, but may even take on other sharks*.

2 Sharks have sensitive snouts equipped with **pimple-sized nodules** called **ampullae of Lorenzini**. These can **sense the tiniest of electrical impulses, allowing sharks to locate prey** even in total darkness.

3 A *shark's eyes sit on the sides of its head*, giving it amazingly wide vision. Hammerhead sharks have **the best vision** of all—their wide-set eyes allow them to **see a full 360 degrees around them**.

4 Sharks shed their teeth. They have **up to 15 rows of spare teeth**, so when an old, blunt tooth falls out, a new one takes its place. **Shark teeth also naturally contain fluorine**, the ingredient we put into toothpaste to prevent cavities.

5 The ancient ancestors of *sharks first evolved around 420 million years ago*. Since then, sharks have **survived five planet extinction events**, including the one that destroyed all the dinosaurs 65 million years ago.

6 A *line of sensory cells called a lateral line runs along a shark's body* from head to tail. Present in all fish, these cells are filled with tiny hairs that can **detect the smallest of vibrations** in the water.

7 Sharks have an incredible sense of smell. They can **detect a single drop of blood in the water** from approximately ½ mile (1 km) away.

Shark skeleton

Sharks belong to a group called cartilaginous fish, along with their close relatives the rays. Shark skeletons are not made out of bone, but of cartilage—a rubbery tissue that is much lighter and more flexible. As well as a long spine, a shark's skeleton has arches to keep the gills open, and cartilage rods to support the fins. Unlike sharks, the majority of fish are bony fishes, which have have a flexible, bony backbone, and bony spines supporting their fins.

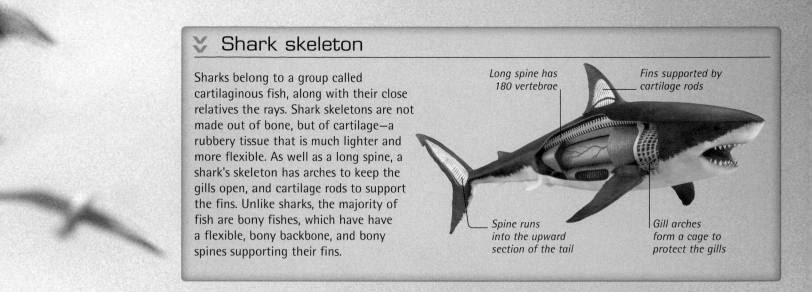

Long spine has 180 vertebrae

Fins supported by cartilage rods

Spine runs into the upward section of the tail

Gill arches form a cage to protect the gills

8 *Great white sharks have to keep moving to stay alive.* Swimming forces water through their mouth, and out of the gills, which extract oxygen. *If the sharks remain stationary, not enough water passes through their gills—meaning they could drown.*

9 *All sharks are carnivores, but not all are aggressive predators. The **biggest shark is the whale shark**, a gentle giant that feeds by filtering food particles from the water. It can reach lengths of **up to 66 ft (20 m)**—almost three times a long as a great white. The smallest is the tiny lanternshark, which is no bigger than a guinea pig.*

10 *Some sharks are not fussy about what they swallow when searching for prey. **Tiger sharks are sometimes called the "garbage cans" of the ocean**— they have been found with **car tires, license plates, and even porcupines** in their stomachs.*

11 *Sharks' jaws are only very loosely connected to their skull, so they **can protrude forward to grab prey.** Once the shark has captured its meal, **it holds the animal locked in its teeth** and shakes its head from side to side to tear off tasty chunks.*

12 *During World War II, pilots from the 1st American volunteer group **painted fearsome shark eyes and teeth on the noses of their aircraft** in order to try and scare their enemies. Nicknamed the Flying Tigers, the group of pilots flew missions over Burma (present-day Myanmar) and China.*

13 *Shark skin is made up of tiny interlocking teeth.* Called denticles, these **tough, ridged scales** allow the shark to swim smoothly and silently through the water. *Scientists are developing **artificial shark skin** that may be used in high-performance wetsuits to allow divers to swim faster.*

13½ *Sharks may seem scary, but really they should be more scared of us. Shark attacks on humans are very rare—causing around 6 deaths a year—but humans hunt around 100 million sharks every year.* Many species are now endangered.

SPREAD THE WORD

From time-worn tablets to modern mobile messages, the written word has allowed humans to communicate for thousands of years. Our ancestors used a range of symbols and codes—some of which we still have not cracked.

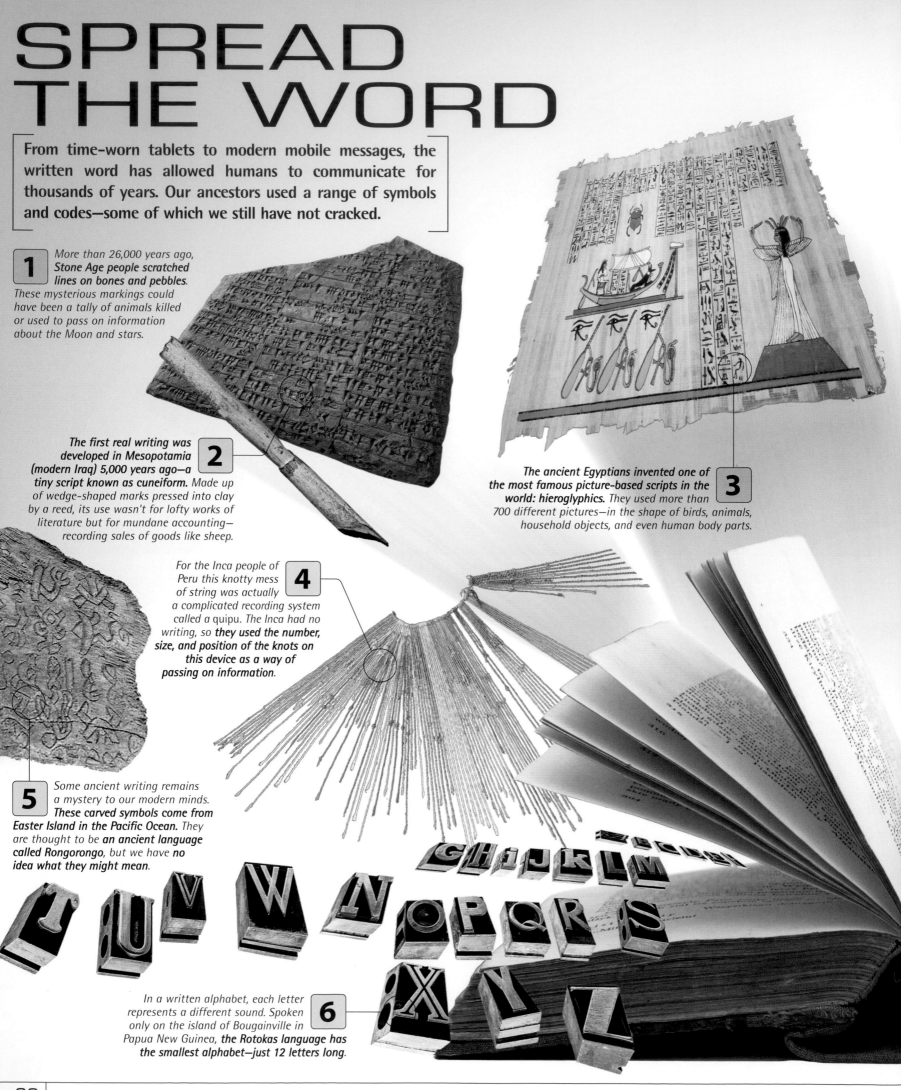

1 More than 26,000 years ago, *Stone Age people scratched lines on bones and pebbles.* These mysterious markings could have been a tally of animals killed or used to pass on information about the Moon and stars.

2 The first real writing was developed in Mesopotamia (modern Iraq) 5,000 years ago—a tiny script known as cuneiform. Made up of wedge-shaped marks pressed into clay by a reed, its use wasn't for lofty works of literature but for mundane accounting—recording sales of goods like sheep.

3 The ancient Egyptians invented one of the most famous picture-based scripts in the world: hieroglyphics. They used more than 700 different pictures—in the shape of birds, animals, household objects, and even human body parts.

4 For the Inca people of Peru this knotty mess of string was actually a complicated recording system called a quipu. The Inca had no writing, so **they used the number, size, and position of the knots on this device as a way of passing on information.**

5 Some ancient writing remains a mystery to our modern minds. **These carved symbols come from Easter Island in the Pacific Ocean.** They are thought to be **an ancient language called Rongorongo,** but we have **no idea what they might mean.**

6 In a written alphabet, each letter represents a different sound. Spoken only on the island of Bougainville in Papua New Guinea, **the Rotokas language has the smallest alphabet—just 12 letters long.**

Some modern languages use characters, rather than an alphabet. **7** **Mandarin, the script used by more than 88 million Chinese speakers, has over 100,000 characters—**symbols that represent a word or phrase. Most people know up to 4,000 of them—more than enough to read a book or newspaper.

8 Today, paper is made of a mixture of pulped wood and water. **The parchment used by our ancestors was made out of dead animal skins.** These were stretched into thin sheets, with excess animal hair scraped off by hand.

First sold in the 1940s, the ballpoint pen is now the world's most popular handwriting tool. **9** It was invented by László Bíró, a busy Hungarian newspaper editor who dreamed of a pen that did not smudge and could write for hours without running out of ink.

10 **An average pencil contains enough "lead" (graphite) to draw a line 35 miles (56 km) long.** It lasts longer than a pen—one pencil can write more than 60 times as many words as a single ballpoint pen before it runs out.

Scientists have **encoded an entire book,** including pictures, on DNA, the genetic code found in every body cell. Just **one teaspoon of DNA could hold every book, poem, letter, or shopping list that's ever been written,** with plenty of room to spare. **11**

In the braille alphabet, **12** used by people who are blind, the letters consist of raised dots, which are "read" with the fingertips. **Braille letters take up much more space than printed ones—a single "Harry Potter" title in braille is 10 volumes long.**

Experts say that **textspeak—the use of slang, initials, and emoticons for messaging on smartphones—may become a new written language.** **13** In 2015, the Oxford English Dictionary named the "Face With Tears of Joy" emoji as its word of the year.

13½ You might have heard that **normal pens do not work in space, but astronauts don't use pencils either.** If the pencil lead broke it could be dangerous—floating into a piece of machinery or someone's eye. Specially designed pens are used instead.

1 Cave paintings on the walls of caves in Chauvet, France, date back more than 30,000 years. **This rock art shows pictures of mammoths, lions, rhinos, galloping bisons, and other animals.** Some people believe these paintings were used in ceremonies to bring good luck in hunting. We will never know.

2 Prehistoric painters **used powdered minerals, charcoal, soil, and burned bones to make their paint colors.** Animal fats were one of the earliest ways of binding the pigments into a sticky paint. Later, paints were mixed with egg yolk, until oil paints were used in the 15th century.

3 Ancient Egyptian painting has a very distinctive style because scribes had to follow a strict set of rules. Look closely and you'll see that **people's eyes and shoulders always face the front, but the other parts of the body are shown side on.** The size of the figures was also symbolic, with the most important people shown the biggest. **In ancient Egypt, art was very exclusive—only to be seen by the wealthy, the gods, or the dead.**

4 More than 8,000 life-size human sculptures make up the impressive terra-cotta army that was discovered in China in 1974. **Made 2,200 years ago, every figure is different.** The statues guard the tomb of Qin Shi Huangdi, the First Emperor. Records say that it took 700,000 men to build the massive tomb.

5 In 1911, the world was stunned when **the famous** Mona Lisa, **painted by Italian artist Leonardo da Vinci in 1503, was stolen** by a small-time Italian criminal. Vincenzo Peruggia got a job at the Louvre in Paris, where the priceless portrait hangs, and walked out with it wrapped in his smock. He was caught two years later, when he tried to sell it.

6 The stunning biblical scenes on the ceiling of the Sistine Chapel in the Vatican were painted by Italian Renaissance artist Michelangelo. He worked on the 60-ft-(18-m-) high ceiling from a wall platform for over four years. **Today, more than 25,000 people view the chapel every single day.**

7 Dutch painter **Vincent Van Gogh is best known for his series of paintings of sunflowers.** Although he painted more than 900 canvases in just 10 years, **he only sold a single painting in his lifetime.** His paintings, with their distinctive style of coarse brushstrokes and rich colors, sell for millions today.

PICTURE PERFECT

If every picture is worth a thousand words, the world has a giant library chronicling the history of art. From careful carvings to bold brushstrokes, different styles have emerged and evolved throughout history.

8 In the 1900s, some artists moved away from painting what they could see, and instead used shapes and colors to represent emotions or ideas. **This is known as abstract art.** It is not always clear how to interpret abstract art. In 1961 **Henri Matisse's Le Bateau was hung upside down in the Museum of Modern Art, New York, for 47 days** before anyone noticed.

9 In the 1920s, the Surrealist art movement turned the world on its head. **Surrealism means "more than real."** Artists often painted in a dreamlike state and produced impossible and absurd objects such as furry teacups and flying fish. One of the best-known Surrealists was the **Spanish artist Salvador Dalí, famous for his lobster telephones and melting watches.**

10 US artist Jackson Pollock took a unique approach to painting in 1947—ditching the easel and **flinging, pouring, and dripping paint on canvases instead.** This energetic style of art caught on and was soon dubbed "action painting," a movement where **the act of painting is more important than the finished result.**

11 Completed in 2004, the world's **largest statue is a stone Buddha in China** measuring 1,365 ft (416 m) tall. However, some sculptures are not even visible to the naked eye. The **world's smallest sculpture of a human form**, Trust by Jonty Hurwitz, was tiny enough to fit on an ant's head, but was accidentally crushed by a photographer's finger in 2015.

12 Art collecting is big business and great works go for eye-popping prices. The **most expensive painting sold at auction** is Nude, Green Leaves and Bust (1932) by Spanish artist Pablo Picasso, which fetched $106.5 million in 2010.

13 **Opinions differ on what is truly art** in the modern world. Creatives have pushed the artistic limits by displaying **a dead cow cut in half (Damien Hirst)**, exhibiting an unmade bed (Tracey Emin), and using dried elephant poop as paint (Chris Ofili).

13½ Are art critics really the ultimate judges of artistic talent? Do they know how to tell good art from bad? In 1964, six paintings by an unknown artist called Pierre Brassau went on display in Göteborg, Sweden. They received praise from critics but the artist was then revealed to be a chimpanzee from a nearby zoo.

A STING IN THE TAIL

Scorpions are nocturnal predators and use their pincers and venomous sting to hunt and kill their prey—they can eat their own weight in insects every day. They live mostly in rain forest and hot countries, in trees and on rocks and sand.

1 Scorpions are invertebrates—they do not have bony internal skeletons. Instead, *their bodies are supported by a hard, outer casing*, or exoskeleton. A scorpion's exoskeleton *glows bright blue-green under ultraviolet light*—but nobody knows why.

2 There are nearly **2,000 different species of scorpions**, from the tiny Microtityus minimus, *just ⅓ in (9 mm) long*, to this **Emperor scorpion**—at 8¼ in (21 cm) long, *as big as a brown rat*. One of the world's largest scorpions, it is native to West Africa.

3 The scorpion doesn't have a system of arteries and veins, like humans. Instead *its tubular heart pumps blood into the body cavity* where all the other organs are floating. **Scorpions and many other arthropods have blue blood.**

4 An Emperor scorpion's **powerful pincers are its main weapon**: it uses sheer strength to catch and crush its prey. Generally, **scorpions with big, muscular pincers deliver a less potent sting** than those with smaller pincers and bigger, fatter tails.

5 Scorpions can't eat solid food, so they **use their clawlike mouthparts, called chelicerae**, to tear off small pieces of their prey. The food is covered in digestive juices from the scorpion's stomach, which then **sucks up the liquid mush**.

6 The scorpion's **simple brain is connected to a nerve cord** that runs along the length of its body. The nerve cord runs through the animal's belly and connects to nerves that work the legs.

Pincer muscle

7 **Sensitive hairs cover the scorpion's legs**, enabling it to sense vibrations in the air. Underneath its body, a special pair of comblike sense organs called pectines pick up vibrations from the ground, and detect temperature and humidity.

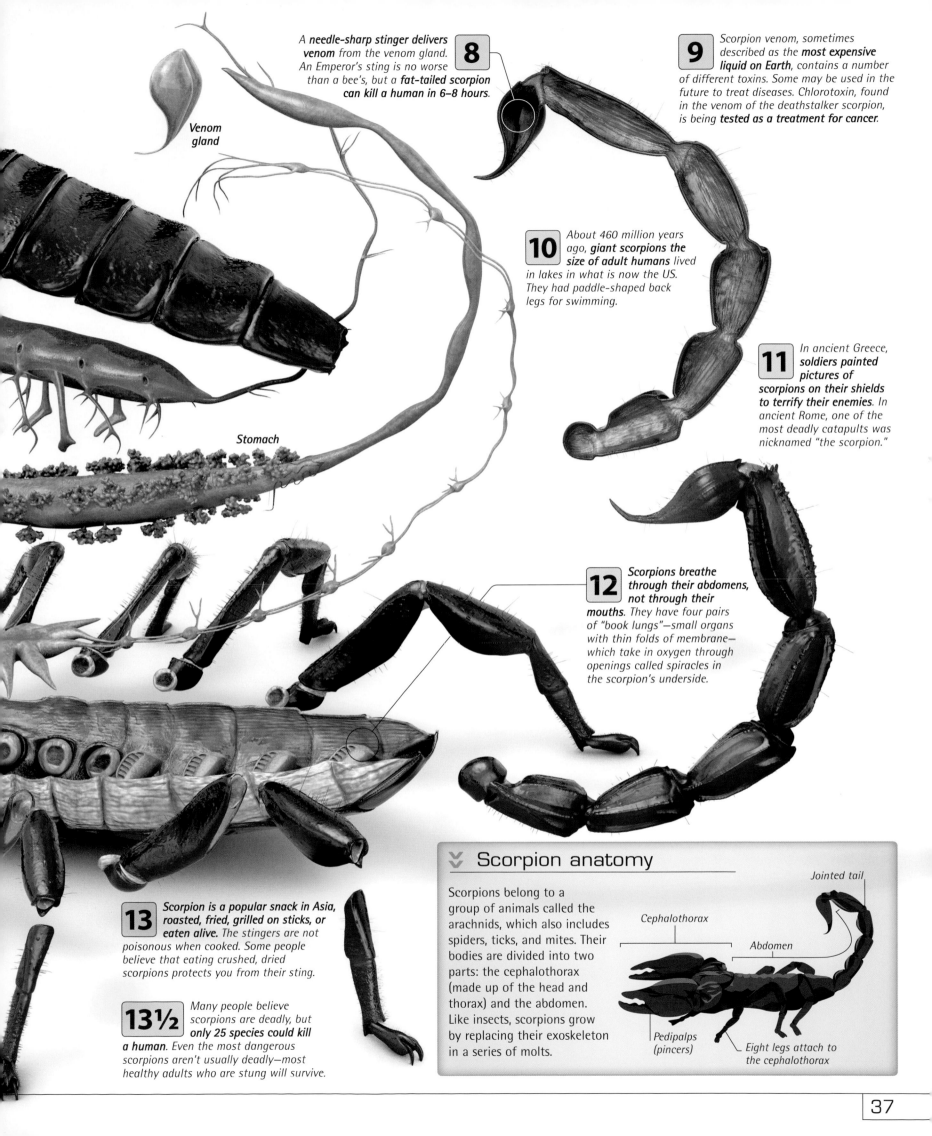

A needle-sharp stinger delivers **venom** from the venom gland. An Emperor's sting is no worse than a bee's, but a **fat-tailed scorpion can kill a human in 6–8 hours.**

8

Venom gland

9 Scorpion venom, sometimes described as the **most expensive liquid on Earth**, contains a number of different toxins. Some may be used in the future to treat diseases. Chlorotoxin, found in the venom of the deathstalker scorpion, is being **tested as a treatment for cancer.**

10 About 460 million years ago, **giant scorpions the size of adult humans** lived in lakes in what is now the US. They had paddle-shaped back legs for swimming.

Stomach

11 In ancient Greece, **soldiers painted pictures of scorpions on their shields to terrify their enemies.** In ancient Rome, one of the most deadly catapults was nicknamed "the scorpion."

12 **Scorpions breathe through their abdomens, not through their mouths.** They have four pairs of "book lungs"—small organs with thin folds of membrane—which take in oxygen through openings called spiracles in the scorpion's underside.

13 **Scorpion is a popular snack in Asia, roasted, fried, grilled on sticks, or eaten alive.** The stingers are not poisonous when cooked. Some people believe that eating crushed, dried scorpions protects you from their sting.

13½ Many people believe scorpions are deadly, but **only 25 species could kill a human.** Even the most dangerous scorpions aren't usually deadly—most healthy adults who are stung will survive.

⌄ Scorpion anatomy

Scorpions belong to a group of animals called the arachnids, which also includes spiders, ticks, and mites. Their bodies are divided into two parts: the cephalothorax (made up of the head and thorax) and the abdomen. Like insects, scorpions grow by replacing their exoskeleton in a series of molts.

Cephalothorax

Jointed tail

Abdomen

Pedipalps (pincers)

Eight legs attach to the cephalothorax

MAKING WAVES

From deep underground to high in the sky, water is everywhere imaginable on Earth—even inside your own body. The planet contains 332 million cubic miles (1.3 billion cubic km) of water, essential to the survival of living things.

1 Just **3 percent of all Earth's water is freshwater**—the water we need to survive. Most of this is trapped as solid ice in glaciers and icecaps, leaving **only 1 percent of freshwater available for us to drink.**

2 The ocean is not the only place where the water is salty. In some large landlocked lakes like the Dead Sea in the Middle East, **the water is so salty you can sit back and easily float on its surface.**

3 Earth is the only planet in our Solar System known to have liquid water, although water is found far out in the vast reaches of space. Twelve billion light-years away, a massive cloud of mist surrounds a black hole. This contains enough water to fill Earth's oceans 140 trillion times.

4 The roots of **plants suck up water from the earth and release it into the atmosphere in a process known as transpiration.** A large oak tree can transpire as much as 88 gallons (400 liters) of water—the equivalent of five bathtubfuls—into the atmosphere in a single day.

5 The **longest river in the world is the Nile**, which snakes across Africa for an estimated 4,258 miles (6,853 km). However, **the Amazon river in South America actually contains more water,** and makes up 20 percent of all the freshwater discharged into the sea.

6 Earthquakes and volcanic eruptions can trigger large tsunami **waves**—one of the world's most destructive forces. These waves can rise to around 115 ft (35 m)—the same height as a 10-story apartment building.

7 Clouds may look light and fluffy, but they actually contain large amounts of water. **The average cumulus (fair weather) cloud weighs around 1.1 million lb (500,000 kg)**—the same as two large airplanes.

8 New technology is constantly being invented to help our access to drinking water. **High-tech water bottles can extract water purely from the air around them,** and tiny nanoparticles can be used to rid dirty water of deadly contaminants.

9 Oceans cover more than **70 percent of the planet.** Their surface and deepwater currents continually circulate water around the globe—a journey that can take 1,000 years.

10 The **average adult human is made up of 65 percent water**—around 85 pints (40 liters). Water is found inside every single cell—even in **hard bones,** which are up to **20 percent water.**

The water cycle

The total amount of water found on Earth never alters, but moves between sea, air, and land in a continuous cycle. Sun-warmed water evaporates into the air, forming water vapor. Water vapor also enters the atmosphere from plants through transpiration. As water vapor rises, it is cooled and turns back into water droplets. Clouds form, which are blown around by winds. As the water droplets get heavier, they fall as rain, snow, and hail.

3 *The water in the air forms clouds*

4 *Water falls to earth as rain*

2 *Trees release water into the atmosphere*

1 *Water from the oceans evaporates into the air*

5 *The surface rain water flows into rivers and the ground. The cycle begins again*

11 *Many animals can move through the water much faster than we can due to their streamlined flippers and fins. US founding father **Benjamin Franklin invented the first pair of swimming flippers** in the 1750s, although these went on the hands rather than the feet.*

12 *One of the most famous deities associated with water is the **Greek god Poseidon**—king of the ocean. **When angry, he would shipwreck his enemies** and was known as "Earth-Shaker" due to his ability to cause catastrophic earthquakes.*

13 *There are **more archaeological artifacts underwater than in all the world's museums**. Hoards of treasure are also believed to be lost in the oceans—**an estimated $8 (£6) for every person in the world**, if it were all extracted.*

13½ *Is it possible to walk on water? Surfing may be the closest humans have come to mastering the waves, but many creatures in the animal kingdom are able to achieve this impressive feat. **Fishing spiders** and insects such as water striders can run over the **surface of water** because of their small size.*

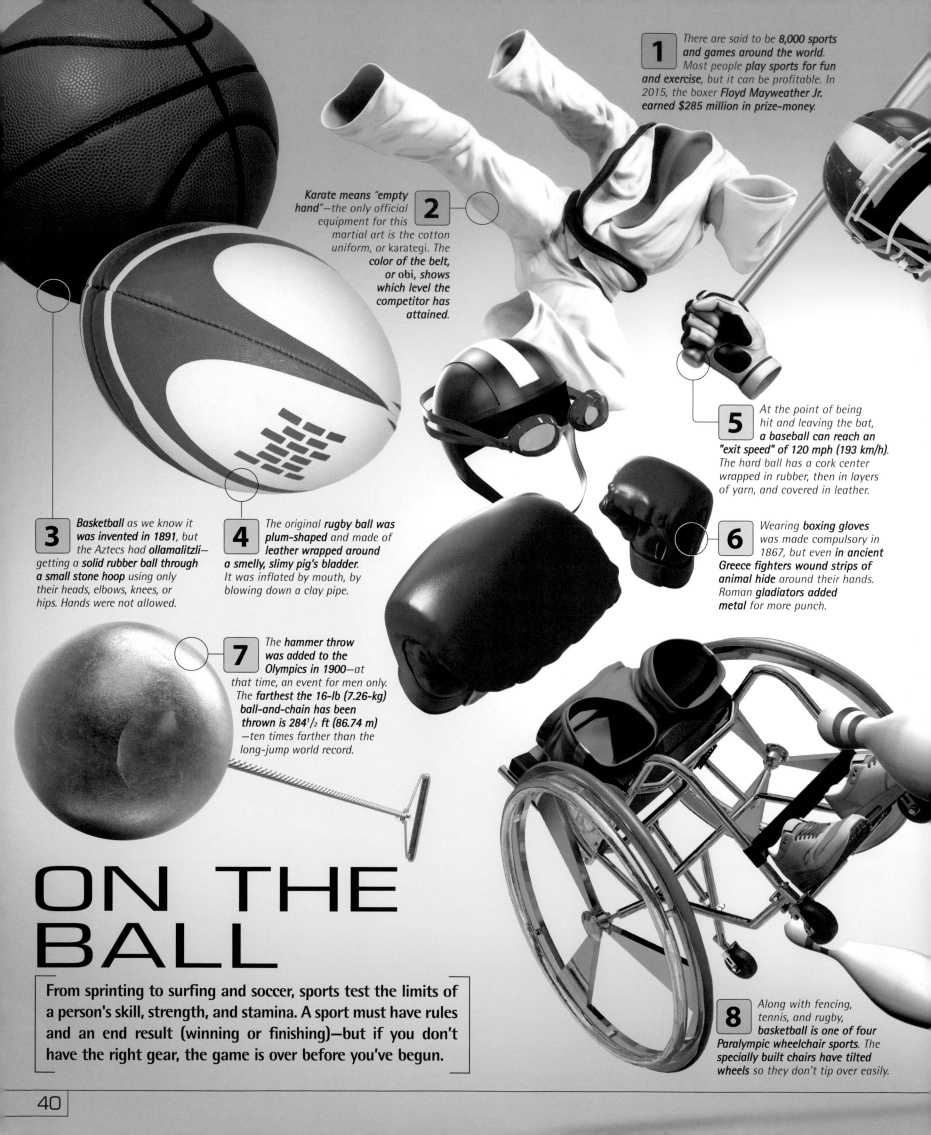

1 There are said to be **8,000 sports and games around the world**. Most people **play sports for fun and exercise**, but it can be profitable. In 2015, the boxer *Floyd Mayweather Jr.* earned $285 million in prize-money.

2 Karate means *"empty hand"*—the only official equipment for this martial art is the cotton uniform, or karategi. The **color of the belt, or obi, shows which level the competitor has attained.**

5 At the point of being hit and leaving the bat, **a baseball can reach an "exit speed" of 120 mph (193 km/h).** The hard ball has a cork center wrapped in rubber, then in layers of yarn, and covered in leather.

3 **Basketball** as we know it **was invented in 1891,** but the Aztecs had **ollamalitzli**—getting a **solid rubber ball through a small stone hoop** using only their heads, elbows, knees, or hips. Hands were not allowed.

4 The original **rugby ball was plum-shaped** and made of **leather wrapped around** a smelly, slimy pig's bladder. It was inflated by mouth, by blowing down a clay pipe.

6 Wearing **boxing gloves** was made compulsory in 1867, but even **in ancient Greece fighters wound strips of animal hide** around their hands. Roman **gladiators added metal** for more punch.

7 The hammer throw was added to the Olympics in 1900—at that time, an event for men only. The **farthest the 16-lb (7.26-kg) ball-and-chain has been thrown is 284$^1/_2$ ft (86.74 m)** —ten times farther than the long-jump world record.

ON THE BALL

From sprinting to surfing and soccer, sports test the limits of a person's skill, strength, and stamina. A sport must have rules and an end result (winning or finishing)—but if you don't have the right gear, the game is over before you've begun.

8 Along with fencing, tennis, and rugby, **basketball is one of four Paralympic wheelchair sports.** The specially built chairs have tilted wheels so they don't tip over easily.

9 The *pads for American football* are made of *shock-absorbing foam covered in plastic.* They *protect the sternum (breast bone)* as well *as the shoulders*: vital when a 360-lb (165-kg) player bears down on you.

Billiard ball

When invented by 12th-century monks, **tennis was played by hitting the ball with your hands.** It's far less painful to use today's strong, lightweight **carbon-fiber or graphite racquets.** **10**

Golf ball

Shuttlecock

11 **Carbon-fiber running blades** *have enabled amputee sprinters to* **run the 100-m sprint in under 11 seconds.** *As the "foot" strikes the ground, the blade is compressed like a spring, then bounces back to push the runner forward. Spikes can be fitted to the blade to grip the running track.*

Surfboard

12 Evidence of *pins and balls found in Egypt* suggests that bowling was enjoyed *as long ago as 3200* BCE. Modern **ten-pin** bowling started in *the US in 1841—* to avoid a ban on nine-pin bowling!

Soccer is the most-watched sport, with 3.2 billion people watching the 2014 World Cup. *Originally, the men of entire towns would play, chasing an inflated pig's bladder as an excuse for a mass brawl.* **13**

Cricket ball

13½ *It is said that a marathon is based on the* **distance** *that a messenger ran from the* **Battle of Marathon to Athens** *in 490* BCE—roughly 25 miles (40 km). In fact, *the marathon was set at the* **1908 Olympics** *to 26 miles, 385 yards: the distance from Windsor Castle to the Olympic stadium in London.*

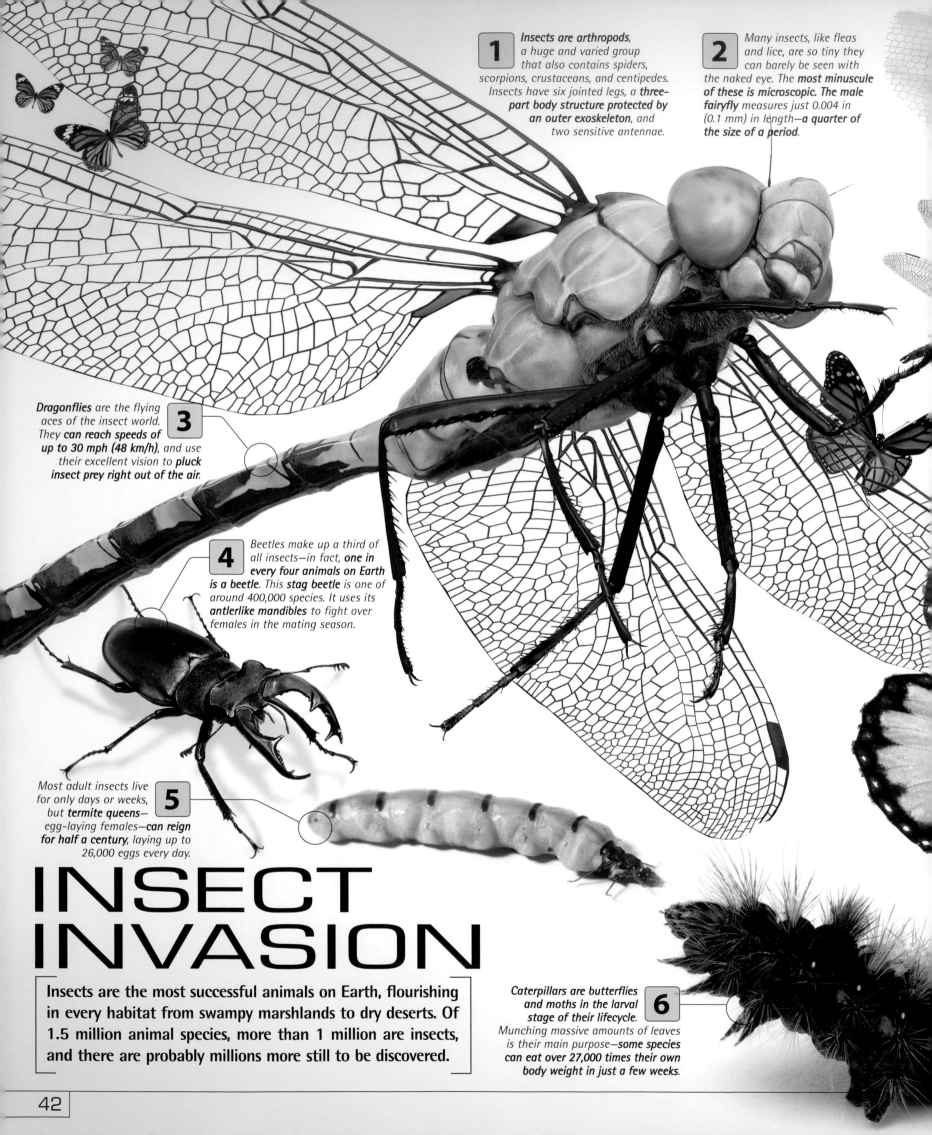

1 Insects are arthropods, a huge and varied group that also contains spiders, scorpions, crustaceans, and centipedes. Insects have six jointed legs, a **three-part body structure protected by an outer exoskeleton**, and two sensitive antennae.

2 Many insects, like fleas and lice, are so tiny they can barely be seen with the naked eye. The **most minuscule** of these is microscopic. The male fairyfly measures just 0.004 in (0.1 mm) in length—**a quarter of the size of a period.**

3 *Dragonflies* are the flying aces of the insect world. They **can reach speeds of up to 30 mph (48 km/h)**, and use their excellent vision to **pluck insect prey right out of the air.**

4 Beetles make up a third of all insects—in fact, **one in every four animals on Earth is a beetle**. This **stag beetle** is one of around 400,000 species. It uses its **antlerlike mandibles** to fight over females in the mating season.

5 Most adult insects live for only days or weeks, but **termite queens**— egg-laying females—**can reign for half a century**, laying up to 26,000 eggs every day.

INSECT INVASION

Insects are the most successful animals on Earth, flourishing in every habitat from swampy marshlands to dry deserts. Of 1.5 million animal species, more than 1 million are insects, and there are probably millions more still to be discovered.

6 Caterpillars are butterflies and moths in the larval stage of their lifecycle. Munching massive amounts of leaves is their main purpose—**some species can eat over 27,000 times their own body weight in just a few weeks.**

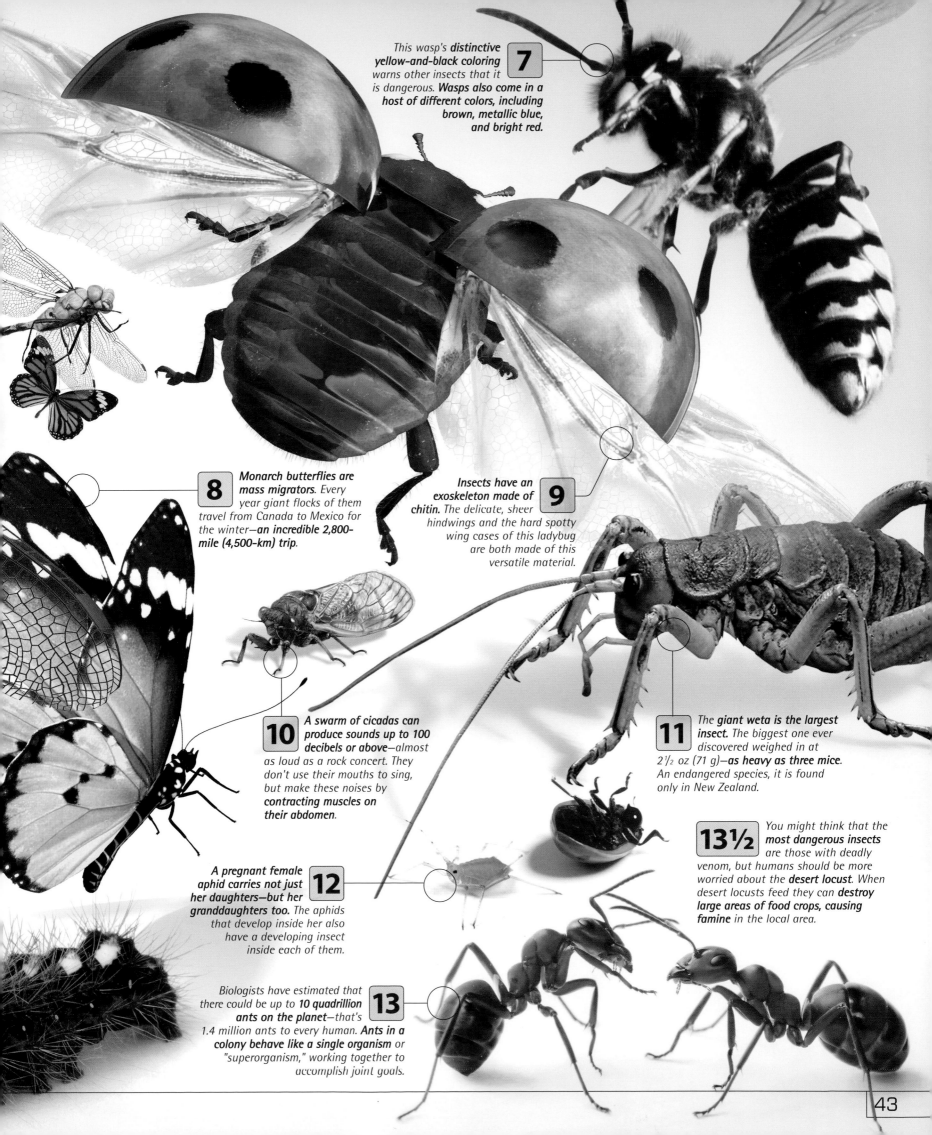

7 This wasp's *distinctive yellow-and-black coloring* warns other insects that it is dangerous. *Wasps also come in a host of different colors, including brown, metallic blue, and bright red.*

8 *Monarch butterflies are mass migrators.* Every year giant flocks of them travel from Canada to Mexico for the winter—*an incredible 2,800-mile (4,500-km) trip.*

9 *Insects have an exoskeleton made of chitin.* The delicate, sheer hindwings and the hard spotty wing cases of this ladybug are both made of this versatile material.

10 *A swarm of cicadas can produce sounds up to 100 decibels or above*—almost as loud as a rock concert. They don't use their mouths to sing, but make these noises by *contracting muscles on their abdomen.*

11 *The giant weta is the largest insect.* The biggest one ever discovered weighed in at 2¹/₂ oz (71 g)—*as heavy as three mice.* An endangered species, it is found only in New Zealand.

12 *A pregnant female aphid carries not just her daughters—but her granddaughters too.* The aphids that develop inside her also have a developing insect inside each of them.

13¹/₂ You might think that the *most dangerous insects* are those with deadly venom, but humans should be more worried about the *desert locust*. When desert locusts feed they can *destroy large areas of food crops, causing famine* in the local area.

13 Biologists have estimated that there could be up to *10 quadrillion ants on the planet*—that's 1.4 million ants to every human. *Ants in a colony behave like a single organism* or "superorganism," working together to accomplish joint goals.

FAMOUS PHARAOH

The name of Tutankhamun is world famous for the stunning treasures in his tomb, placed there to ease his journey to the next world. Life was often short in ancient Egypt and people believed in an afterlife, where they would live on forever.

1 *Ancient Egypt was a civilization that thrived on the banks of the Nile* for more than 3,000 years, from around 3,000 BCE. At the top of Egyptian society was the pharaoh—a ruler worshipped as a living god.

2 *Tutankhamun became pharaoh in 1336 BCE and died ten years later.* His mummy was found wearing a **solid gold death mask, weighing 22$\frac{1}{2}$ lb (10.2 kg)**. It is thought to be an actual portrait of his face.

3 *Tutankhamun's tomb lay undisturbed in the Valley of the Kings, near modern-day Luxor, for 3,000 years,* before British archaeologist Howard Carter discovered it in 1922. Carter spent 17 years cataloging the many treasures he found inside.

4 *Making a mummy took 70 days.* The internal organs were removed and **the body was washed and covered in natron** (a type of salt) to dry it out. The organs were preserved and then **placed back in the body**, packed with linen and straw.

5 *The ancient Egyptians mummified the bodies of pharaohs* **so that they could live again in the afterlife.** They believed the dead journeyed to the realm of the god Osiris, who would judge **whether they were worthy of eternal life.**

6 *The preserved body was wrapped in linen bandages. Unwrapped, these* **could stretch for 1 mile (1.6 km)**. In 19th-century England, **public unwrappings of mummies** were sometimes held at scientific societies.

7 *Tutankhamun's body was laid inside three coffins,* each fitting inside the next, which were then placed in a stone sarcophagus. The **innermost coffin was made of solid gold** and weighed a whopping 240 lb (110 kg).

8 *The two outer coffins were made of* **wood lined with gold leaf.** Some historians think that the **middle coffin and several other objects in the tomb were secondhand**—originally made for other royal figures.

9 *Tutankhamun is world famous today, but in life he was an insignificant ruler.* **He became pharaoh at about the age of nine and died aged only 19.** He may have been **murdered by a rival** who then seized the throne, but no one knows for sure.

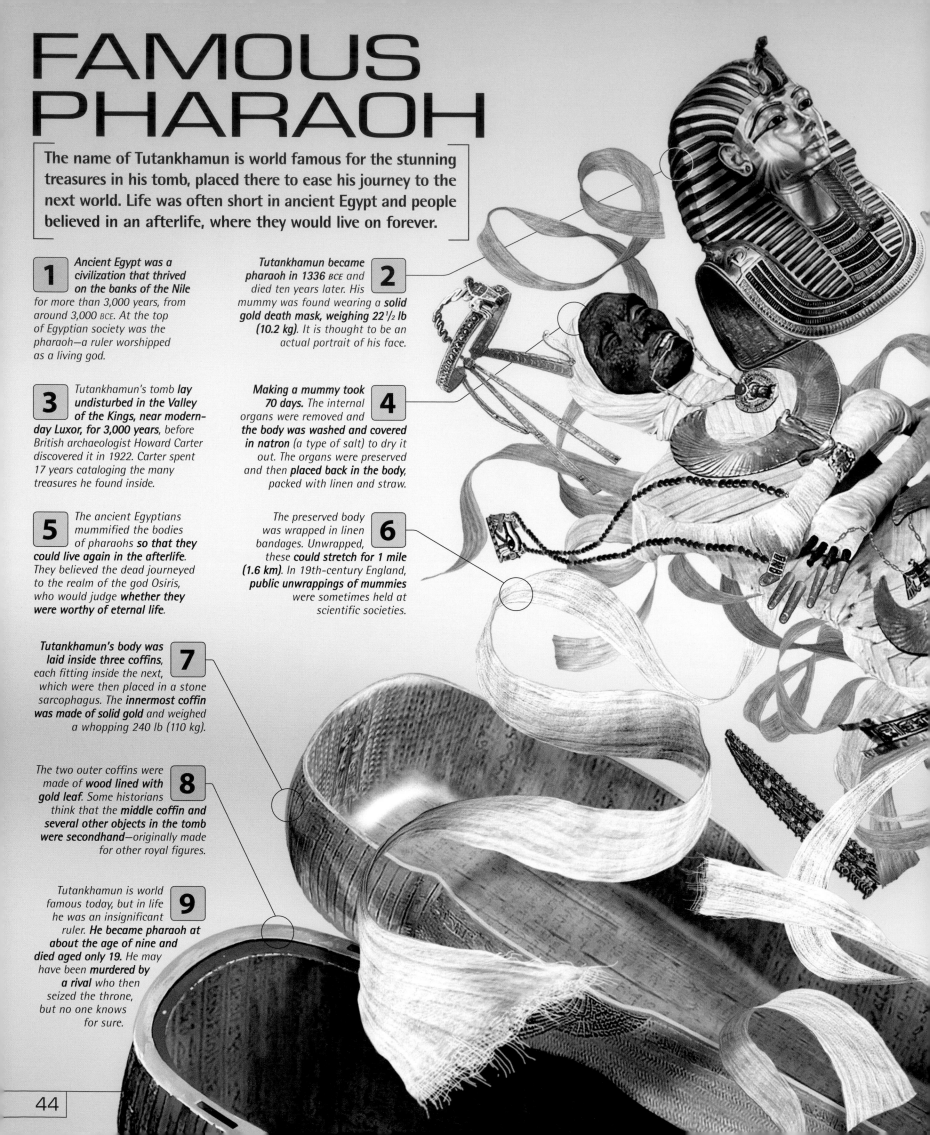

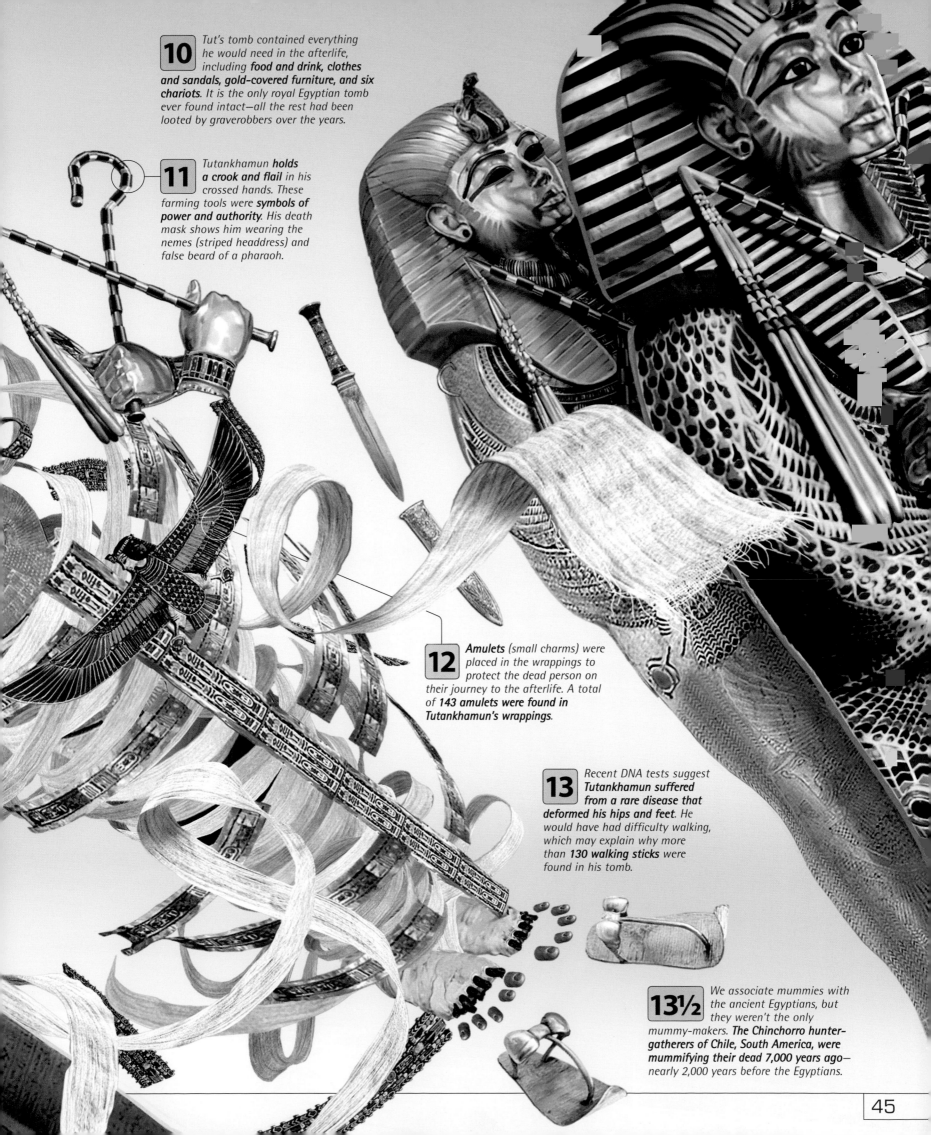

10 Tut's tomb contained everything he would need in the afterlife, including **food and drink, clothes and sandals, gold-covered furniture, and six chariots**. It is the only royal Egyptian tomb ever found intact—all the rest had been looted by graverobbers over the years.

11 Tutankhamun **holds a crook and flail** in his crossed hands. These farming tools were **symbols of power and authority**. His death mask shows him wearing the nemes (striped headdress) and false beard of a pharaoh.

12 **Amulets** (small charms) were placed in the wrappings to protect the dead person on their journey to the afterlife. A total of **143 amulets were found in** Tutankhamun's wrappings.

13 Recent DNA tests suggest **Tutankhamun suffered from a rare disease that deformed his hips and feet.** He would have had difficulty walking, which may explain why more than **130 walking sticks** were found in his tomb.

13½ We associate mummies with the ancient Egyptians, but they weren't the only mummy-makers. **The Chinchorro hunter-gatherers of Chile, South America, were mummifying their dead 7,000 years ago**—nearly 2,000 years before the Egyptians.

HEARD THE BUZZ?

We mostly think of flies as pests that buzz, carry dirt, and annoy us—like the housefly shown here. But there are more than 160,000 species of flies and while a few are dangerous, most cause no trouble. Some are actually very useful.

1 Flying insects have been around a long time, **the first true flies appearing 250 million years ago.** A true fly has one pair of wings, rather than two pairs like many other insects.

2 This housefly beats its wings up to 200 times a second, and can reach **speeds of 5 mph (8 km/h)** whether moving up and down, sideways, or backward.

3 A housefly's bristly body **may carry as many as 29 million germs,** picked up when it lands on dirt or rotten food. Serious fly-borne diseases include cholera and typhoid.

4 The most dangerous of all flies is the mosquito. This **bloodsucking insect carries malaria,** a disease that causes more than **400,000 deaths a year.**

5 The biggest flies in the world are the timber flies of Central and South America. These can reach a **whopping 3 in (8 cm) in length**—that's bigger than your palm.

6 Flies can walk on ceilings because **their feet have sticky pads and tiny claws** that fix onto most surfaces. They also **have taste buds on their feet and legs.**

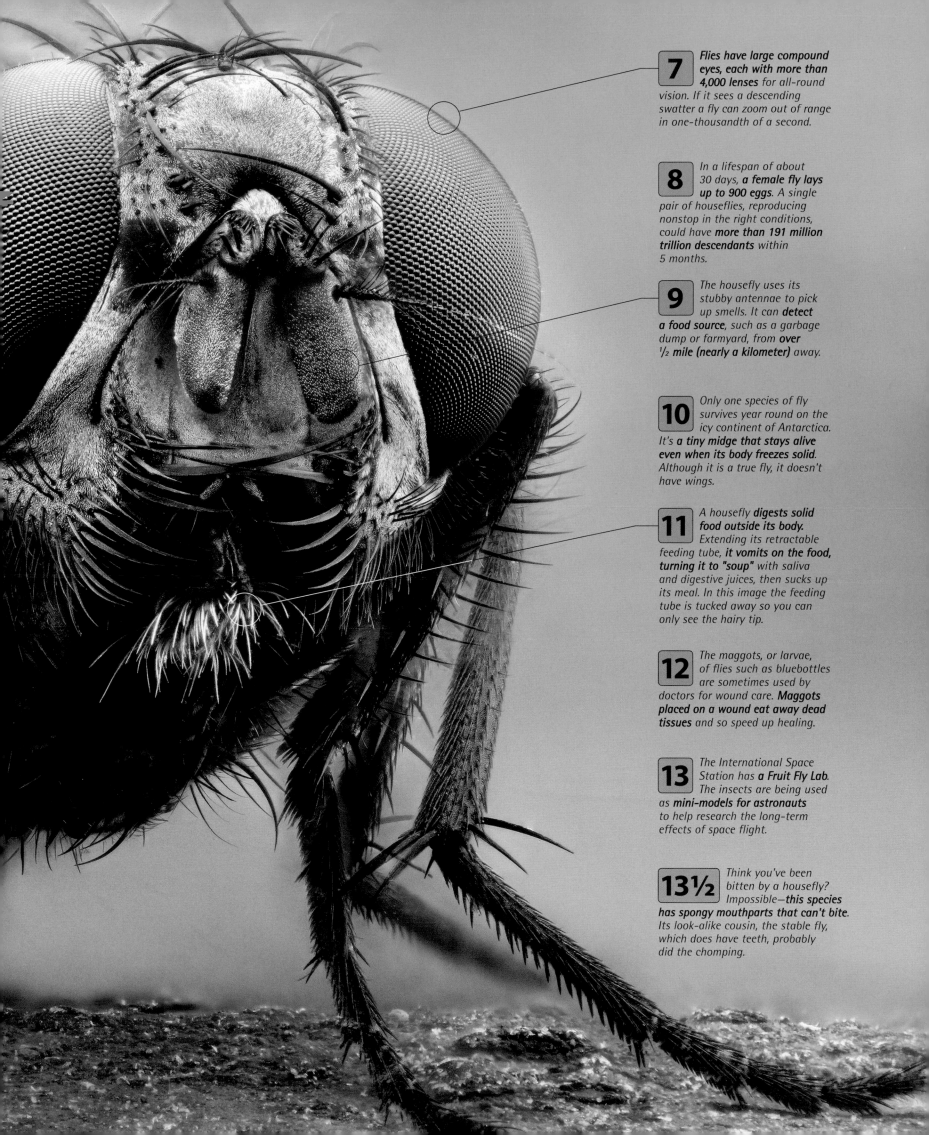

7 Flies have large compound eyes, each with more than **4,000 lenses** for all-round vision. If it sees a descending swatter a fly can zoom out of range in one-thousandth of a second.

8 In a lifespan of about 30 days, **a female fly lays up to 900 eggs.** A single pair of houseflies, reproducing nonstop in the right conditions, could have **more than 191 million trillion descendants** within 5 months.

9 The housefly uses its stubby antennae to pick up smells. It can **detect a food source**, such as a garbage dump or farmyard, from **over ¹/₂ mile (nearly a kilometer)** away.

10 Only one species of fly survives year round on the icy continent of Antarctica. It's **a tiny midge that stays alive even when its body freezes solid.** Although it is a true fly, it doesn't have wings.

11 A housefly **digests solid food outside its body.** Extending its retractable feeding tube, **it vomits on the food, turning it to "soup"** with saliva and digestive juices, then sucks up its meal. In this image the feeding tube is tucked away so you can only see the hairy tip.

12 The maggots, or larvae, of flies such as bluebottles are sometimes used by doctors for wound care. **Maggots placed on a wound eat away dead tissues** and so speed up healing.

13 The International Space Station has **a Fruit Fly Lab.** The insects are being used as **mini-models for astronauts** to help research the long-term effects of space flight.

13½ Think you've been bitten by a housefly? Impossible—**this species has spongy mouthparts that can't bite.** Its look-alike cousin, the stable fly, which does have teeth, probably did the chomping.

BIG IDEAS

Philosophy means "love of wisdom" in Greek. It's an area of study that asks lots of questions about existence and reality to deepen our understanding. Here are just a few of the big ideas history's biggest minds have puzzled over.

1 Philosophy began with the ancient Greeks. Perhaps their greatest thinker was **Socrates, who wanted people to understand the truth about themselves.** In 399 BCE, he was sentenced to either exile or death for corrupting young people with his ideas. Choosing death, **he drank the poison hemlock.**

2 Ancient Greek philosopher **Plato was concerned with the question of "What is beauty?"**—something still debated today. He also believed in **the importance of thinking things through—by reasoning.** In 387 BCE Plato opened Europe's first university, called The Academy, in Athens.

3 Aristotle was a pupil of Plato. A great scholar, he taught **the use of reason to work things out in a systematic way.** Aristotle was also a great scientist, and was fascinated by animal life. **He had one of the first zoos**—a collection of many exotic animals.

4 Chinese philosopher **Confucius developed a system for leading a good life** known as the Five Virtues. By 136 BCE, his code had become China's religion, called Confucianism. **For 2,000 years Chinese officials had to take an exam based on Confucius's ideals.**

5 The Buddhist religion is based on the teachings of the Buddha (c.563–c.483 BCE), who reflected under a lotus tree for 49 days until he achieved "enlightenment." **Buddhism is also very much a philosophy and one of its main ideas is the Middle Way**—that truth cannot be found in the unbending beliefs of religions, or in doubting everything, but in between.

6 The son of an Italian count, Thomas Aquinas lived from c.1225–74 and was a Dominican monk. **At a time when religion clashed with science and philosophy he taught that they could all work together** to help each other. He was later made a saint for his great work as a scholar of the Church.

7 In 1641 the great French philosopher and mathematician René Descartes wrote **"I think therefore I am."** He had once **doubted everything,** including his own existence. But he reasoned that if he could think, and doubt, then he could be certain he existed.

8 In the 18th century a cultural movement called **the Enlightenment swept across Europe**. It called for people to think things out for themselves, and its ideas included freedom of expression. German philosopher Immanuel Kant's rallying cry was, **"Dare to know! Have courage to use your own reason!"**

9 Englishman John Locke was another Enlightenment thinker. He believed **people should have the right to control their own bodies**. His ideas, known as "natural law," were **written into the US Declaration of Independence** of 1776.

10 You can still find the 18th-century British philosopher **Jeremy Bentham** at University College London. His skeleton, dressed in his own clothes and topped with a wax model of his head, is kept in a cabinet there. He thought we should aim for **"the greatest happiness of the greatest number."**

11 **How do you decide what to do in life?** German philosopher Friedrich Nietzsche thought each person should make their own choices, rather than listening to others. **He wanted people to experience life to the full—to be a "Superman"!** Nietzsche did not imagine anyone soaring through the air wearing a cape but rather becoming a great artist, thinker, or leader.

12 French philosopher Jean-Paul Sartre (1905–80) believed we can choose between two ways of life. Either we live the way everyone thinks we should, or **we can be "different,"** living the life that feels just right for us and finding meaning in it. It's up to us to decide.

13 Simone de Beauvoir **(1908–86) was a French philosopher and pioneer of feminism.** She argued that society expects women to behave in a certain way, and that there is a difference between being born female and conforming to society's ideas of what a woman should be.

13½ **Philosophy asks lots of questions, but where are the answers?** You won't find any definite answers. Philosophy is not like a science in which things can often be proved without doubt. A dozen philosophers may give a **dozen different answers** to the same question, or no answer at all.

GRAB A BITE

Food is the vital fuel we need to power our bodies. Each tasty morsel we eat gives us energy, keeps us warm, and allows our body to grow and regenerate. The classic American hamburger combines many of the essential food groups.

Balanced diet

There are five main food groups: carbohydrates (starchy foods like pasta, rice, and potatoes); proteins (meat, eggs, beans, and lentils); milk and dairy products; fruit and vegetables; and fats and sugars. Advice varies from country to country, but most experts agree that at least half of a healthy meal should be made up of fruit and vegetables, and that fats and sugars should be eaten more sparingly.

Fruit and vegetables

Dairy

Fats and sugars

Protein

Carbohydrates

The food wheel shows what proportion of your daily diet should come from each food group.

1 Bread is made from wheat, a staple food. **Staples are filling foods that form a large part of people's diets.** They vary from country to country, but include wheat, corn, and rice. Together this trio provides *more than half of the world's energy intake.*

2 *Around 9 billion burgers are served in US restaurants every year.* The fast food chain McDonald's alone sells 75 burgers every second of every day.

3 Mayonnaise is a sauce made from combining egg yolks and oil. **One tablespoon of mayonnaise contains around 90 calories—** that's the same as a small box of strawberries.

4 **Mustard** may taste sharp, but it actually **contains added sugar,** like many processed foods. A tablespoon of tomato ketchup contains *more sugar than a chocolate-chip cookie.*

5 *Every year, the world throws away* **around 1.4 billion tons of food.** *That's about one-third of all the food that gets produced. At the same time, one in nine people don't have enough to eat.*

6 Fruits and vegetables may be packed with vital **vitamins and minerals,** but they also contain a lot of water. We get around **20 percent of our water** intake from food.

8 Humans began milking cows around 3000 BCE and since then milk has been used to make all kinds of dairy products, like this cheese. **The French eat the most cheese—an average of 60 lb (26.8 kg) each in 2015.**

10 Today we associate ketchup with tomatoes, but back in the 1700s it was *usually made from mushrooms, seafood, or nuts.*

13½ *Despite rumors,* there is *no evidence that eating cheese before bed gives you nightmares.* However, high-fat foods are *hard for your body to digest, so a cheesy snack right before bedtime might lead to a disturbed night's sleep.*

7 *Pickling, salting, drying, and freezing* are just some of the ways we prevent food from going bad. This pickle has been *left in vinegar or salty water to preserve it.*

9 Cooked meat provides more energy than raw meat, and is easier to digest. Learning to cook meat may have given us bigger brains. Our *ancestors invented cooking 1.8 million years ago and experienced a surge in brain size.*

11 In 2013, scientists unveiled the *first burger to be grown in a lab.* Developed from the cells of cows, the meat patty cost a staggering *$325,000,* and received mixed reviews from food critics.

12 *In the future, we could all be eating insects.* They are less damaging to the environment than livestock and require less land and resources. In fact, *2 billion people across the world already eat insects* as part of their regular diet.

13 Ancient foods from our prehistoric past are sometimes dug up today. While excavating a tomb in Georgia, archaeologists found the world's oldest honey, *still edible after being preserved for more than 5,000 years.*

GET THE MESSAGE

I've got something to tell you, but how can I get my message across? From sending a letter as the ancient Romans did, to banging on a drum to warn of invading armies, there are so many more ways of communicating than sending a text.

1 In ancient Greece, *carrier pigeons were used to announce Olympic victors,* but in more modern times they have saved lives. During World War I, despite being badly injured, pigeon **Cher Ami flew 25 miles (40 km) to carry a message that saved 194 American soldiers.** He was awarded a medal for bravery.

2 As far back as 800 BCE, guards along the Great Wall of China sent **smoke signals to warn of invasions.** In ancient Greece, a **smoke alphabet was devised** to spell out specific messages.

3 Semaphore—holding out your arms in particular positions to spell out letters—is another ancient message system: in the 4th century BCE, the ancient Greeks built **towers with movable "arms" to send semaphore messages.** Modern semaphore systems use flags. At sea, the flags are red and yellow; on land, they are blue and white.

4 *Electronic communication kicked off with the telegraph* in 1816. Users tapped out messages, which were sent as electrical signals along wires. **In 1858, the first transatlantic message was sent via a cable under the ocean.** It was quicker than sending a ship (a 10-day trip), but still took 16 hours to transmit by Morse code.

5 **Morse code uses short and long signals (dots and dashes) to represent letters.** It was invented to send telegraph messages quickly. At first, messages were heard and written down, but a machine was invented to type out the messages using holes to show where the dots and dashes fell.

6 The **first phone call was made in 1876.** The oldest existing phone directory, from 1878, lists 391 people's names, but not their numbers: instead, you **called the operator and asked to be connected.**

7 When the US's parcel post started in 1913, **almost anything could be sent by mail**. In Ohio, a baby boy was sent to his grandparents at a cost of 15 cents.

8 The first radio signals were sent and received in 1895, but it took another 11 years for **the first radio entertainment program to be broadcast, from Massachusetts, US**, by Canadian inventor Reginald Fessenden. Today the most popular station is the BBC World Service, with many millions of listeners worldwide.

9 Hand-held two-way radios were invented in the 1930s, but the first to be known as a **walkie-talkie was actually worn as a backpack**. Developed by the US Army during World War II, the 5-lb (2-kg) metal box had a telephone receiver to make and receive calls.

10 In 1926, Scottish inventor John Logie Baird pioneered the mechanical "televisor." American Philo Farnsworth demonstrated his **all-electronic TV in 1934**—the same year as the first TV station launched. **The first advertisement followed in 1941**. It was for a watch company, and was aired in New York, US, before a baseball game.

11 Sent into space in 1962, the **Telstar communications satellites relayed TV and phone signals** across the Atlantic. Two Telstars are still up in orbit today, although they are no longer in use—but there are **more than 2,000 other satellites** up there doing the job.

12 Launched in 1984, the DynaTAC was the first commercially available mobile phone. It was **the size of a brick, weighed 2 lb (1 kg), and cost a hefty $3,995 (£3,200)**.

13 The **World Wide Web was launched in 1991**. Back then, most people had no idea what it was, but today there are more than 3 billion Internet users and 1 billion websites in the world. **Email is 20 years older than the WWW**: the first email was sent in the 1970s.

13½ You might think that mobile phones are quite modern, but being able to phone on the move is an old idea: **car phones date back to 1946!** They comprised a hefty handset attached to a 80-lb (36-kg) box that fixed into the car. They were more popular than mobile phones in the 1980s, but are now defunct.

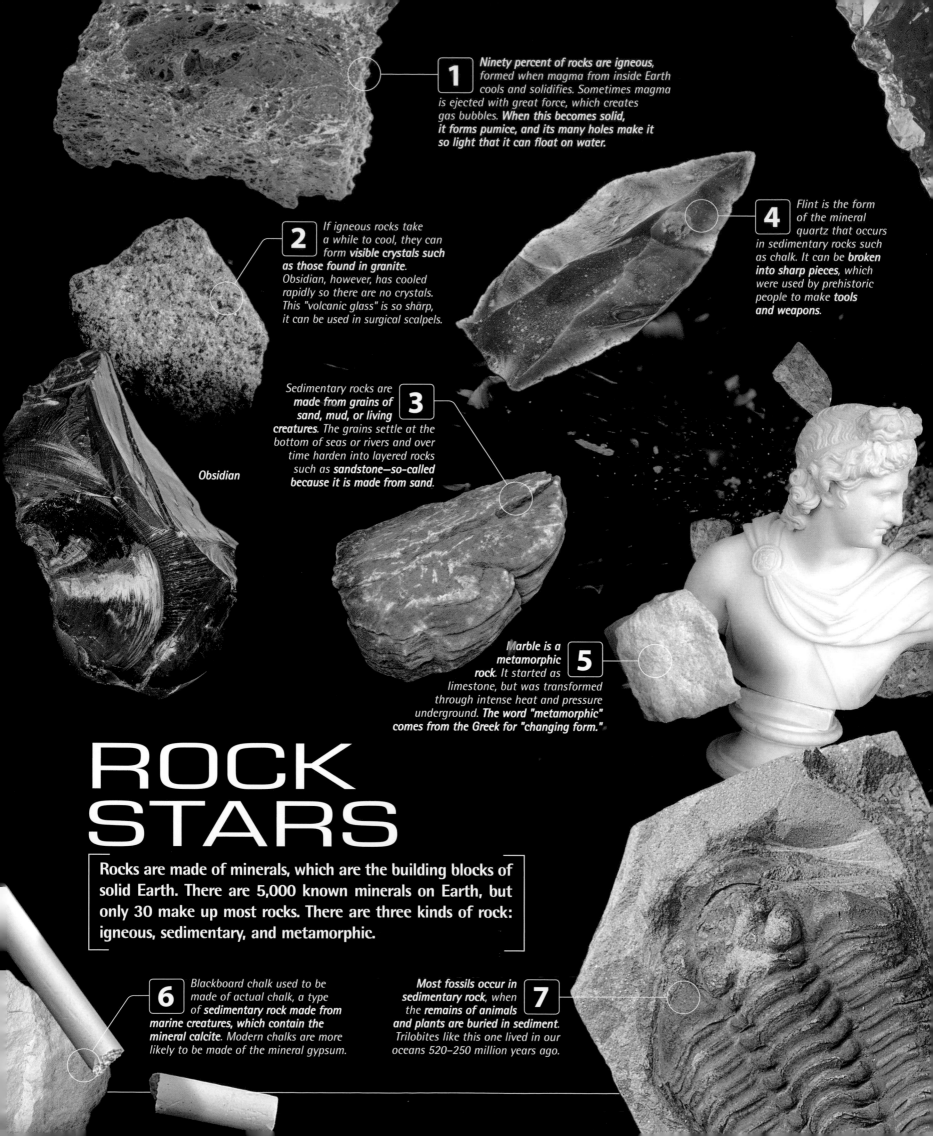

1 Ninety percent of rocks are igneous, formed when magma from inside Earth cools and solidifies. Sometimes magma is ejected with great force, which creates gas bubbles. **When this becomes solid, it forms pumice, and its many holes make it so light that it can float on water.**

2 If igneous rocks take a while to cool, they can form **visible crystals such as those found in granite.** Obsidian, however, has cooled rapidly so there are no crystals. This "volcanic glass" is so sharp, it can be used in surgical scalpels.

Obsidian

4 Flint is the form of the mineral quartz that occurs in sedimentary rocks such as chalk. It can be **broken into sharp pieces,** which were used by prehistoric people to make **tools and weapons.**

3 Sedimentary rocks are **made from grains of sand, mud, or living creatures.** The grains settle at the bottom of seas or rivers and over time harden into layered rocks such as **sandstone—so-called because it is made from sand.**

5 *Marble is a metamorphic rock.* It started as limestone, but was transformed through intense heat and pressure underground. **The word "metamorphic" comes from the Greek for "changing form."**

ROCK STARS

Rocks are made of minerals, which are the building blocks of solid Earth. There are 5,000 known minerals on Earth, but only 30 make up most rocks. There are three kinds of rock: igneous, sedimentary, and metamorphic.

6 Blackboard chalk used to be made of actual chalk, a type of **sedimentary rock made from marine creatures, which contain the mineral calcite.** Modern chalks are more likely to be made of the mineral gypsum.

7 *Most fossils occur in sedimentary rock,* when the remains of animals and plants are buried in sediment. Trilobites like this one lived in our oceans 520–250 million years ago.

8 *Amethyst is the purple variety of quartz*—one of the most abundant minerals on Earth. A quartz crystal vibrates if an electric current passes through it, and *quartz is used in watches* because these vibrations can be used to keep a steady time.

Prized for centuries, semiprecious **lapis lazuli was used for making beads in Neolithic times** (3000 BCE) and later was ground up to make eyeshadow and paint. **The color "azure" is named after lazuli.** **9**

Many minerals occur in glittering crystals, which **form as liquid chemicals turn solid.** Their **10** shape depends on the way their atoms cling together. The mineral **crocoite**—made up of lead and chromium—has **long, four-sided crystals that are usually vivid red.**

The **cube-shaped crystals of pyrite shine a pale yellow, giving this iron mineral the nickname of "fool's gold."** Pyrite is named **11** from the Greek word for fire because it sparks when you hit it against steel, and in the 16th century it was used in guns to create a spark for firing.

12 Around **45,000 meteorites (space rocks) have been found on Earth.** Most are stony meteorites: just **five percent of them are iron, such as this octahedrite.** The long crystals formed when the meteorite slowly cooled. It is made of the same minerals (iron and nickel) as found in Earth's core, but **40 minerals have been found in meteorites that don't occur on Earth.**

There are **two different minerals we know as jade: jadeite and nephrite.** In ancient China, nephrite jade was **13** believed to **protect dead bodies and ensure immortality,** and so was used to make burial suits for royalty.

13½ You might think that **all rocks are hard,** but some are not. Clay is a type of sedimentary rock: just **add water and you can make it soft** enough to mold into plates, pots, and pipes. Bake it, however, and it will be fixed into the shape you've made (unless you drop it).

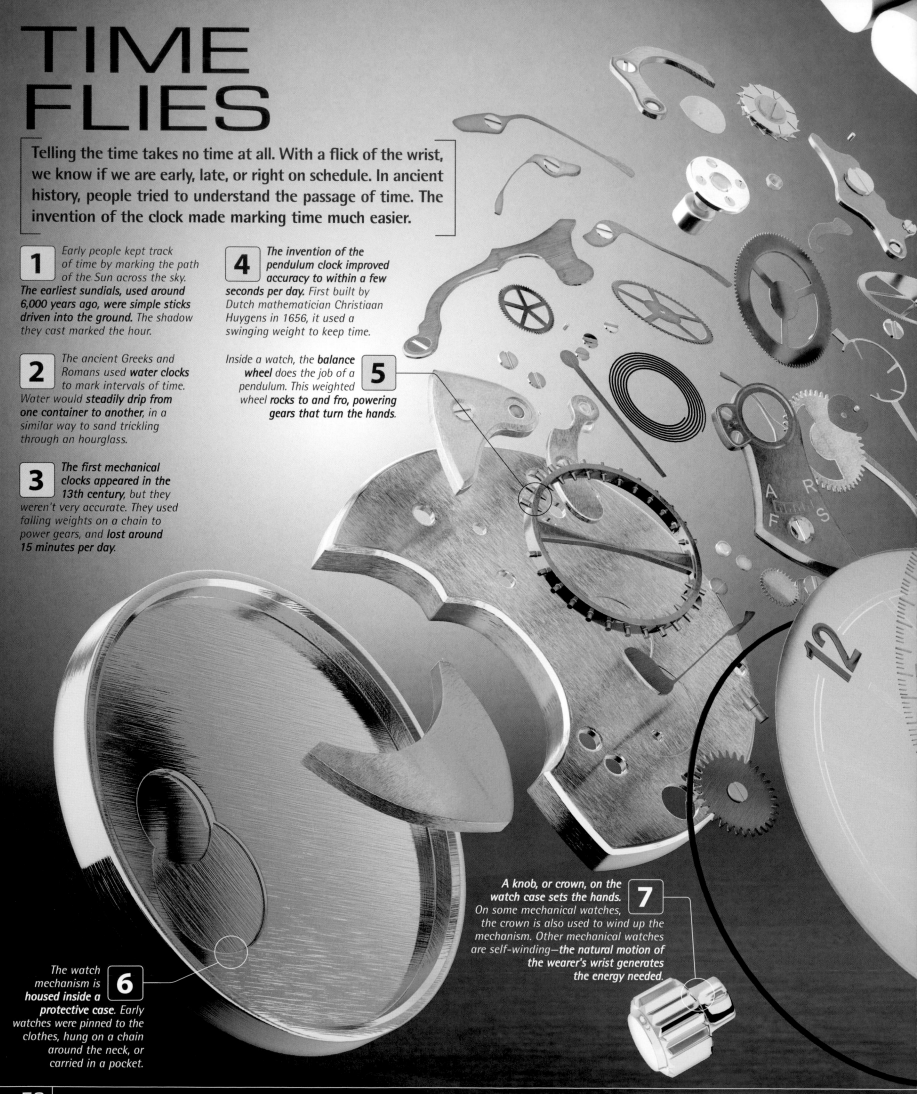

TIME FLIES

Telling the time takes no time at all. With a flick of the wrist, we know if we are early, late, or right on schedule. In ancient history, people tried to understand the passage of time. The invention of the clock made marking time much easier.

1 Early people kept track of time by marking the path of the Sun across the sky. *The earliest sundials, used around 6,000 years ago, were simple sticks driven into the ground.* The shadow they cast marked the hour.

2 The ancient Greeks and Romans used **water clocks** to mark intervals of time. Water would **steadily drip from one container to another,** in a similar way to sand trickling through an hourglass.

3 *The first mechanical clocks appeared in the 13th century,* but they weren't very accurate. They used falling weights on a chain to power gears, and **lost around 15 minutes per day.**

4 *The invention of the pendulum clock improved accuracy to within a few seconds per day.* First built by Dutch mathematician Christiaan Huygens in 1656, it used a swinging weight to keep time.

Inside a watch, the **balance wheel** does the job of a pendulum. This weighted wheel **rocks to and fro, powering gears that turn the hands.** **5**

6 The watch mechanism is **housed inside a protective case.** Early watches were pinned to the clothes, hung on a chain around the neck, or carried in a pocket.

A knob, or crown, on the watch case sets the hands. On some mechanical watches, the crown is also used to wind up the mechanism. Other mechanical watches are self-winding—**the natural motion of the wearer's wrist generates the energy needed.** **7**

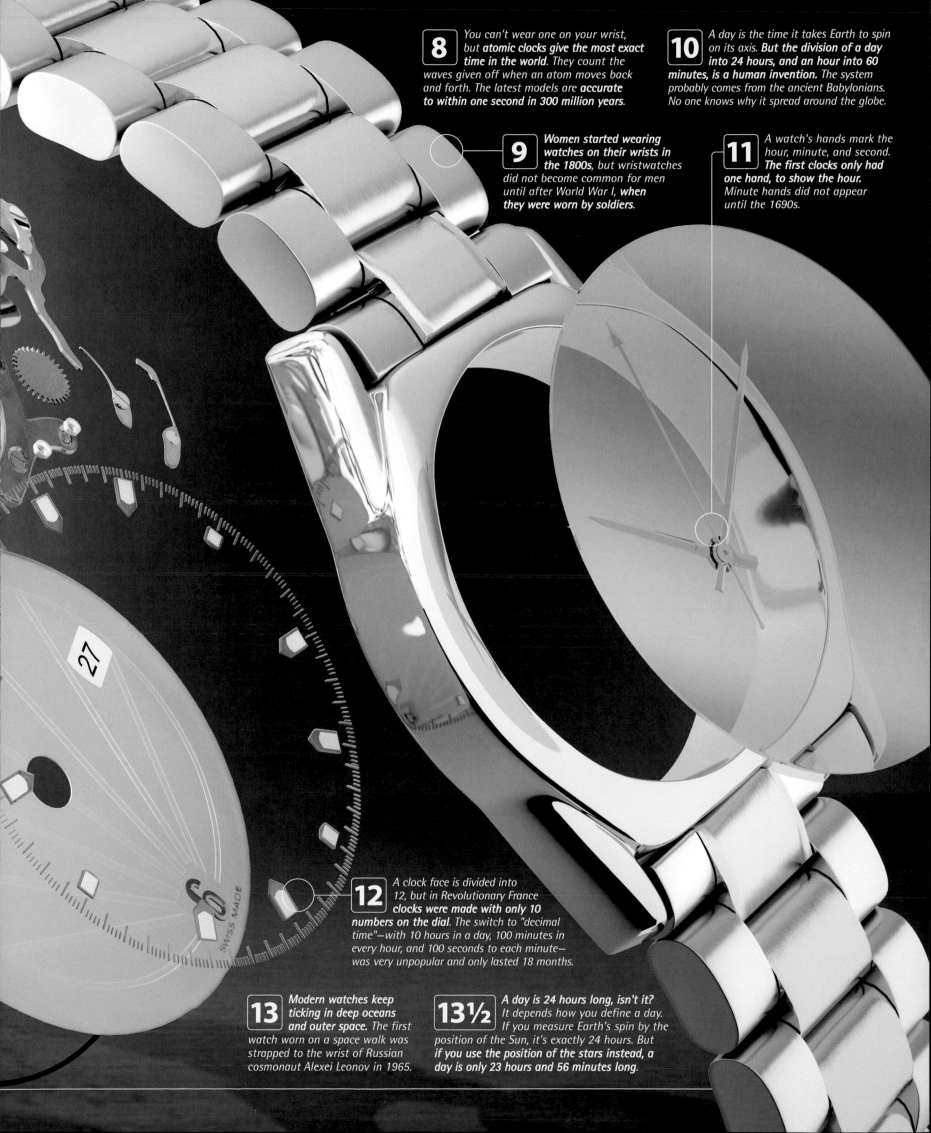

8 You can't wear one on your wrist, but **atomic clocks give the most exact time in the world.** They count the waves given off when an atom moves back and forth. The latest models are **accurate to within one second in 300 million years.**

10 A day is the time it takes Earth to spin on its axis. **But the division of a day into 24 hours, and an hour into 60 minutes, is a human invention.** The system probably comes from the ancient Babylonians. No one knows why it spread around the globe.

9 **Women started wearing watches on their wrists in the 1800s,** but wristwatches did not become common for men until after World War I, **when they were worn by soldiers.**

11 A watch's hands mark the hour, minute, and second. **The first clocks only had one hand, to show the hour.** Minute hands did not appear until the 1690s.

12 A clock face is divided into 12, but in Revolutionary France **clocks were made with only 10 numbers on the dial.** The switch to "decimal time"—with 10 hours in a day, 100 minutes in every hour, and 100 seconds to each minute— was very unpopular and only lasted 18 months.

13 **Modern watches keep ticking in deep oceans and outer space.** The first watch worn on a space walk was strapped to the wrist of Russian cosmonaut Alexei Leonov in 1965.

13½ A day is 24 hours long, isn't it? It depends how you define a day. If you measure Earth's spin by the position of the Sun, it's exactly 24 hours. But **if you use the position of the stars instead, a day is only 23 hours and 56 minutes long.**

Invertebrates are animals without backbones, such as insects, worms, snails, and other creepy-crawlies. **A whopping 97 percent of all animal species are invertebrates.**

1

Vertebrates are animals with backbones. Half of all vertebrate species are fishes. Sailfish hunt in groups. **They attack together, slashing with their swordlike bills to injure as many fish as possible.**

2

3 Owls see prey in dim light with their huge eyes. Their eyes cannot move, though, so **these birds turn their heads up to 270 degrees from side to side** to look around.

Mantis shrimps have the most sophisticated color vision of any animal. They watch for prey on coral reefs, then smash their victims to pieces with clublike claws.

4

Green lynx spider

5 Many plant-eating insects have ravenous appetites. **A locust swarm, which consists of at least 40 million insects, eats the same amount of food in one day as about 35,000 people.**

ANIMAL KINGDOM

The dazzling diversity of the animal kingdom covers 1.5 million species, from huge whales to microscopic worms. Animals live across all the continents and in every ocean, displaying amazing survival skills and surprising behaviors.

Many animals go to extreme lengths to avoid being eaten. **The porcupine fish swallows seawater to inflate into a spiky ball more than twice its usual size.**

6

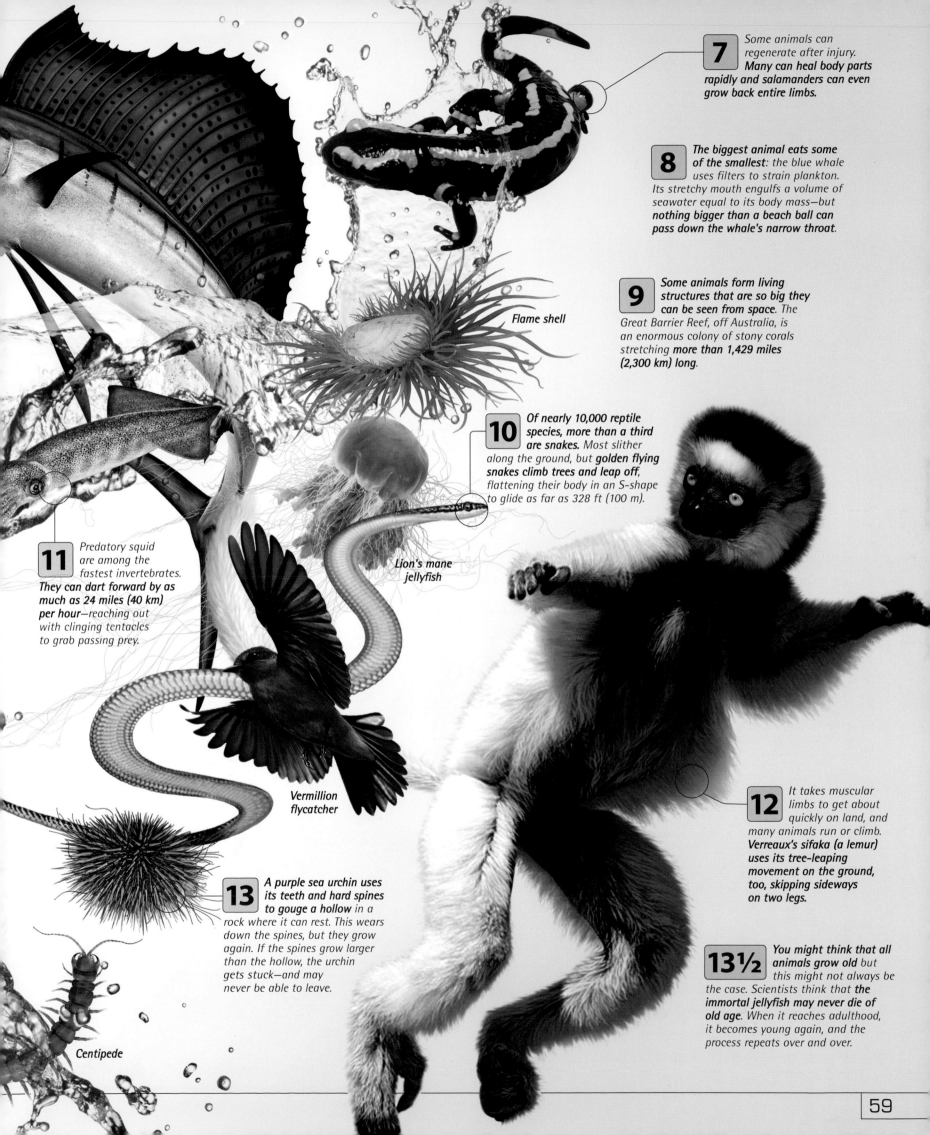

7 Some animals can regenerate after injury. **Many can heal body parts rapidly and salamanders can even grow back entire limbs.**

8 The biggest animal eats some of the smallest: the blue whale uses filters to strain plankton. Its stretchy mouth engulfs a volume of seawater equal to its body mass—but **nothing bigger than a beach ball can pass down the whale's narrow throat.**

9 Some animals form living structures that are so big they can be seen from space. The Great Barrier Reef, off Australia, is an enormous colony of stony corals stretching **more than 1,429 miles (2,300 km) long.**

Flame shell

10 Of nearly 10,000 reptile species, more than a third are snakes. Most slither along the ground, but **golden flying snakes climb trees and leap off,** flattening their body in an S-shape to glide as far as 328 ft (100 m).

Lion's mane jellyfish

11 Predatory squid are among the fastest invertebrates. **They can dart forward by as much as 24 miles (40 km) per hour**—reaching out with clinging tentacles to grab passing prey.

Vermillion flycatcher

12 It takes muscular limbs to get about quickly on land, and many animals run or climb. Verreaux's sifaka (a lemur) uses its tree-leaping movement on the ground, too, skipping sideways on two legs.

13 A purple sea urchin uses its teeth and hard spines **to gouge a hollow** in a rock where it can rest. This wears down the spines, but they grow again. If the spines grow larger than the hollow, the urchin gets stuck—and may never be able to leave.

13½ You might think that all animals grow old but this might not always be the case. Scientists think that **the immortal jellyfish may never die of old age.** When it reaches adulthood, it becomes young again, and the process repeats over and over.

Centipede

1 For over 500 years, the city of *Rome in Italy sent its armies to conquer and control* the lands around the Mediterranean Sea and much of Western Europe. By the beginning of the 2nd century CE, the *Roman Empire extended from Scotland in the north to Syria in the east*.

2 The Romans built nearly *80,000 miles (130,000 km) of roads* so the army could move around the Empire quickly to wherever it was needed. Wherever they went, the soldiers brought with them the benefits of Roman living, such as *sewage systems, public baths, and underfloor heating*.

3 Our word century—100 years—comes from the Latin *centum*, meaning 100. However, *there were only 80 men in a military century*, and the commander of this military unit was called a centurion.

To wear the armor of a legionary soldier, you had to be a Roman citizen. *Soldiers signed up from about the age of 20 for 25 years* and were not allowed to marry. If they made it to retirement, they were *given a plot of land*. **4**

5 A legionary's gladius (short sword) *could slice through bone and muscle*. It was a thrusting sword, ideal when the legionaries were at *close quarters with the enemy*. Very often, their opponents had slashing blades that were too long to use efficiently in close combat.

6 Soldiers wore a crest of dyed red *horsehair or feathers on their helmets*. The crest usually went from front to back, but centurions wore them sideways so that their men could identify them in battle.

7 Our word salary comes from *sal, the Roman for salt*, which has given rise to speculation that the soldiers were paid in salt. The Romans built their first and busiest main road, the Via Salaria ("Salt Road"), from Rome to the Adriatic Sea, where the precious preservative was collected and traded.

8 A Roman soldier's *gear weighed about 90 lb (40 kg)—as much as a 12-year-old child*. As well as his armor, weapons, shield, and woolen cloak, a legionary carried digging tools, a water bottle, and cooking pans.

ROMANS RULE

The world has rarely seen such a highly trained army as that of the mighty Roman Empire. Each legionary (infantry soldier) was a mean fighting machine. As a whole, the army was organized, disciplined, and almost unbeatable.

9 Noncitizens living within the Roman Empire joined the army as cavalry and **archers** and were granted citizenship on retirement. Called auxiliaries, they made up about 60 percent of the total fighting force of around 450,000 men.

10 Every soldier carried a scutum (curved shield) that covered his body. When attacking a fortress, **soldiers advanced together holding their shields over their heads**. This was known as a testudo (tortoise) because **the cluster of shields resembled a tortoise's shell**.

11 This shield is decorated with **a design of eagle's wings and lightning bolts**—emblems of mighty Jupiter, king of the Roman gods. The city of Rome was under Jupiter's special protection. Each unit bore its own set of symbols on its shields.

12 Discipline was harsh. The **worst punishments were for desertion**, when the soldier could be **beheaded, crucified, or thrown off a high rock**. If a whole unit mutinied, it could be **"decimated."** From the Latin meaning "remove one-tenth," this punishment involved **executing one in every 10 soldiers at random**.

13 Army boots had to be tough because **Roman soldiers marched up to 20 miles (30 km) a day** in them. They had thick soles studded with nails, and were open at the sides like sandals.

13½ Carvings of Roman soldiers show them with bare feet, but in fact **they wore socks with their sandals in cold regions**. A letter to a soldier serving on Hadrian's Wall in northern Britain refers to socks—and to his request for **two pairs of underwear**.

1 Seeds *need warmth and moisture before they will germinate* (begin to grow). Even if a seed is planted upside down, it will still *sprout the right way up.*

Sunflower seeds

2 Some seeds, like this cherry "pit", are *surrounded by juicy fruit*. Animals eat the fruit and spread the seeds by *pooing them out far from the parent plant.*

SUPER SEEDS

Seeds are survival capsules for plants. Each seed, however tiny, contains the beginnings of a new plant and a food store that can keep it alive—sometimes for many years—until conditions are just right for it to grow.

3 These *spiky burdock seeds*, or burs, *hook onto the fur of animals* in order to travel away from the original plant. A Swiss engineer came up with the idea for Velcro when he spotted them tangled in his dog's fur.

4 Seeds are the original space travelers. In 1946, *corn seeds* traveling on a US V2 rocket became *the first organisms to be launched into space.*

5 Larger than a human head, *the seeds of the coco de mer palm are the biggest of any plant*. They can weigh as much as 55 lb (25 kg).

Custard apple

6 These explosive seedpods belong to the *Himalayan balsam*, which ejects its seeds violently. The pods burst open when touched and *can fire the seeds up to 39 ft (12 m) away.*

7 *Castor beans* contain the *deadly poison ricin*. In 1978, Bulgarian Georgi Markov was assassinated by being jabbed with an umbrella that *injected a tiny ricin bullet* into his body.

8 The **lotus** is a water plant that produces seeds in a **large, flattened seedhead**. The seeds fall into the water and are washed away. The dried, empty seedpods **can spark horror in those suffering from trypophobia**—fear of holes.

Lotus seedpod

9 Horse chestnut seeds are used in the game of conkers. The shiny brown seeds are **dried and threaded onto a string**. Players take turns to try and **smash each other's conkers** with their own.

Acorn

10 The **squirting cucumber** contains a sticky surprise. When the fruit of the plant is ripe, it bursts, **ejecting the seeds everywhere in a stream of thick liquid.**

11 In 2012, Russian researchers **grew a plant using 32,000-year-old campion seeds.** The seeds were found in Siberia, preserved deep in the frozen earth, where they are believed to have been **stashed by an ice-age squirrel.**

12 Lightweight **dandelion seeds** are easily scattered by the wind. Each is attached to a feathery parachute that can carry it at least **6 miles (10 km) from the original plant.**

13 Each seed of a pomegranate fruit is surrounded in a **fleshy covering known as an aril.** The leathery outer skin of the fruit splits open so that **birds can eat the sweet, juicy arils** and carry away the seeds.

Pomegranate aril

13½ Don't worry if you swallow a seed: **it won't grow into a plant in your stomach.** Your body might be warm and moist, but a seed needs oxygen and sunlight to germinate.

1 Music is much more than just sound. **It's one of the few activities that uses your whole brain,** including the parts that control emotion and memory. This is why **music can bring tears to your eyes,** or make you want to jump up and dance with joy.

2 We know that **early people made music using drums, rattles, and flutes** crafted from wood, seeds, and animal skin. A **40,000-year-old whistle made of the hollow toe bone of a reindeer** was found at one prehistoric site in France.

3 Classical music is a European style that developed in the 1600s. Perhaps **the greatest classical composer of all was the Austrian prodigy Wolfgang Amadeus Mozart.** In 1764, he wrote his first symphony aged just eight. When he died aged 35, he had composed more than 600 works.

4 For big music you need an **orchestra, which is usually made up of 70 to 100 instrumentalists,** playing string, percussion, brass and woodwind instruments, and keyboard. The loudest instruments sit behind the quieter ones to balance the sound. In 2016, **an orchestra with a record-breaking 7,548 musicians** played in a football stadium in Frankfurt, Germany.

5 The world's most expensive instrument is **a violin handmade in 1721 by Italian Antonio Stradivari, which was auctioned for nearly $16 million** in 2011. This mastercraftsman made 600 instruments, known as "Strads," famous for the quality of their sound. **To this day, his skill has never been matched.**

6 Mainstream music styles often have their roots in folk music. **A big influence on popular music today is blues,** which began as the songs of black slaves in the southern US, who sung as they labored. Blues bands played banjos, guitars, and harmonicas, and sometimes **instruments made from everyday objects, such as washtubs, pitchers, and bottles.**

7 Whenever there's a party, there's music! One of the biggest parties in the world is the Mardi Gras carnival in Rio de Janeiro, Brazil. **Every year about 300 bands take to the streets playing samba—a traditional music of Brazil—**to get two million revelers each day dancing to the beat.

DON'T STOP THE MUSIC

The world of music is like a giant jukebox of different genres. From classical and country to rock and reggae, you'll find a style that sounds like music to your ears. Happy, sad, excited, or chilled, there's nothing like music for creating a mood.

8 Traditional guitars make a beautiful sound but are too quiet to be lead instruments. In the 1940s, however, **electrical amplification was added and the guitar got a whole lot louder.** One of the first was a solid wooden post known as "the log."

9 The title of King of Rock-and-Roll goes to Elvis Presley. From the 1950s, his unique mix of country, rhythm, and blues revolutionized pop music. **The best-selling solo artist of all time, Elvis is estimated to have sold over one billion records.** Although he died in 1977, he lives on through the 80,000 people who make a living impersonating him.

10 People love to sing, as demonstrated by the popularity of karaoke. *Meaning "empty orchestra," the sing-along machine was invented in 1971 by Japanese drummer Daisuke Inoue.* One of the most-played karaoke songs today is Let It Go, from the 2013 film Frozen.

11 In 1977, a spacecraft was launched to explore the Universe. In case it should ever be found by an alien life form, the craft took with it **a gold-plated disk of sounds and images to show the diversity of life on Earth, including music.** The broad selection of styles ranged from Azerbaijani bagpipes to singing from Zaire, as well as the rock-and-roll music of Chuck Berry.

12 The **best-selling album of all time is Michael Jackson's Thriller.** Since its release in 1982, it has sold **more than 65 million copies.** The zombie dance sequence for the title track remains one of the best-known music videos ever.

13 Music makes money, and **the market in the US is more than triple that of any other country, worth more than $15 billion in 2016.** Live music ticket sales contribute the largest share. In 2016, top-seller Bruce Springsteen grossed $268.3 from his world tour, closely followed by Beyoncé at $256.4 million.

13½ In 1993, a study claimed that **listening to Mozart made people brainier.** Parents played his work to their children even before they were born. The "Mozart effect" was short-lived, however, because it was later proved that his music had **no lasting effect on listener intelligence.**

GOING SUPERSONIC

Since the invention of powered vehicles, people have used them to travel faster and faster. In the last 70 years, transportation has gone supersonic—faster than the speed of sound, known as Mach 1, more than 760 mph (1,230 km/h).

1 The first person to fly at supersonic speeds was American pilot *Charles "Chuck" Yeager*. He *"broke the sound barrier"* on October 14, 1947, in a bullet-shaped aircraft called *X-1*, at an altitude of 8½ miles (13.7 km).

2 On October 15, 1997—50 years and one day after Chuck Yeager broke the sound barrier—*British pilot Andy Green became the first person to break the sound barrier in a land vehicle*. The car, called Thrust SSC, was powered by two jet engines.

3 *Only two supersonic passenger planes have been in service so far.* These were the Russian Tupolev Tu-144 and the British-French Concorde. The Tu-144 made its last commercial flight in 1978, and Concorde's last flight was in 2003.

4 One reason Concorde was withdrawn from service was due to the *high cost of fuel*. During its regular 3½-hour flight from London, UK, to New York, US, Concorde burned through about 24,000 gallons (90,000 liters) of fuel—about *240 gallons (900 liters) for each of the 100 passengers.*

5 As an airplane approaches supersonic speeds, it creates *waves of air pressure that form a short-lived cloud*, called a vapor cone. At supersonic speeds, *a loud sound, called a sonic boom, will be heard by people on the ground.*

6 At supersonic speed, *air resistance creates a lot of heat, which makes the metal fuselage (skin of the airplane) expand by several inches.* A Concorde engineer once placed his cap in the gap that appeared in his aircraft when it expanded. The cap stuck when the aircraft cooled.

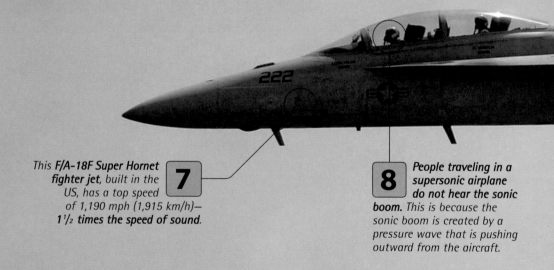

7 This *F/A-18F Super Hornet fighter jet*, built in the US, has a top speed of 1,190 mph (1,915 km/h)— 1½ times the speed of sound.

8 *People traveling in a supersonic airplane do not hear the sonic boom.* This is because the sonic boom is created by a pressure wave that is pushing outward from the aircraft.

⌄ Sonic boom

Moving objects push the air in front of them out of the way, creating pressure waves like the water wave in front of a moving boat. The wave travels away at the speed of sound—but if the object is moving faster than that, the pressure wave bunches up into a shock wave, which is heard as a sonic boom.

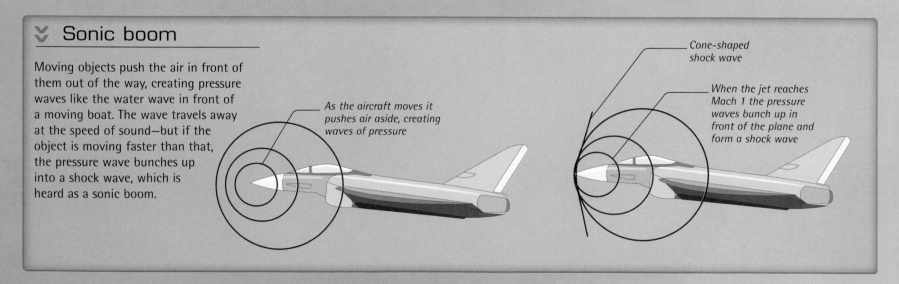

As the aircraft moves it pushes air aside, creating waves of pressure

Cone-shaped shock wave

When the jet reaches Mach 1 the pressure waves bunch up in front of the plane and form a shock wave

13½ It may seem that a sonic boom is a one-off sound, which happens only when the airplane passes the speed of sound. **In fact, the sonic boom is a continuous booming sound** that is produced as long as the airplane is supersonic.

13 While "supersonic" is anything faster than Mach 1, "hypersonic" means faster than Mach 5 (five times the speed of sound). **The fastest ever airplane is NASA's unmanned experimental X-43.** In 2004, it reached **"high hypersonic" speeds of Mach 9.6**—almost 10 times the speed of sound.

12 On October 14, 2012, Austrian daredevil Felix Baumgartner became **the first person to break the sound barrier while falling freely** through the air. Baumgartner jumped from a capsule at the incredible altitude of 24 miles (39 km) and **reached a speed of 844 mph (1,358 km/h)—more than Mach 1**—before landing safely with a parachute.

11 Meteors (shooting stars) are tiny rocks that enter Earth's atmosphere from space. They hit the atmosphere at extremely high speeds, and **always create a sonic boom**—although they are so high up it is rarely heard at ground level.

9 When a whip makes a cracking sound, it is because the very tip, called the cracker, is moving faster than the speed of sound. **The cracking sound is actually a sonic boom**—a miniature version of the loud sound made by a supersonic aircraft.

10 The vapor cone forms around the aircraft at "transonic speed" (just below the speed of sound). The air pressure changes rapidly from high to low around the fast-moving airplane, making the water vapor in the air condense into a cloud.

FEEDING TIME

Animals need to eat food—and other living things provide their breakfast, lunch, and dinner. All plants and animals depend on one another to stay alive, linked in food chains where each organism provides energy for the next.

1 *Rabbits are herbivores, eating greenery in summer and surviving on twigs, bark, and pine needles in winter. Rabbits' teeth are constantly growing—up to 5 in (12 cm) a year—but they get worn down by the silica granules in the grass they eat.*

2 *Plants are rich in nutrients, but tough to digest. A rabbit's digestive system is 16 ft (5 m) long and works hard to get nourishment from grass. Rabbits even eat their own droppings so the meal travels through the gut twice.*

3 *Food chains start with plants using sunlight's energy, carbon dioxide from the air, and water to make food. Each year, this process—called photosynthesis—removes more than 100 billion tons of carbon from the air.*

4 *Many plants make poisons to deter plant-eaters. Clover leaves release deadly cyanide when crushed, which repels snails and herbivorous insects.*

Pyramid of numbers

Energy gets passed through a food chain as food-producing plants are eaten by herbivores, and then herbivores are eaten by carnivores. But growth and movement use up energy, and some things end up dying and decomposing without being eaten, so the amount of energy reduces as it passes up the chain. This results in a "pyramid of numbers" within an ecosystem: there are lots of plants, but fewer herbivores and even fewer carnivores because there's less energy to support them. Top predators are the rarest of all.

Top predators are fewest in number in an ecosystem.

There are fewer carnivores than herbivores.

There are fewer herbivores than plants.

Plants are the most numerous.

8 Top predators are those that are not preyed upon by other animals. This red-tailed hawk is a **top predator** in the North American fields and deserts where it lives. It **swoops down** on prey and sinks its razor-sharp talons into the animal's head and neck.

9 Meat is so rich in nutrients that **carnivores need to eat less frequently than herbivores**. Birds of prey may kill every few days—but **big snakes can go for months without feeding**.

10 **Many animals eat lots of different species**, so individual food chains come together to form a complex food web. As well as snakes, this red-tailed hawk eats rats, mice, voles, birds, and rabbits.

11 Many animals are neither strictly herbivores nor carnivores: they are **omnivores that eat a variety of foods**. Brown bears are the largest omnivores, with a diet ranging from berries, nuts, and leaves to salmon and cattle.

7 **Snakes do not chew their food**, so they must swallow prey whole. Their highly flexible jaws can **open wider than their head**, but it can still take more than two hours to swallow a rabbit.

12 When a living thing dies or an animal poops, the **nutrients it contains are recycled**, courtesy of **decomposers such as bacteria and fungi** breaking down the waste. Without decomposers, the planet would be covered in dead things and dung.

6 Rattlesnakes locate their next meal by **using heat-sensitive pits on the side of their head to pick up tiny changes in temperature**. They can sense a rabbit's body warmth from 3 ft (1 m) away.

13 A lot of the energy in an animal's food is used for growth. But **some is lost as heat**. Small, warm-blooded animals can lose more than 90 percent of their energy as heat.

5 Snakes are predators of live prey. Venomous snakes use a toxic bite to immobilize and kill victims. **This rattlesnake's venom can kill a rabbit within 10 minutes.**

13½ We like to think that **humans are at the top of the food chain**—but humans are omnivores (we eat plants and meat), which puts us **somewhere in the middle**. With the advantages of civilization and technology, we eat what we want and don't often get eaten ourselves, but **true top predators eat only meat**.

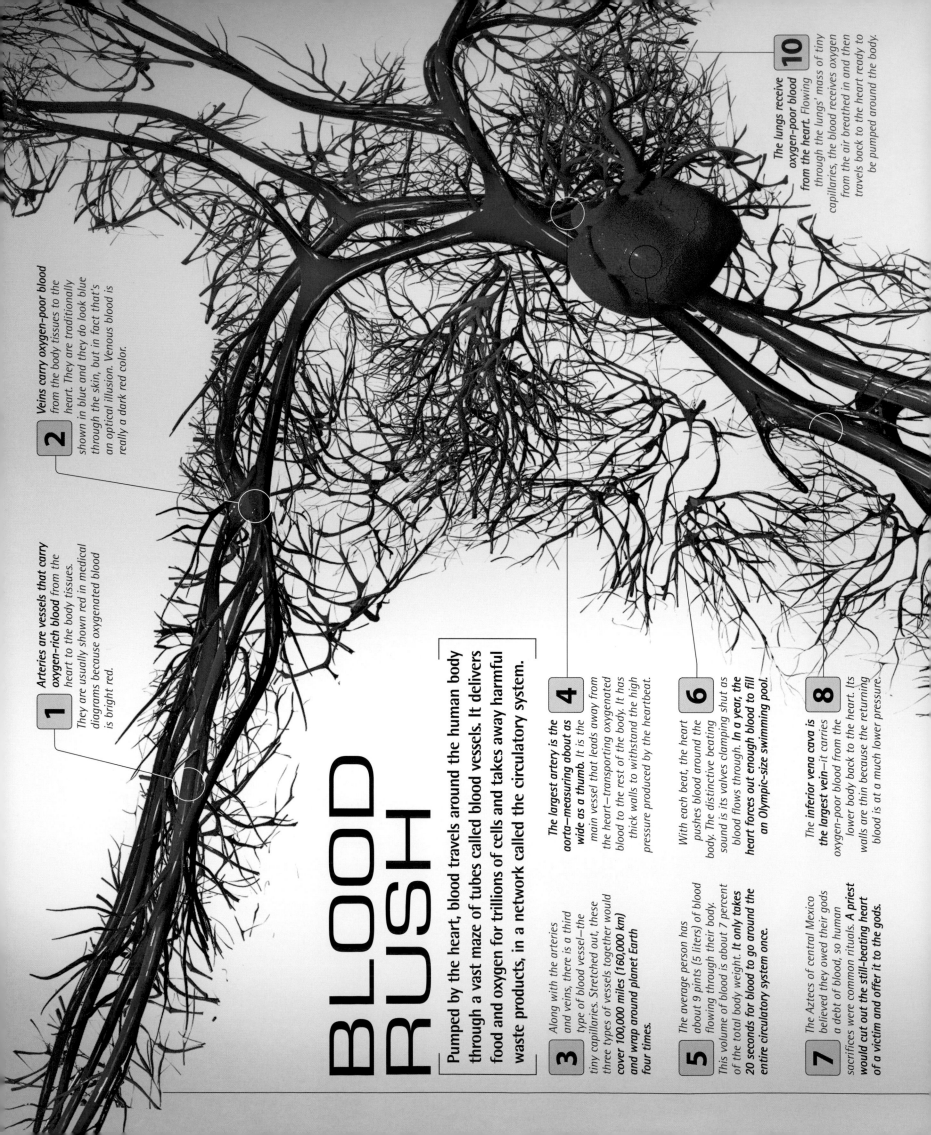

BLOOD RUSH

Pumped by the heart, blood travels around the human body through a vast maze of tubes called blood vessels. It delivers food and oxygen for trillions of cells and takes away harmful waste products, in a network called the circulatory system.

1 *Arteries are vessels that carry oxygen-rich blood from the heart to the body tissues.* They are usually shown red in medical diagrams because oxygenated blood is bright red.

2 *Veins carry oxygen-poor blood from the body tissues to the heart.* They are traditionally shown in blue and they do look blue through the skin, but in fact that's an optical illusion. Venous blood is really a dark red color.

3 Along with the arteries and veins, there is a third type of blood vessel—the tiny capillaries. Stretched out, these three types of vessels together would cover 100,000 miles (160,000 km) and wrap around planet Earth four times.

4 *The largest artery is the aorta—measuring about as wide as a thumb.* It is the main vessel that leads away from the heart—transporting oxygenated blood to the rest of the body. It has thick walls to withstand the high pressure produced by the heartbeat.

5 The average person has about 9 pints (5 liters) of blood flowing through their body. This volume of blood is about 7 percent of the total body weight. **It only takes 20 seconds for blood to go around the entire circulatory system once.**

6 With each beat, the heart pushes blood around the body. The distinctive beating sound is its valves clamping shut as blood flows through. **In a year, the heart forces out enough blood to fill an Olympic-size swimming pool.**

7 The Aztecs of central Mexico believed they owed their gods a debt of blood, so human sacrifices were common rituals. **A priest would cut out the still-beating heart of a victim and offer it to the gods.**

8 *The inferior vena cava is the largest vein—it carries oxygen-poor blood from the lower body back to the heart.* Its walls are thin because the returning blood is at a much lower pressure.

10 *The lungs receive oxygen-poor blood from the heart.* Flowing through the lungs' mass of tiny capillaries, the blood receives oxygen from the air breathed in and then travels back to the heart ready to be pumped around the body.

11 Every year, about 108 million units (1 pint/525 ml) of blood are donated to blood banks worldwide to help patients. **Red blood cells have a shelf-life of up to 35 days, while platelets last up to a week.** *Every two seconds, someone in a medical emergency needs blood.*

» Blood breakdown

Blood is a mixture of blood cells and plasma—a fluid which is 90 percent water and more than 100 other dissolved substances, such as food, waste, and salt. There are three types of blood cells: red blood cells, which carry oxygen; white blood cells, which defend the body by destroying invading germs and bacteria; and platelets, which help the blood clot after an injury and heal the site of a wound. A single drop of blood contains 250 million red blood cells, 375,000 white blood cells, and 12 million platelets.

Plasma
This fluid is 54 percent of your bloodstream.

White blood cells
Along with platelets, white blood cells make up 1 percent of your blood.

Curved cells
Red blood cells are curved so they have more surface area for taking in oxygen.

Red blood cells
These cells account for 45 percent of your blood.

12 Blood, including white blood cells, is made in the bone marrow, a jellylike tissue found inside hollow bones. Two million blood cells die every second, and **each blood cell can live for about 120 days.**

13 Bloodletting (deliberately removing blood from a patient) was a common practice in early medicine and continued right up to the 1800s. When US president **George Washington** (1732–99) became ill, he asked for bloodletting to cure him. **Almost half his blood supply was removed by the time he died.**

13½ We always *associate blood with the color red*, but in the animal kingdom, crabs have **blue blood**, earthworms and leeches have **green blood**, and cockroaches have **colorless blood.**

9 Blood travels through **tiny capillaries**, where oxygen and nutrients in the blood seep into the body cells. Capillaries are only **one-tenth the width of a human hair** and are virtually invisible to the naked eye, but they **make up 98 percent of the total length of the circulatory system.**

1 More than 60 percent of the planet is covered by ocean more than 1 mile (1,600 m) deep. **The deepest point is the Mariana Trench— 36,070 ft (10,994 m) below the surface.** That's so deep that Mount Everest would fit inside and still not break the surface.

2 This **wood-eating shrimp** makes an unexpected home at the bottom of the Mariana Trench, where food is hard to come by. **It survives on fragments of wood and coconut shells that drift down to its depths.**

Bomber worm

3 **Deep-sea anglerfish have a luminous lure to attract prey.** Only the females have lures; the tiny males are less than a tenth of their size.

4 **The barbeled dragonfish's snakelike body is 83 percent water,** which allows it to stay buoyant under extreme pressure. Ocean **pressure compresses the air inside organisms,** so rather than using gassy swim bladders to stay afloat, deep-sea fish have lighter skeletons and are filled with more water.

5 Massive monsters lurk in the ocean depths. **The largest invertebrate, the colossal squid, makes its home in the deep and can grow up to 46 ft (14 m) long—the length of a bus.** Its eyeballs are the size of footballs—the biggest in the animal kingdom.

OCEAN DEPTHS

Here is a world that's as black as midnight, bitterly chilled, and under pressure that would crush a car. But life still thrives at the bottom of the ocean. In the deepest waters bizarre animals live out their strange lives.

6 **Hagfishes** are slimy scavengers that burrow into dead animals using their suckerlike mouths. **They can even tie their bodies into a knot**—giving them the leverage to tear scraps of food off a corpse.

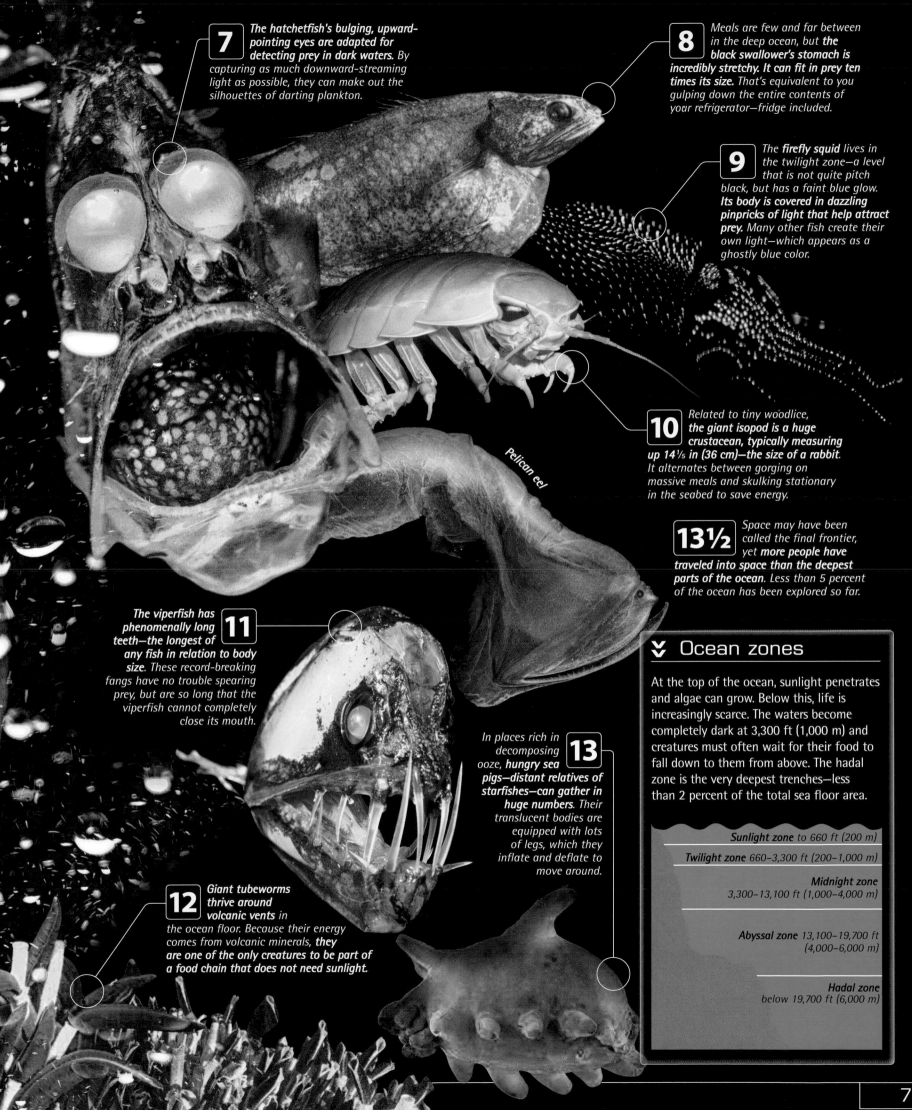

7 The hatchetfish's bulging, upward-pointing eyes are adapted for detecting prey in dark waters. By capturing as much downward-streaming light as possible, they can make out the silhouettes of darting plankton.

8 Meals are few and far between in the deep ocean, but **the black swallower's stomach is incredibly stretchy. It can fit in prey ten times its size.** That's equivalent to you gulping down the entire contents of your refrigerator—fridge included.

9 The **firefly squid** lives in the twilight zone—a level that is not quite pitch black, but has a faint blue glow. **Its body is covered in dazzling pinpricks of light that help attract prey.** Many other fish create their own light—which appears as a ghostly blue color.

10 Related to tiny woodlice, **the giant isopod is a huge crustacean, typically measuring up 14⅕ in (36 cm)—the size of a rabbit.** It alternates between gorging on massive meals and skulking stationary in the seabed to save energy.

Pelican eel

13½ Space may have been called the final frontier, yet **more people have traveled into space than the deepest parts of the ocean.** Less than 5 percent of the ocean has been explored so far.

11 The viperfish has phenomenally long teeth—the longest of any fish in relation to body size. These record-breaking fangs have no trouble spearing prey, but are so long that the viperfish cannot completely close its mouth.

13 In places rich in decomposing ooze, **hungry sea pigs—distant relatives of starfishes—can gather in huge numbers.** Their translucent bodies are equipped with lots of legs, which they inflate and deflate to move around.

12 **Giant tubeworms thrive around volcanic vents in** the ocean floor. Because their energy comes from volcanic minerals, **they are one of the only creatures to be part of a food chain that does not need sunlight.**

⌄ Ocean zones

At the top of the ocean, sunlight penetrates and algae can grow. Below this, life is increasingly scarce. The waters become completely dark at 3,300 ft (1,000 m) and creatures must often wait for their food to fall down to them from above. The hadal zone is the very deepest trenches—less than 2 percent of the total sea floor area.

Sunlight zone to 660 ft (200 m)

Twilight zone 660–3,300 ft (200–1,000 m)

Midnight zone 3,300–13,100 ft (1,000–4,000 m)

Abyssal zone 13,100–19,700 ft (4,000–6,000 m)

Hadal zone below 19,700 ft (6,000 m)

HOT ROCKS

A volcanic eruption occurs when molten rock from inside the Earth breaks through the surface. Sometimes it gently oozes out, but every so often it erupts with explosive force, throwing up burning rocks, boiling lava, and billowing gases.

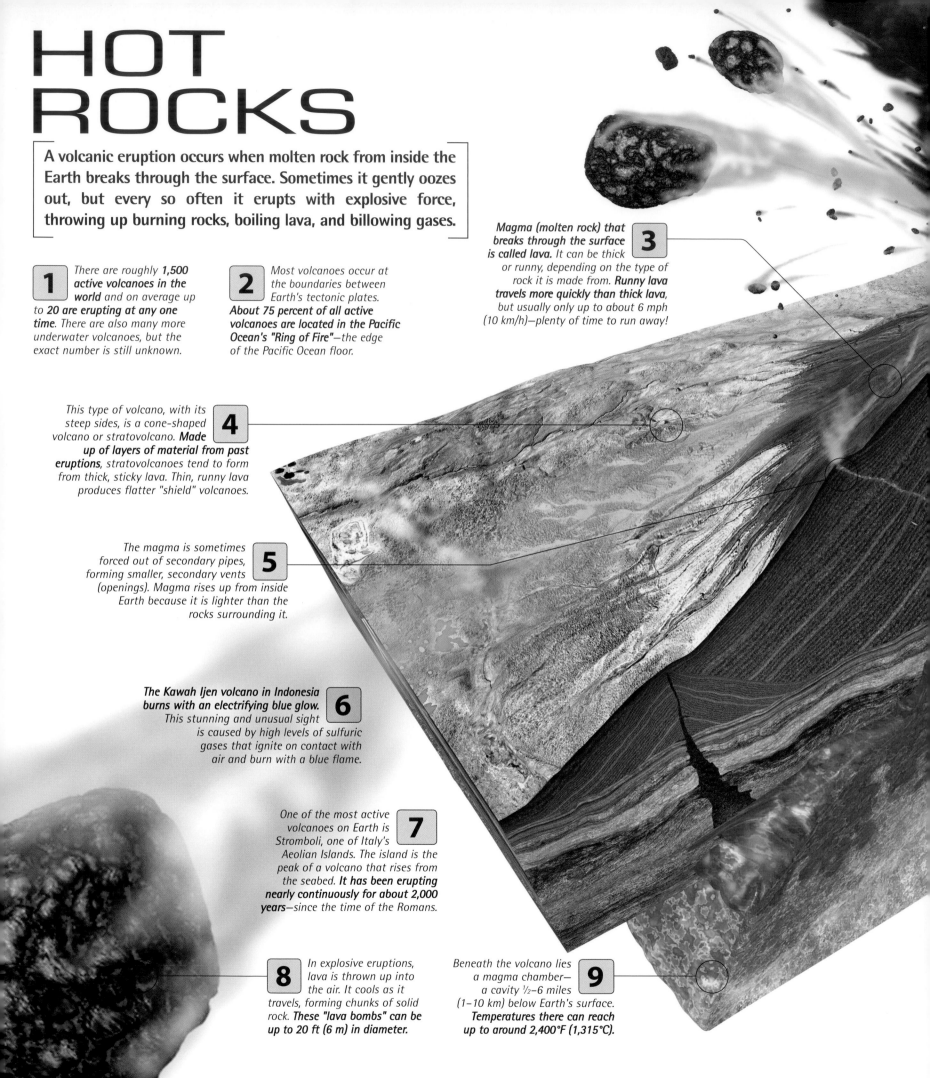

1 There are roughly *1,500 active volcanoes in the world* and on average up to *20 are erupting at any one time*. There are also many more underwater volcanoes, but the exact number is still unknown.

2 Most volcanoes occur at the boundaries between Earth's tectonic plates. **About 75 percent of all active volcanoes are located in the Pacific Ocean's "Ring of Fire"**—the edge of the Pacific Ocean floor.

3 Magma (molten rock) that breaks through the surface is called lava. It can be thick or runny, depending on the type of rock it is made from. **Runny lava travels more quickly than thick lava,** but usually only up to about 6 mph (10 km/h)—plenty of time to run away!

4 This type of volcano, with its steep sides, is a cone-shaped volcano or stratovolcano. **Made up of layers of material from past eruptions,** stratovolcanoes tend to form from thick, sticky lava. Thin, runny lava produces flatter "shield" volcanoes.

5 The magma is sometimes forced out of secondary pipes, forming smaller, secondary vents (openings). Magma rises up from inside Earth because it is lighter than the rocks surrounding it.

6 The Kawah Ijen volcano in Indonesia **burns with an electrifying blue glow.** This stunning and unusual sight is caused by high levels of sulfuric gases that ignite on contact with air and burn with a blue flame.

7 One of the most active volcanoes on Earth is Stromboli, one of Italy's Aeolian Islands. The island is the peak of a volcano that rises from the seabed. **It has been erupting nearly continuously for about 2,000 years**—since the time of the Romans.

8 In explosive eruptions, lava is thrown up into the air. It cools as it travels, forming chunks of solid rock. **These "lava bombs" can be up to 20 ft (6 m) in diameter.**

9 Beneath the volcano lies a magma chamber—a cavity ½–6 miles (1–10 km) below Earth's surface. **Temperatures there can reach up to around 2,400°F (1,315°C).**

10 The **ash cloud** blasted up in an eruption contains gases from within the magma chamber and **tiny fragments of solidified magma**. A big eruption can cause an **ash column that reaches 37 miles (60 km) into the air.**

11 A pyroclastic flow is a dangerous feature of some explosive eruptions. This deadly avalanche of hot gas, ash, and rocks can race down the volcano at **speeds of over 310 mph (500 km/h), heated to more than 1,470°F (800°C).**

12 Some volcanoes are so huge and powerful they are known as "supervolcanoes"—**capable of eruptions 1,000 times bigger than anything seen in recent times.** Yellowstone National Park, US, is the site of one of these—it last erupted 640,000 years ago, blasting ash across half of the United States.

13 The **largest volcano on Earth is Tamu Massif,** an extinct shield volcano under the Pacific Ocean that is more than 2½ miles (4 km) high. But it is dwarfed by **Olympus Mons** on the planet Mars, which at 16 miles (25 km) high is the **largest volcano in our Solar System.**

13½ You might think that volcanoes take years to appear, but you'd be wrong. The Parícutin volcano in Mexico appeared in a farmer's field overnight. **Within 24 hours, it had created a 164-ft (50-m) cone and within a week it had grown to 492 ft (150 m).**

SKY LIGHTS

Auroras are magnificent displays of light that appear in the night sky over Earth's two magnetic poles. The shape of an aurora can vary from vertical shafts of light to long curving arcs and bands that sweep across the sky like curtains.

1 Auroras that occur around the north magnetic pole are called *Aurora Borealis—the northern lights*. This aurora was captured over Manitoba, northern Canada, just south of the Arctic Circle. The lights are also frequently seen in *Alaska, Scandinavia, Iceland, Greenland, and northern Russia*.

2 Auroras take their name from the *Roman goddess of the dawn*, whose job it was to fly across the sky to announce the arrival of the Sun. "Borealis" comes from the Greek name for the North Wind, while "Australis" means "of the south."

3 The lights around the south magnetic pole are called the *Aurora Australis*. These happen just as often as the northern lights, but fewer people see them, because **they mostly occur over Antarctica and the Southern Ocean**. Occasionally they are visible from southern parts of Chile, Argentina, New Zealand, and Australia.

4 A *Babylonian clay tablet* from 568 BCE is probably the **first written account** of an aurora. **Recorded by the official astronomers of King Nebuchadnezzar II,** it describes a "red glow" in the night sky.

5 Auroras are caused by the reaction of charged particles from the Sun with gases in Earth's atmosphere. These solar particles enter Earth's atmosphere in rings around each of its poles, where they make the gases in the air glow in vibrant colors.

6 Italian astronomer *Galileo Galilei,* who came up with the name "Aurora Borealis," **thought an aurora showed reflected sunlight.** It was only in 1908 that Norwegian scientist Kristian Birkeland realized the lights were caused by charged particles entering the atmosphere, although his theory was not proven until almost 60 years later.

7 Huge eruptions from the Sun can cause spectacular auroras here on Earth. One such eruption in March 1989, was as powerful as **thousands of nuclear bombs exploding at the same time** and sent a one-billion-ton cloud of particles hurtling toward Earth. **The northern lights were visible as far south as Florida and Cuba.**

⌄ How an aurora works

Earth's magnetic field extends out into space for tens of thousands of miles. It forms a protective cage around our planet, called the magnetosphere. Energetic particles from the Sun are mostly deflected by the magnetosphere, and a few trickle down into the atmosphere, but some become trapped. When the magnetosphere is disturbed by a blast from the Sun in a solar storm, the trapped particles are accelerated down into the atmosphere in ring-shaped zones surrounding the north and south magnetic poles.

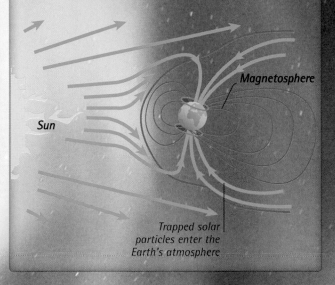

Sun

Magnetosphere

Trapped solar particles enter the Earth's atmosphere

8 The color of an aurora depends on which gas the solar particles are reacting with. **Oxygen produces the distinctive yellow-greenish light of this image,** but also glows red when the reaction occurs at higher altitudes. Nitrogen produces pink and blue lights.

9 In Norse mythology, the Aurora Borealis was said to be **a bridge of colored fire that connected Earth to Asgard,** the home of the gods. The bridge was known as Bivröst (meaning "Moving Way"), and it was guarded by the god Heimdall.

12 Astronauts on the **International Space Station get a stunning side-on view of auroras.** The station orbits at the same altitude at which the lights usually occur, so **astronauts see them as towering peaks clinging to Earth.**

11 Auroras are not just an Earthly phenomenon: they can **also be seen on other planets, including Mars, Jupiter, and Saturn.** A far-away brown dwarf (a world bigger than a planet but smaller than a star) hosts the **most powerful auroras ever seen—one million times brighter than our northern lights.**

10 The dazzling displays of the auroras can take place at dizzying heights— **up to 620 miles (1,000 km) above Earth.** Most occur at heights of around 50–75 miles (80-120 km) up.

13 Neon lights glow for the same reason as auroras. A tube or bulb is filled with gas that glows when an electric current runs through it. Neon gas produces an orange light, mercury glows blue, and sodium emits bright yellow.

13½ Auroras may look the most stunning against the background of the night sky, but **auroras don't just happen at night.** They are too faint to see by eye, but scientists know **they exist in the daytime as well,** because they have sent infrared cameras into the sky on a balloon.

1 More movie tickets are sold in India than anywhere else. In 2016, Indians bought nearly 2.3 billion tickets. Chinese audiences snapped up 1.2 billion, and US movie fans also purchased 1.2 billion.

2 Movies make **most money through the box office,** but they also earn big bucks from DVD and home broadcast sales and toys and other merchandising. The **top earner of all time was Avatar in 2009,** with global sales of $2.78 billion.

3 What's all the hype about opening weekend? **A movie may make a third of its entire earnings in the first weekend.** Star Wars: The Force Awakens broke all records with a $529-million opening weekend in 2015.

4 Movies may make mega money, but **many cost a fortune to make.** The most expensive film produced so far is Pirates of the Caribbean: At World's End. It cost the Disney studio $300 million in 2007. **The price of special effects alone was $1 million a minute.**

5 Still thinking big? The **largest movie screen in the world** is in Jiangsu, China, at 113 ft (34.6 m) wide and 88 ft (26.8 m) high. That's **as wide as a Boeing 737's wing span.**

6 China has been building movie screens at the super-speedy rate of up to 27 a day. With nearly 40,000 screens in total, **China will soon grab the record from the US to have the most screens globally.**

7 Movie trailers have been around since 1913. These movie ads used to run (or "trail") after the feature movie, until someone figured out most of the audience had already gone home.

MAKING MOVIES

A movie screen is like a window through which we can escape into new and magical worlds—just one reason why people love going to the movies. For those who work in the film industry, the big screen is big business.

11 What's next? We may soon experience 3D without glasses, 4D (3D combined with simulated effects such as rain and strobe lights), and **virtual reality, where the film surrounds you** and you sit in 360° swivel chairs.

12 It may be hard to figure out which movie genre is most popular, but we do know that **action films make people eat more snacks.** A study showed that the fast pace of these blockbusters caused viewers to eat more than twice as much food than when watching a talk show—even when the sound was muted.

10 Film studios have used all kinds of tricks to attract audiences, from movie **random seats** (during a scary movie **would vibrate** to jolt a cinemagoer's bottom) to Smell-o-Vision (**foul odors were pumped into the cinema**). Neither have taken off.

9 3D movies have been around longer than you might think—first becoming highly popular in the 1950s. The glasses you wear to watch these movies work by showing each eye a slightly different picture. Your brain then automatically puts these images together. Today, they are more popular than ever, with more than 75,000 3D screens worldwide.

8 The sound effects added to a movie often have unusual origins—coconuts are used to sound like a horse trotting, and gloves flapping to imitate bird flight. **The iconic sound of the lightsabers in Star Wars was made from the noise produced when a microphone was put too close to a TV.**

13½ You may think that Hollywood is the **biggest movie industry in the world, but in fact India produces the most films**—up to 2,000 a year. Best known are the Hindi-language Bollywood blockbusters from Mumbai. Next in line is Nigeria, with the US in third place.

13 Not everyone **munches on popcorn at the movies**. The Chinese love pickled plums, and other favorite movie snacks include dried sardines in Japan, reindeer jerky in Norway, chewy dried cuttlefish in South Korea, salted liquorice in the Netherlands, and samosas in India.

NOBLE KNIGHT

In medieval Europe, a knight was a soldier who fought on horseback for a king or lord. This formidable warrior swore to protect his lord, and defend the Church, women, and the weak. His steel armor was his own personalized fortress.

1 Armor was originally made of mail—interlocking iron rings. Small steel plates were gradually added to protect vulnerable areas. By the 15th century, **full steel plate armor** had become the norm. A complete suit would have weighed about 55 lb (25 kg).

2 The piece of armor that protected the knight's lower face and neck was called a "bevor," *from an old French word meaning "to dribble."* It had air holes to breathe through, but the knight's breath would have condensed inside, **making it very wet.**

3 The long sword had a double-edged blade and tapered to a point. *In the skilled grasp of a knight, it was capable of **cutting off a limb or even the enemy's head** in one slice.*

4 Warhorses had their own armor called barding. *If the knight could only afford one piece, it would be the **protective headpiece on the horse's ears and muzzle.** A knight usually had horses for several different functions: two warhorses, a palfrey to travel on, and packhorses to carry his belongings.*

7 The squire became a knight in a **special ceremony called dubbing.** He would be granted a plot of land by his lord or the king, and in return promised to perform certain duties, including military service.

5 Becoming a knight took years of training. **At the age of seven a well-born boy would be sent away from home to become a page to a knight.** He would run errands and learn about horsemanship and weaponry.

6 **At 14, the page became a squire.** He was trusted to look after the knight's horse and weapons, and helped him put on his armor. After about seven years of service, a squire could become a knight himself.

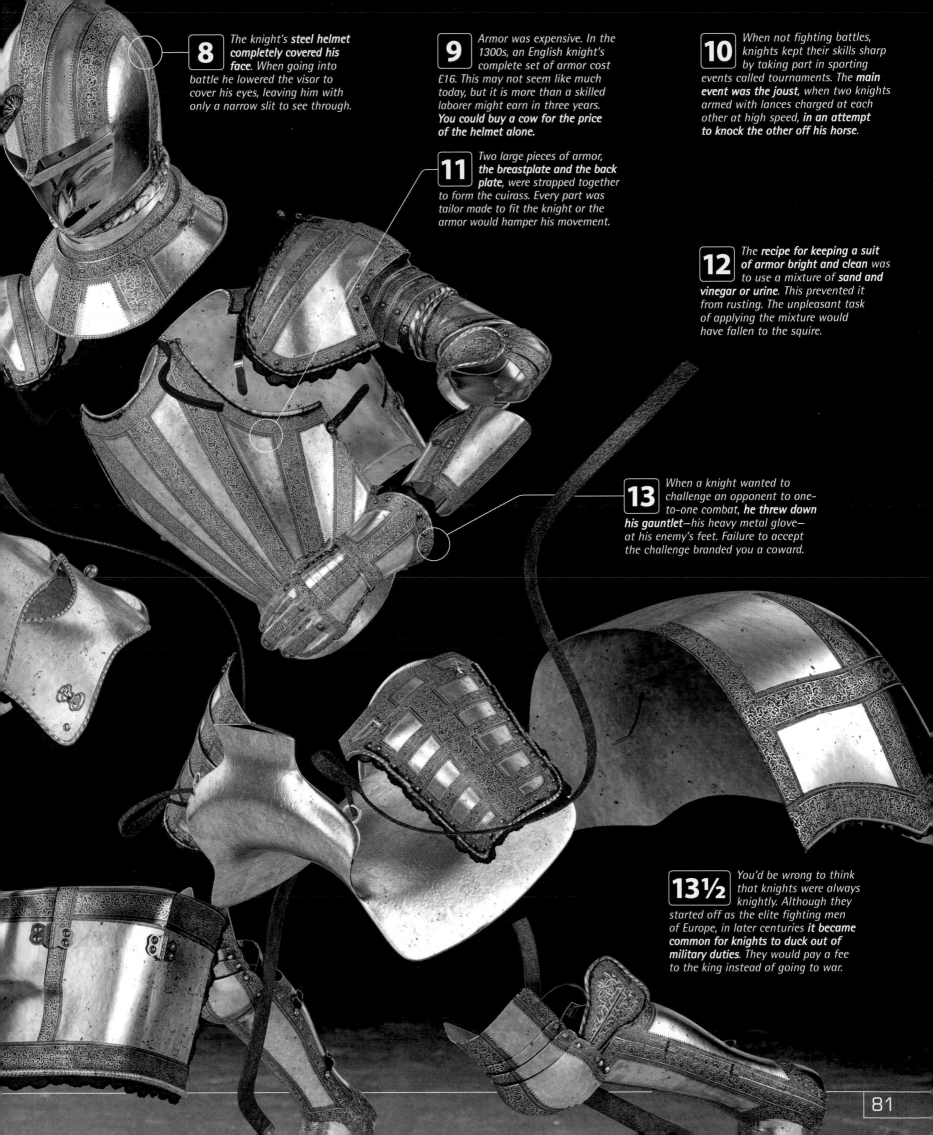

8 The knight's **steel helmet completely covered his face**. When going into battle he lowered the visor to cover his eyes, leaving him with only a narrow slit to see through.

9 Armor was expensive. In the 1300s, an English knight's complete set of armor cost £16. This may not seem like much today, but it is more than a skilled laborer might earn in three years. **You could buy a cow for the price of the helmet alone.**

10 When not fighting battles, knights kept their skills sharp by taking part in sporting events called tournaments. The **main event was the joust**, when two knights armed with lances charged at each other at high speed, **in an attempt to knock the other off his horse.**

11 Two large pieces of armor, **the breastplate and the back plate**, were strapped together to form the cuirass. Every part was tailor made to fit the knight or the armor would hamper his movement.

12 The **recipe for keeping a suit of armor bright and clean** was to use a mixture of **sand and vinegar or urine**. This prevented it from rusting. The unpleasant task of applying the mixture would have fallen to the squire.

13 When a knight wanted to challenge an opponent to one-to-one combat, **he threw down his gauntlet**—his heavy metal glove—at his enemy's feet. Failure to accept the challenge branded you a coward.

13½ You'd be wrong to think that knights were always knightly. Although they started off as the elite fighting men of Europe, in later centuries **it became common for knights to duck out of military duties**. They would pay a fee to the king instead of going to war.

IN A SPIN

Maneuvering easily through the skies, helicopters are vital for surveillance, search and rescue, and other operations. Many, like this Seahawk SH-60, are used by the military, launching into the air from enormous aircraft carriers.

1 Helicopter flight was child's play in ancient China. Inspired by the spinning seeds of the maple tree, *Chinese children began to play with "bamboo-copters" around 2,400 years ago*—small rotors that flew up into the air when spun.

2 Helicopters' long rotor blades are the key to how they fly. When these whirl round at high speed, they push down on the air below them. This creates enough lift to get the heavy metal body of the aircraft off the ground.

3 *Italian inventor Leonardo da Vinci was the first person to sketch the idea for a manned helicopter, in the late 15th century.* However, his model would never have worked. The first real helicopter did not fly until 1939—more than 450 years later.

4 Helicopters can reach speeds of around 250 mph (400 km/h), but cannot travel as fast as powerful planes. However, they are much niftier—able to take off and land vertically, fly backward, forward, sideways, hover over a spot, and land in a space as small as a tennis court.

5 *The Seahawk's exterior has a special protective coating to prevent it from rusting in the salty sea air.* The helicopter can be used for many naval missions, including carrying cargo, search and rescue, and warfare.

6 *The two turbine engines on either side of the helicopter power the rotor blades*, spinning them as fast as 200 revolutions per minute. They are similar to car engines, but more powerful.

7 The tail rotor may look insignificant, but it is needed to offset the rotating force caused by the main rotor blades. *Without it, the body of the helicopter would spin around in the opposite direction from the rotor blades—making it impossible to fly.*

8 For easy storage at sea, the tail section of the Seahawk can be collapsed and folded back into the body. The rotor blades can also be pushed together—*reducing this flatpack flier to around half of its original size.*

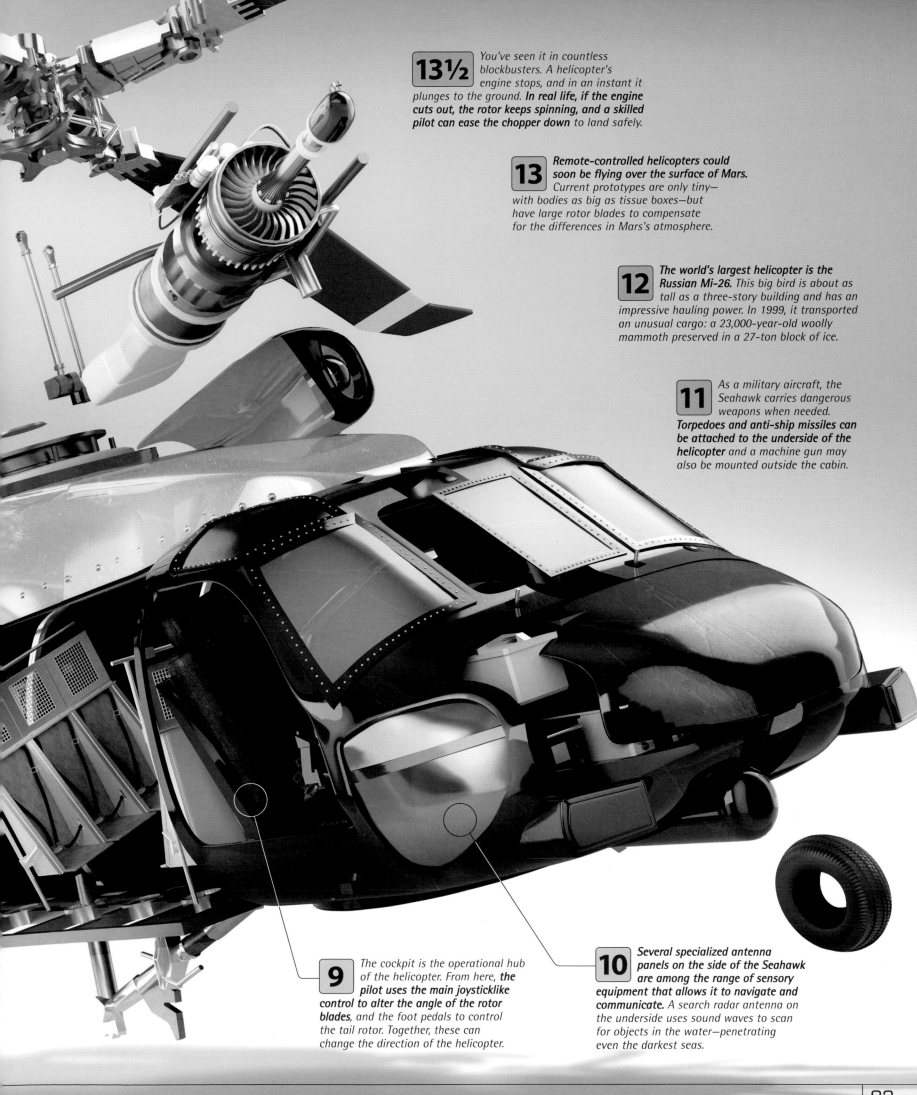

13½ You've seen it in countless blockbusters. A helicopter's engine stops, and in an instant it plunges to the ground. *In real life, if the engine cuts out, the rotor keeps spinning, and a skilled pilot can ease the chopper down* to land safely.

13 Remote-controlled helicopters could soon be flying over the surface of Mars. Current prototypes are only tiny—with bodies as big as tissue boxes—but have large rotor blades to compensate for the differences in Mars's atmosphere.

12 *The world's largest helicopter is the Russian Mi-26.* This big bird is about as tall as a three-story building and has an impressive hauling power. In 1999, it transported an unusual cargo: a 23,000-year-old woolly mammoth preserved in a 27-ton block of ice.

11 As a military aircraft, the Seahawk carries dangerous weapons when needed. *Torpedoes and anti-ship missiles can be attached to the underside of the helicopter* and a machine gun may also be mounted outside the cabin.

9 The cockpit is the operational hub of the helicopter. From here, **the pilot uses the main joysticklike control to alter the angle of the rotor blades,** and the foot pedals to control the tail rotor. Together, these can change the direction of the helicopter.

10 *Several specialized antenna panels on the side of the Seahawk are among the range of sensory equipment that allows it to navigate and communicate.* A search radar antenna on the underside uses sound waves to scan for objects in the water—penetrating even the darkest seas.

WHAT'S THE MATTER?

Matter is all the "stuff" in the Universe—including you. On our planet, it exists in three main states: solid, liquid, and gas. Many substances can exist in all three states, changing from one to the other when they are heated or cooled.

1 *All matter is made of extremely tiny particles that are always vibrating to and fro or moving around.* **The state of a substance—solid, liquid, or gas—depends on how the particles are moving.**

2 *The particles that make up* **solid matter,** *such as the metal of this teaspoon,* **cannot move around freely.** *They vibrate to and fro, but remain locked together.* **That is why a solid has a definite shape.**

3 *The* **particles that make up liquid matter are close together, but can move around** *and slip past each other. Liquids have* **a definite volume but no definite shape.** *Tea will take on the shape of the cup it is in.*

4 *The particles that make up gases* **are far apart and move freely in all directions.** *They do not have a fixed shape or volume, and* **will spread out to fit a container.** *This process, called diffusion, explains* **how a smell spreads rapidly across a room.**

5 *When a liquid is warm, some of the particles of which it is made leave the surface liquid and become an invisible* **vapor—a gas that can easily become liquid again.** *This process is called evaporation.*

6 *As the water vapor from the tea cools, some of the vapor's particles join together, or condense, to form tiny liquid droplets.* **Steam is a mist made up of these droplets suspended in air.**

7 *Much of the matter around us is not purely solid, liquid, or gas, but a mixture of two or more states.* **Lemon peel, for example, feels like a solid, but it is actually a mixture of solids and liquids.**

8 *All matter was* **created at the very start of time,** *when the Universe began, 13.8 billion years ago. Scientists call this moment "the Big Bang."*

9 *Liquids are held together by the attraction between their particles. At the surface of a liquid the particles are more attracted to other surface particles.* **This is known as surface tension and is what makes liquids form drops.**

⌄⌄ Three states

When a solid such as ice is heated, its particles vibrate faster, and they break apart from each other. The solid loses its shape and becomes liquid. If the heating continues, the particles may break apart altogether, and escape to form a gas. These steps also run in reverse: from gas to liquid to solid. These three diagrams show the movement of particles in each of the three states.

The particles of a solid do not move about.

The particles of a liquid move closely past each other.

The particles of a gas are completely free of each other.

*You may think that there are only three states of matter, but **there is a fourth state**. It is called plasma, and it occurs at very high temperatures, such as in stars, lightning, and neon signs. In fact, **plasma makes up 99.9 percent of matter in the Universe**.* **13½**

13 *Some liquids are thin and runny, and flow easily. Others are thick and sticky, and flow slowly. **How a liquid flows is called its viscosity.** Pitch is a liquid that is so viscous that it **takes 10 years to form a single drop**.*

12 *All water on Earth has existed for millions of years. **The rain that falls today is the same water that the dinosaurs drank.** Water moves from the ground to the air to the ground again in the water cycle. It changes from solid to liquid to gas, over and over again.*

Most liquids shrink as they are cooled. However, water expands as it freezes into ice. **11** ***This change of state from liquid to solid can burst water pipes and split rock.***

Water is highly unusual in that it occurs abundantly on our planet in all three states: **10** *liquid water, gaseous vapor, and solid ice. No other planet in our solar system has liquid water—they are either too hot or too cold.*

OUR STAR

Earth's nearest star is a gigantic spinning ball of flaming hydrogen and helium. Its gravity shapes the entire Solar System and its blazing surface bathes the planets around it in light, powering all life on Earth.

1 The Sun *sits at the center of the Solar System*—the family of planets, moons, asteroids, and comets that *formed from the same cloud of dust as the Sun 4.6 billion years ago.*

2 The Sun measures *870,000 miles (1.4 million km) in diameter.* Accounting for *99.8 percent of the mass of our Solar System,* it is so huge that it could fit *1.3 million Earths inside.*

3 Compared with other stars, however, *the Sun isn't particularly big.* It is a dwarf star—relatively small and dim. The *largest star known, UY Scuti,* could hold 3 billion Suns.

4 Throughout history, *the Sun has been feared and worshipped.* The ancient Egyptians had a sun god called Ra, while the Aztecs worshipped a deity called Tonatiuh.

5 Every second the Sun *releases 400 trillion watts* of energy—that's *a million times more energy than everyone on Earth uses in one year.*

6 The Sun is 93 million miles (150 million km) from Earth but it *takes just eight minutes for energy from the Sun to reach us.* By contrast it takes up to *100,000 years for energy from the Sun's core to reach its surface.*

7 A stream of particles is continually ejected from the Sun. This *solar wind* streams off the Sun at up to 560 miles/s (900 km/s) and *carries a million tons of gas into space every second.*

8 The upper atmosphere, or corona, is *not visible to the eye* but shows up in this ultraviolet view. It is *500 times hotter than the visible surface* but scientists don't understand why.

9 *This intensely bright region is called a facula.* These areas are associated with sunspots, temporary cooler regions that *vary in number over an 11-year cycle.*

10 The surface of the Sun looks *granulated or bubbly,* like orange peel. The individual granules are *cells of rising gas* each about 600 miles (1,000 km) wide.

11 This *gigantic jet of glowing gas* is called a prominence. It *extends about 186,000 miles (300,000 km)* into space—that's about 25 times the diameter of Earth.

12 This prominence erupted in August 2012, in an event known as a *coronal mass ejection (CME).* A big CME can blast *a billion tons of particles* into space.

13 The Sun is *halfway through its life.* In about 5 billion years, it will expand into a red giant, *engulfing Mercury and Venus,* before throwing off its outer layers, leaving a tiny dense core behind.

13½ The Sun may seem special to us, but it's a *fairly typical star—just one of billions* in our galaxy alone, which in turn is one of a likely *2 trillion galaxies in the observable universe.*

⊻ Inside the Sun

The source of the Sun's energy is its core, which contains more than half the Sun's mass. In the core, more than 600 tons of hydrogen are converted into helium every second, at a temperature of 27 million°F (15 million°C). The energy produced in these nuclear reactions is slowly transferred outward toward the Sun's visible surface.

In the convection zone currents of gas carry energy toward the surface

The radiation zone is a deep layer where energy travels by radiation

Hot, dense core

Visible surface is called the photosphere

GET CRACKING

For most amphibians, reptiles, fish, and invertebrates, eggs are a vital part of their lifecycle—encasing and protecting their fragile young before they are born. Some animals lay enormous numbers, but others focus their efforts on a few.

Frogspawn

1 The eggs we eat come from domestic chickens, but they don't contain baby birds because they are unfertilized. *Globally, we consume more than 1 billion hens' eggs every year.*

2 Ostriches lay the biggest eggs of any animal. *The largest one on record weighed a whopping 5 lb 11 oz (2.6 kg)*—about as heavy as a brick.

3 Most eggs are camouflaged, but not those of the great tinamou. **It is thought that its glossy green eggs may attract other female tinamous** who help keep the eggs safe by nesting in numbers.

4 *Bird eggs need to remain at a constant warm temperature in order to hatch.* Most parent birds achieve this by taking up a protective perch atop their eggs—incubating the developing bird inside.

5 Nile crocodile eggs don't have a gender when they are first laid. The embryos form based on the temperature around them—any eggs below 88°F (31°C) become females and the warmer ones develop into males.

6 The soft, leathery eggs of many reptiles like this corn snake are not as hard as those of birds. Birds' eggs may be harder because they have to bear the weight of the adult birds that incubate them.

7 Some animals really are born in a dump. **Several species of reptiles and birds bury their eggs under rotting vegetables** that give off heat as they decompose.

Slug

8 Unobtrusive insects are often the biggest breeders. **The Australian ghost moth can lay 29,000 eggs at one time.** However, it does not stick around to care for its children, but scatters the eggs at random as it flies.

Leopard gecko

9 When breaking out of their protective prisons, **baby birds are aided by a special egg tooth on their bills.** This helps them hack away at the hard eggshell, then it falls off when they no longer need it.

This European cave spider lays its hundreds of eggs in a large silken pouch. It suspends this in the corner of a cave—a spot where it can easily guard its future offspring. **10**

11 The eggs of the horn shark are protected in an unusual corkscrew-shaped package. **These spiral egg cases allow the mother shark to wedge them into crevices** to keep them safe.

After female octopuses have laid their eggs, they cover them with their body to protect them. **One dedicated deep sea octopus was observed brooding her eggs for more than four and a half years**—without once leaving to feed. **12**

Rat snake

Rainbow trout

Leopard tortoise

Most eggs are spherical, but **the murre lays long, pointed eggs**, which don't roll off the cliff ledges where murres nest. **13**

⌄ Inside a bird egg

When an egg leaves the parent bird's body, the embryo inside is just a tiny speck. Nourished by food from the yolk, and the heat from incubation, the developing bird begins to grow. The porous shell lets in air so it can breathe. A chicken fetus will mature for around three weeks before it is ready to hatch.

The yolk provides nourishment

A sac of fluid cushions the developing bird

A waste sac collects the embryo's urine

Air sac

13½ Mammals are normally defined as creatures that give birth to live young. However, **a special group of mammals—called monotremes—lay eggs.** This group consists of echidnas and platypuses—species found only in Australia and New Guinea.

Chinese oak silk moth

FUNNY BONES

Your skeleton provides structure, protects your vital organs, and anchors the muscles that make you move around. Bones are eight times stronger than concrete, but very light—your skeleton only makes up 15 percent of your body weight.

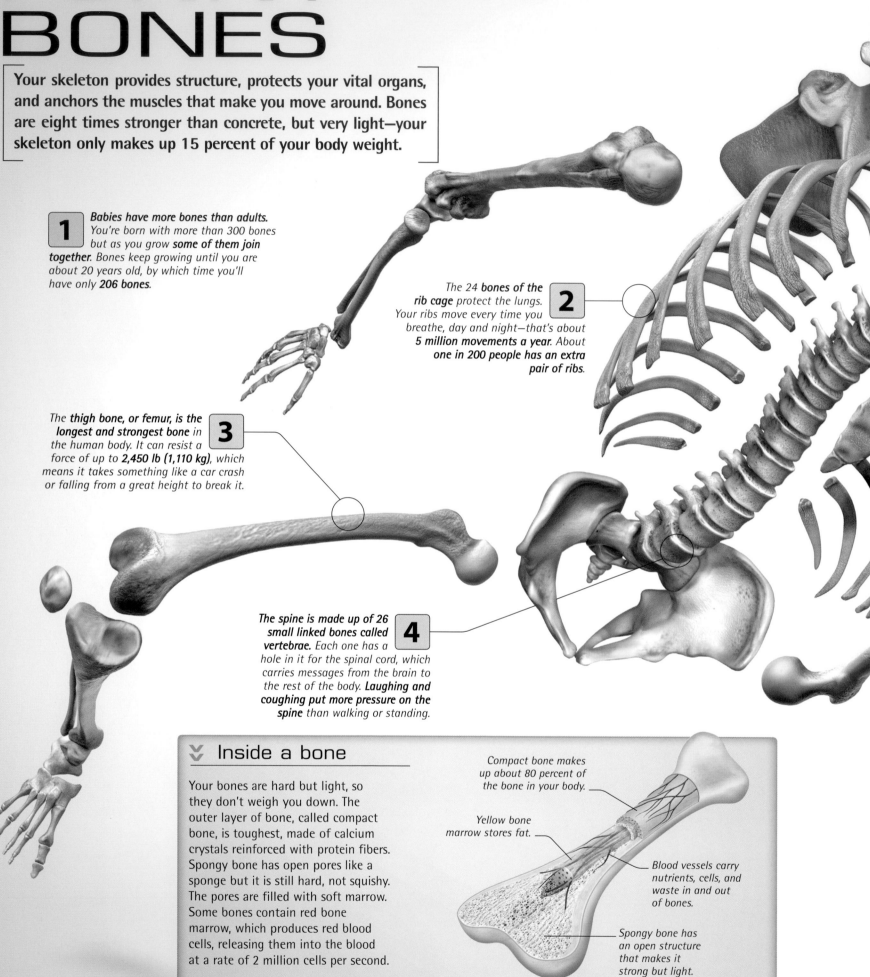

1 *Babies have more bones than adults.* You're born with more than 300 bones but as you grow **some of them join together.** Bones keep growing until you are about 20 years old, by which time you'll have only **206 bones.**

*The 24 **bones of the rib cage** protect the lungs. Your ribs move every time you breathe, day and night—that's about* **5 million movements a year.** *About one in 200 people has an extra pair of ribs.* **2**

*The **thigh bone, or femur, is the longest and strongest bone** in the human body. It can resist a force of up to* **2,450 lb (1,110 kg),** *which means it takes something like a car crash or falling from a great height to break it.* **3**

The spine is made up of 26 small linked bones called **vertebrae.** *Each one has a hole in it for the spinal cord, which carries messages from the brain to the rest of the body.* **Laughing and coughing put more pressure on the spine** *than walking or standing.* **4**

⋎ Inside a bone

Your bones are hard but light, so they don't weigh you down. The outer layer of bone, called compact bone, is toughest, made of calcium crystals reinforced with protein fibers. Spongy bone has open pores like a sponge but it is still hard, not squishy. The pores are filled with soft marrow. Some bones contain red bone marrow, which produces red blood cells, releasing them into the blood at a rate of 2 million cells per second.

Compact bone makes up about 80 percent of the bone in your body.

Yellow bone marrow stores fat.

Blood vessels carry nutrients, cells, and waste in and out of bones.

Spongy bone has an open structure that makes it strong but light.

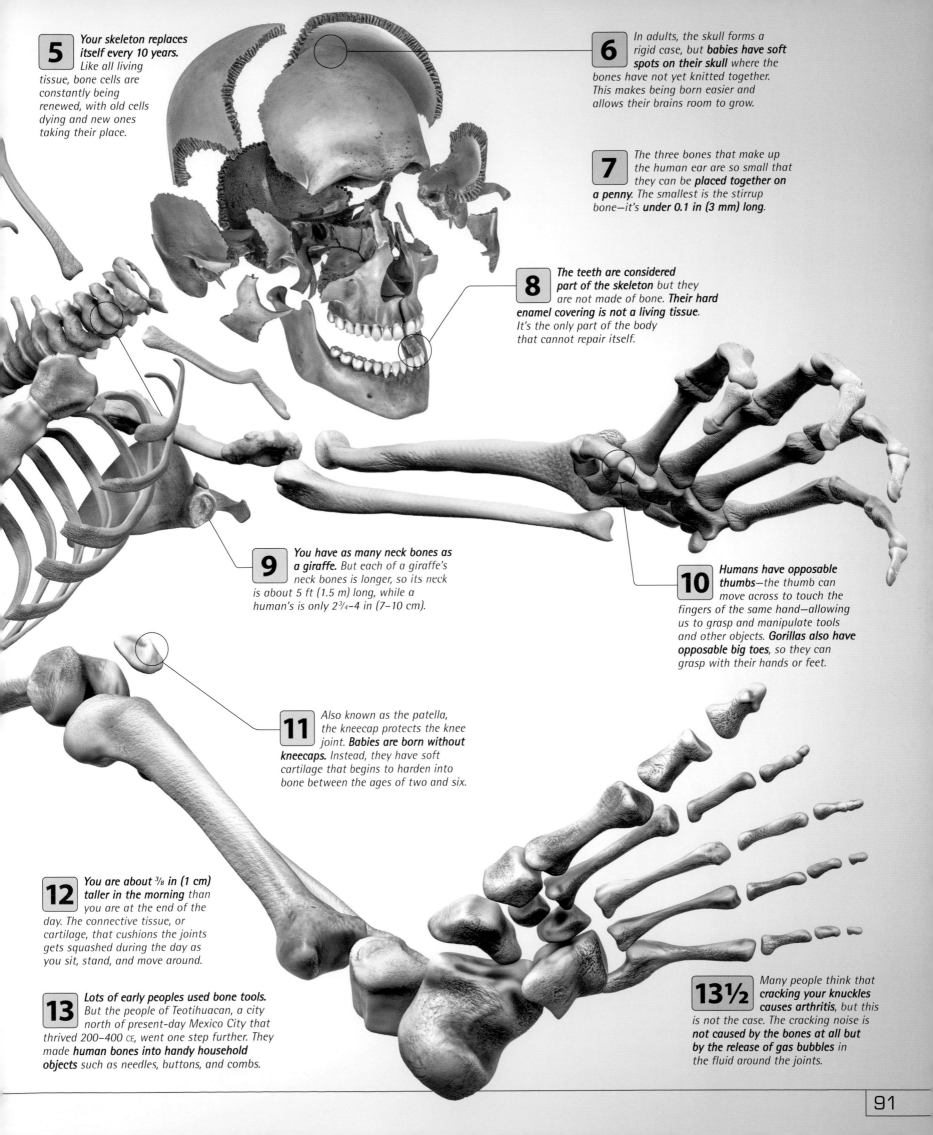

5 Your skeleton replaces itself every 10 years. Like all living tissue, bone cells are constantly being renewed, with old cells dying and new ones taking their place.

6 In adults, the skull forms a rigid case, but **babies have soft spots on their skull** where the bones have not yet knitted together. This makes being born easier and allows their brains room to grow.

7 The three bones that make up the human ear are so small that they can be **placed together on a penny.** The smallest is the stirrup bone—it's **under 0.1 in (3 mm) long.**

8 The teeth are considered **part of the skeleton** but they are not made of bone. **Their hard enamel covering is not a living tissue.** It's the only part of the body that cannot repair itself.

9 You have as many neck bones as **a giraffe.** But each of a giraffe's neck bones is longer, so its neck is about 5 ft (1.5 m) long, while a human's is only 2¾–4 in (7–10 cm).

10 Humans have opposable **thumbs**—the thumb can move across to touch the fingers of the same hand—allowing us to grasp and manipulate tools and other objects. **Gorillas also have opposable big toes,** so they can grasp with their hands or feet.

11 Also known as the patella, the kneecap protects the knee joint. **Babies are born without kneecaps.** Instead, they have soft cartilage that begins to harden into bone between the ages of two and six.

12 You are about ⅜ in (1 cm) taller in the morning than you are at the end of the day. The connective tissue, or cartilage, that cushions the joints gets squashed during the day as you sit, stand, and move around.

13 Lots of early peoples used bone tools. But the people of Teotihuacan, a city north of present-day Mexico City that thrived 200–400 CE, went one step further. They made **human bones into handy household objects** such as needles, buttons, and combs.

13½ Many people think that **cracking your knuckles causes arthritis,** but this is not the case. The cracking noise is **not caused by the bones at all but by the release of gas bubbles** in the fluid around the joints.

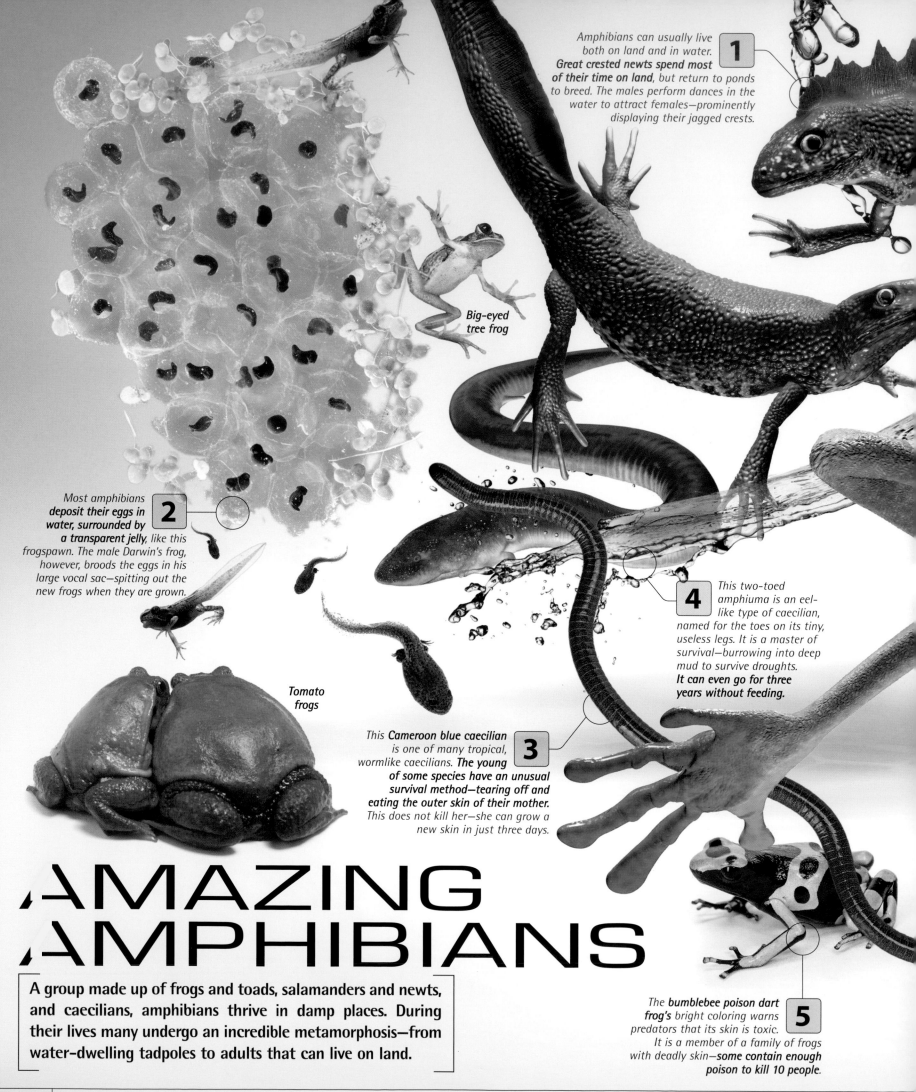

Amphibians can usually live both on land and in water. **1** **Great crested newts spend most of their time on land**, but return to ponds to breed. The males perform dances in the water to attract females—prominently displaying their jagged crests.

Big-eyed tree frog

Most amphibians **deposit their eggs in water, surrounded by a transparent jelly**, like this **2** frogspawn. The male Darwin's frog, however, broods the eggs in his large vocal sac—spitting out the new frogs when they are grown.

Tomato frogs

This two-toed amphiuma is an eel-like type of caecilian, named for the toes on its tiny, **4** useless legs. It is a master of survival—burrowing into deep mud to survive droughts. **It can even go for three years without feeding.**

This **Cameroon blue caecilian** is one of many tropical, wormlike caecilians. **The young of some species have an unusual survival method—tearing off and eating the outer skin of their mother.** This does not kill her—she can grow a new skin in just three days. **3**

AMAZING AMPHIBIANS

A group made up of frogs and toads, salamanders and newts, and caecilians, amphibians thrive in damp places. During their lives many undergo an incredible metamorphosis—from water-dwelling tadpoles to adults that can live on land.

The **bumblebee poison dart frog's** bright coloring warns **5** predators that its skin is toxic. It is a member of a family of frogs with deadly skin—**some contain enough poison to kill 10 people.**

6 The axolotl is one of several salamanders that *do not grow up*. Never leaving the water, it spends all its life with a baby's body resembling a tadpole with legs.

7 Not all amphibians live near water. The vividly colored **red-eyed tree frog** makes its home high up in tropical rain forests. Despite its slimy skin, it can climb expertly through the trees, *using suction pads on its fingers and toes to cling tightly to branches*.

9 You might think that all amphibians lay spawnlike eggs, but **some give birth to live young**. Several caecilian species nourish the young inside their bodies, until they are ready to emerge as miniature adults.

8 Most amphibians have short lifespans, but **the olm can live for a century or more**. This blind, white-bodied salamander spends its life deep in underground caves.

10 Despite their watery births, salamanders have long been associated with fire. *Ancient Greek philosopher Aristotle believed that the salamander was a magical lizard* able to both survive in fire and extinguish it at will.

11 Many frogs and toads communicate with chirps, croaks, or whistles. **The Great Plains toad's deafening trill is so loud it can be heard ½ mile (1 km) away**. It inflates its large vocal sac to amplify the sound.

12 The long tongue of the common toad is a perfect weapon for catching prey, shooting out in just one-fifth of a second. The sticky tip ensures prey can't wriggle away.

13 Amphibians shed their skin very frequently—as often as every day. This thin, moist layer is **rich in protein and many frogs and toads eat it!**

13½ Frogs raining from the sky may seem like fiction, but there have been many reports of these downpours over the years. **Theories suggest that frogs could get picked up by whirlwinds and dropped in other places**, but we don't know if this is how it happens.

您好

1 Around the world today, people speak about 7,000 languages and dialects (regional versions of a language). There are **2,200 languages in Asia and 850 in Papua New Guinea** alone. More than half of the world's population speak one of just 23 languages.

2 Someone who can speak lots of languages is known as a polyglot. *Sir John Bowring—a 19th-century governor of Hong Kong—was said to be able to speak 100 languages,* and had studied many more.

hola

3 We write down language with a **set of letters called an alphabet**. The word comes from "aleph" (meaning ox) and "bet" (house), the first two letters of the ancient Phoenician alphabet. A drawing of an ox head eventually became our letter a, and a house symbol turned into the letter b.

4 Computers have their own languages that we use to tell them what to do. **There are more than 500 of these programming languages,** all made up of complicated lines of typed code.

здравствуйте

5 You won't be at a loss for words with English. **It has a quarter of a million words, probably more than any other language.** Every year, around 1,000 new words are added to the English dictionary.

jambo

6 People who cannot hear spoken words may use hand signals called sign language, to communicate. *As in speech, there are many languages, as well as regional differences.* This could be different signals used in certain areas, or changes in how fast or expressively people sign.

A WAY WITH WORDS

Got something to say? Language enables us to share our thoughts and ideas, to express our feelings, to persuade and to blame, and to shape events around us. It is a powerful tool, but how does it make the world turn?

bonjour

olá

नमस्ते

7 Do you talk to yourself? An *idioglossia* is the name for a language spoken by just one person. A child who grows up in a multilingual household sometimes makes his or her own language. Twins may have their own secret language, called cryptophasia.

8 In some movies, books, and video games, *characters communicate in a fictional language*. Star Trek introduced the Klingon language in its TV show and movies. Klingon has been created so comprehensively that fans of the show can learn the language and speak to each other using it. There is even a Klingon dictionary.

hello

sannu

9 Languages can encompass a wide range of sounds. *Several languages in southern and eastern Africa use clicking sounds as consonants.* In La Gomera in the Canary Islands, some of the inhabitants use a unique language called Silbo Gomera—Spanish, but translated into whistles in order to be heard over long distances.

10 *Robot talkers such as Apple's Siri can speak more than 20 different languages,* and can copy accents and male or female voices. However, their bland and emotionless voices cannot really match the patterns of human speech, because it's not just what you say that conveys meaning, but how you say it.

11 Long before texting, *Morse code was developed to send messages by a series of short or long bursts of electricity,* represented by dots and dashes. Inventor Samuel Morse worked out the most common letters and gave those the shortest pulses. Three dots are used for "S" and three dashes for "O," so SOS became a distress signal because it was quick and easy to send.

merhaba

12 The United Nation's *Universal Declaration of Human Rights has been translated into more than 300 different languages,* making it the most translated document in the world.

مرحبا

13 *"Abracadabra!" is a magic word in any language.* The word first appeared in the journals of a third-century Roman doctor. He urged people with malaria to write down the lucky word on paper, wrap it in cloth, and tie it around their necks for nine days. Sadly, the magical cure did not work.

13½ A language no longer in everyday use is described as dead. *You may think Latin died out after the Roman Empire crumbled, but it is still alive* as the international language of science, law, and especially religion. In the Vatican City, near Rome, there's even a cash machine with instructions in Latin.

DRESS TO IMPRESS

Throughout history, people have used clothing to flaunt their wealth. In the 14th to 16th centuries, the discovery of new worlds brought exotic fabrics to Europe. Opulent fashions, like the 16th-century outfits shown here, really took off.

Linen undergarment

Detachable sleeve

Bum roll

Woolen stockings

Leather shoes

1 *Fashionable nobles wore so many layers of clothing that they required assistance to get dressed. For Queen Elizabeth I (who ruled England from 1558 to 1603), this ritual took more than two hours every day.*

2 *Ladies wore a "pair of bodies"—two garments that laced up tightly to shape the upper body. They were sometimes stiffened with wood, metal, or even whalebone—it was impossible to slouch.*

3 *Clothing contained holes and slashes to allow the contrasting color of the lining to show through. Gowns could have as many as 9,000 small holes.*

4 *Cloth was soaked in urine before being made into clothes because the ammonia in the liquid kept colors bright. Families filled urine pots to give to the fabric industries.*

5 *During Queen Elizabeth I's reign, most ordinary women had only one or two dresses. The queen, however, owned around 3,000 gowns. She was the style icon of her time.*

6 *A stiff, hooped skirt called a farthingale spread out the layers of skirts. The skirt made the wearer around 2ft (60 cm) wider. A padded "bum roll," tied around the waist, widened the hips.*

7 Elaborate neck ruffs were worn by both men and women. English playwright Ben Jonson (1572–1637) observed that *a large ruff made it look like a person was wearing their head on a plate.*

8 In 1571, an English law stated that *all males over six years old, except nobles, had to wear a woolen cap on Sundays.* This law was passed to make plenty of work for those who made the caps.

9 Over his shirt, a man wore a doublet. It was *often padded with horsehair to make him look broader* at the shoulders and narrower at the waist.

Linen undershirt

10 Breeches were puffy, padded garments worn to the knee. One account tells of a man who was *arrested for over-padding his breeches,* inside which were found *two tablecloths, 10 napkins, and four shirts.*

11 The *oldest-known trousers were made in China around 3,300 years ago.* Their shape suggests that they were invented to make horseback riding more comfortable.

12 *Children were dressed as miniature adults* until the 19th century, when clothes for children were first styled. From around 1650 to 1900, *boys wore dresses,* sometimes up to eight years of age.

Leather boots

Woolen hose

13½ You may think that people who lived hundreds of years ago were dirty and smelly, but although they didn't wash their clothes as often as we do, they still wore *clean underclothes each day.*

13 During the Renaissance, *heeled shoes became a status symbol.* This is where the expression "well-heeled," to describe a person of wealth, very likely comes from.

CHOCOLATE CHUNKS

From the bitter beans of the cocoa plant comes the world's sweetest treat—chocolate. For the last century, global demand has grown every year. Today, chocoholics splurge in excess of $100 billion a year on this tasty snack.

1 Chocolate is made from cocoa beans, which are the seeds of the cocoa plant. *About 40 cocoa beans are used to make each bar of chocolate—about one pod's worth.*

2 The colorful pods of the cocoa plant **open to reveal white pulp encasing sweet juice and bitter beans.** *The plant's scientific name—Theobroma cacao—means "food of the gods" in Latin. The small tree thrives in Central and South America.*

3 About five million **chocolate farmers produce 4.2 million tons of cocoa beans a year.** *The Ivory Coast produces the most—30 percent of the world's total.*

4 To make chocolate, cocoa beans are **fermented, dried, cleaned, roasted, and shelled, before being ground down into pure liquid form.** *Cocoa solids and cocoa butter—the two key ingredients of solid chocolate—are then extracted.*

5 **In old black-and-white films, chocolate syrup was used as fake blood.** *Its goopy consistency matched that of real blood.*

6 **Solid chocolate was invented in 1847**, *when Englishman Joseph Fry mixed melted cocoa butter with liquid chocolate. The creamy creation contained added sweet ingredients, including sugar.*

7 Crunchy chocolate critters might not seem the tastiest of treats, but **chocolate-coated scorpions are sold around the world.** The venom is removed before coating—just in case.

8 The ancient civilizations of Central and South America were the very first to enjoy chocolate. Their bitter brew "xocolatl" would have been spicier than today's hot chocolate, because it contained not just cocoa beans, but also chilies and spices. **Aztec emperor Montezuma drank about 50 cups a day from his golden chalice.**

9 Cocoa beans were so highly prized by the ancient Aztecs and Mayas that **they were used as currency.** Considered more valuable than gold, they were exchanged for other goods.

10 Europeans eat almost half of the world's chocolate. **The average Swiss citizen eats about 26 lb (11.9 kg) of chocolate a year**—that's about the same weight as four bricks.

11 There could be **tiny insect parts** hidden in your chocolate bar, because some **bugs can get mashed up with the cocoa beans.** People who are allergic to chocolate may really be reacting to these impurities.

12 **Cocoa powder contains a powerful stimulant** called theobromine—harmless to us, but **highly poisonous to dogs and cats.** Humans would have to consume impossibly huge quantities to be affected.

13½ Despite its name, **white chocolate is not technically chocolate at all.** This is because it does not contain any cocoa solids, only cocoa butter.

13 Chocolate toothpaste is not as unhealthy as you might think. Some studies claim the **theobromine in cocoa powder is better than fluoride at protecting teeth.**

HEAVY METAL

It's impossible to imagine the modern world without metals. These strong, workable materials are all around us, in cars and cans, saucepans and skyscrapers. Pure metals are elements—substances made from only one type of atom.

1 The most familiar kind of metals are known as the transition metals. *Hard and shiny, they can be bent or hammered into shape, and have high melting points.*

2 Most metals are not found in pure form, but locked up in rocks called ores. *To get to the metal, the rocks are smelted—heated with chemicals—to separate the metal from other elements.*

3 Iron is the sixth most common element in the Universe. *Earth's core consists of a gigantic single crystal of iron, up to 10,800°F (6,000°C)— hotter than the surface of the Sun.*

4 Copper was the first metal to be used by humans, *around 10,000 years ago. It was found in pure form and used to make jewelry. The first copper mines date back to the 5th millennium BCE.*

5 Why can't Superman see through lead? *It's because this metal is so dense that his X-ray vision can't penetrate it. Lead lining is often used in hospitals to protect staff from X-ray equipment.*

6 Lead isn't the heaviest metal. *That title goes to osmium, which is twice as dense. A piece of osmium about the size of a microwave oven would weigh as much as a small car.*

Alloy car wheel hubs

Native silver

Galena (lead ore)

Copper

Copper pipe

Steel paperclip

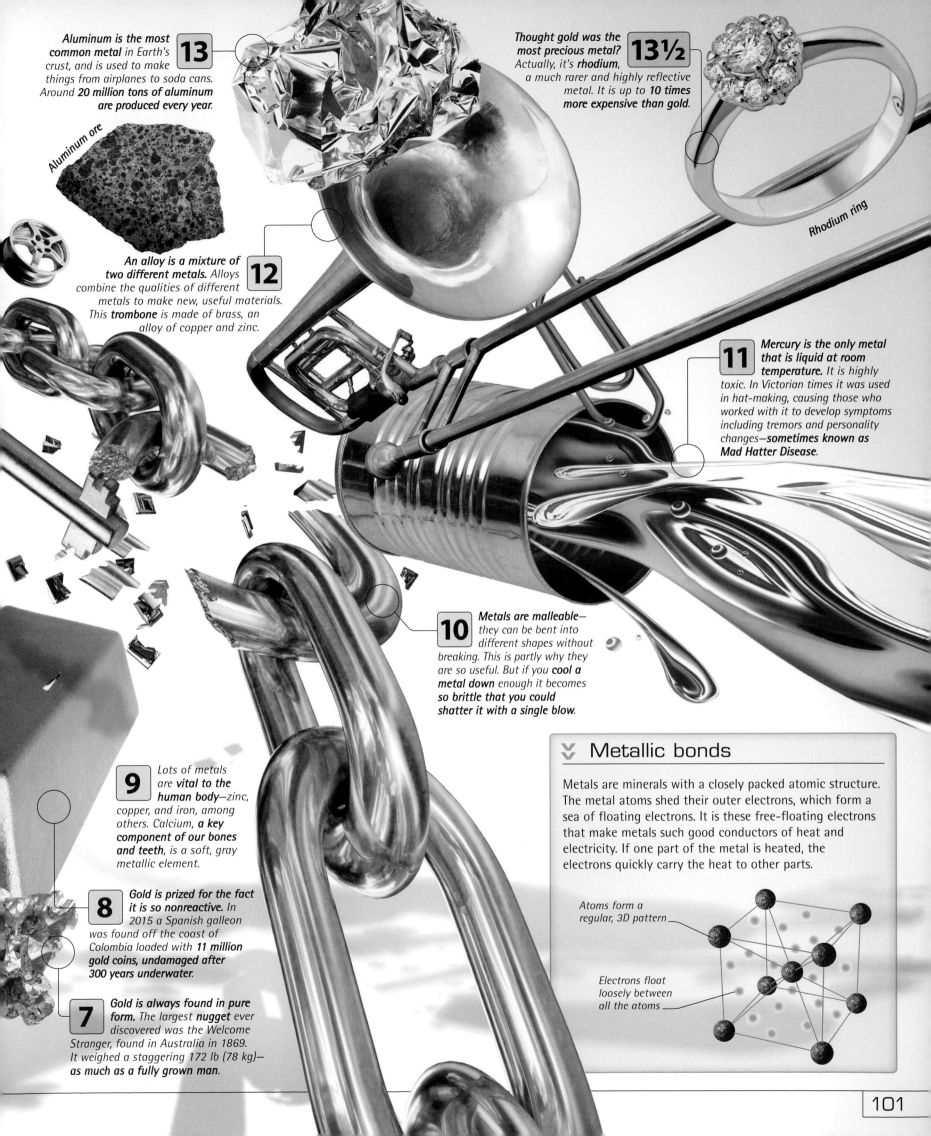

13 Aluminum is the most common metal in Earth's crust, and is used to make things from airplanes to soda cans. Around **20 million tons** of aluminum are produced every year.

Aluminum ore

13½ Thought gold was the most precious metal? Actually, it's **rhodium**, a much rarer and highly reflective metal. It is up to **10 times more expensive than gold**.

Rhodium ring

12 An alloy is a mixture of two different metals. Alloys combine the qualities of different metals to make new, useful materials. This **trombone** is made of brass, an alloy of copper and zinc.

11 Mercury is the only metal that is liquid at room temperature. It is highly toxic. In Victorian times it was used in hat-making, causing those who worked with it to develop symptoms including tremors and personality changes—**sometimes known as Mad Hatter Disease**.

10 Metals are malleable— they can be bent into different shapes without breaking. This is partly why they are so useful. But if you **cool a metal down** enough it becomes **so brittle that you could shatter it with a single blow**.

⌄ Metallic bonds

Metals are minerals with a closely packed atomic structure. The metal atoms shed their outer electrons, which form a sea of floating electrons. It is these free-floating electrons that make metals such good conductors of heat and electricity. If one part of the metal is heated, the electrons quickly carry the heat to other parts.

Atoms form a regular, 3D pattern

Electrons float loosely between all the atoms

9 Lots of metals are vital to the **human body**—zinc, copper, and iron, among others. Calcium, **a key component of our bones and teeth**, is a soft, gray metallic element.

8 Gold is prized for the fact it is so nonreactive. In 2015 a Spanish galleon was found off the coast of Colombia loaded with **11 million gold coins, undamaged after 300 years underwater**.

7 Gold is always found in pure form. The largest **nugget** ever discovered was the Welcome Stranger, found in Australia in 1869. It weighed a staggering 172 lb (78 kg)— as much as a fully grown man.

PLANE CRAZY

Dreams of flying are as old as humankind itself, but the real story of human aviation began around 230 years ago with a hot-air balloon. The 20th-century invention of the powered airplane has helped shape the modern world.

1 The age of flight lifted off in 1783 when the first hot-air balloon, built by the Montgolfier brothers of France, **was flown with a duck, a sheep, and a rooster on board.**

2 In 1903, the Wright brothers achieved the first powered airplane flight in their craft, the Wright Flyer, in North Carolina, US. Astronaut **Neil Armstrong carried a small piece of that original aircraft when he walked on the Moon in 1969.**

3 In 1919, John Alcock and Arthur Brown from the UK were the first to fly **nonstop across the Atlantic.** At one point, Alcock had to clamber out on the plane wings to remove ice from the engine.

4 Amelia Earhart of the US became the **first woman to fly solo across the Atlantic** in 1928. Five years later, she mysteriously disappeared while trying to fly around the world.

5 One of the biggest aircraft, Germany's LZ 129 Hindenburg, **stretched the length of three soccer fields and even had its own post office.** In 1937, the hydrogen gas in the balloon exploded, killing 36 people.

6 World War I saw the **first use of aircraft on a large scale in a war.** In 1944, during World War II, Germany developed the **first operational jet fighter and the most advanced aircraft** of its time—the Messerschmitt Me 262.

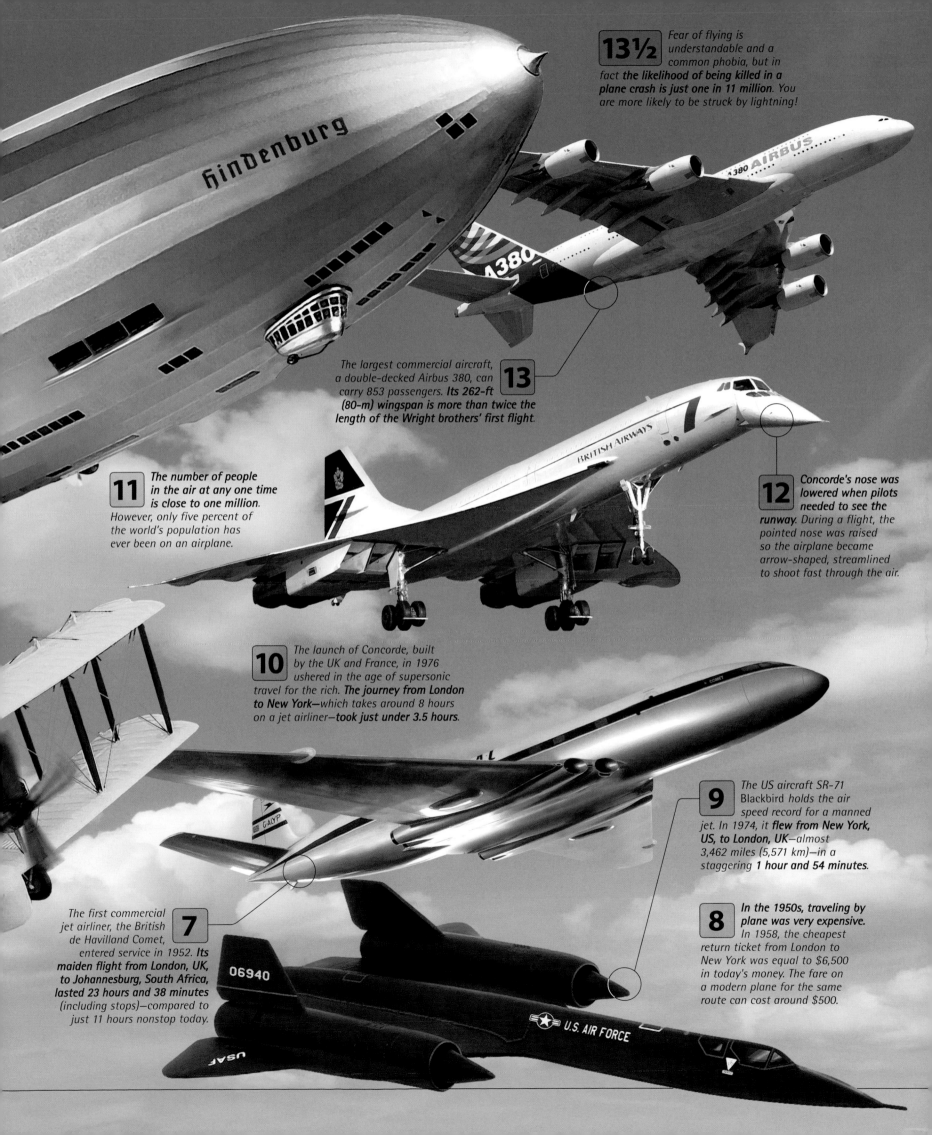

13½ Fear of flying is understandable and a common phobia, but in fact **the likelihood of being killed in a plane crash is just one in 11 million.** You are more likely to be struck by lightning!

The largest commercial aircraft, a double-decked Airbus 380, can carry 853 passengers. **Its 262-ft (80-m) wingspan is more than twice the length of the Wright brothers' first flight.** **13**

11 **The number of people in the air at any one time is close to one million.** However, only five percent of the world's population has ever been on an airplane.

12 Concorde's nose was lowered when pilots needed to see the runway. During a flight, the pointed nose was raised so the airplane became arrow-shaped, streamlined to shoot fast through the air.

10 The launch of Concorde, built by the UK and France, in 1976 ushered in the age of supersonic travel for the rich. **The journey from London to New York—which takes around 8 hours on a jet airliner—took just under 3.5 hours.**

9 The US aircraft SR-71 Blackbird holds the air speed record for a manned jet. In 1974, it **flew from New York, US, to London, UK—almost 3,462 miles (5,571 km)—in a staggering 1 hour and 54 minutes.**

The first commercial jet airliner, the British de Havilland Comet, entered service in 1952. **Its maiden flight from London, UK, to Johannesburg, South Africa, lasted 23 hours and 38 minutes** (including stops)—compared to just 11 hours nonstop today. **7**

8 **In the 1950s, traveling by plane was very expensive.** In 1958, the cheapest return ticket from London to New York was equal to $6,500 in today's money. The fare on a modern plane for the same route can cost around $500.

06940

U.S. AIR FORCE

USAF

BRIGHT SPARKS

Flick a switch and trillions of charged particles move through wires, pushed by the invisible force of electricity. Today, we use electricity to power almost everything, but the first electricity supplies were used only to light electric bulbs.

An electric current is the flow of tiny charged particles. In electricity supplies, those particles are electrons, which are found in every atom and carry a negative charge. **[1]**

The first practical light bulb was **created in 1881 by US inventor Thomas Edison.** Within 25 years it had reached millions of homes. At first, **warning signs were needed**, so people who were used to oil lamps and candles didn't try to light the bulbs with matches. **[2]**

The first light bulbs were "incandescent." They worked by passing an electric current through a thin filament, which **becomes so hot that it glows.** Edison **tried more than 6,000 filament materials, including beard hair,** before deciding on charred bamboo. **[3]**

Incandescent bulbs are still in use today, but with **filaments made of tungsten** (a type of metal) wound into a tight coil. If you could uncoil a modern tungsten light bulb filament, it would be **more than 20 in (50 cm) long.** **[4]**

Edison invented the screw-in base and a whole range of other innovations to make his bulb successful. In total he **filed more than 1,000 patents** for inventions ranging from sockets and switches to power station equipment. **[5]**

Some animals are capable of creating their own electricity. The electric eel—not really an eel at all, but a fish—**stuns its prey with a powerful electric shock of several hundred volts.** **[6]**

Metal is a conductor—its **electrons float free from their atoms and can move**, so electric current can flow. A bulb has a **metallic electrical foot contact** that brings electricity into the light bulb when it is connected to the electricity supply. **[7]**

[8] The longest-burning light bulb has been **glowing for more than 100 years,** since 1901, in Livermore, California, US. It operates on around 4 watts, whereas most incandescent light bulbs operate on 60 watts or 100 watts.

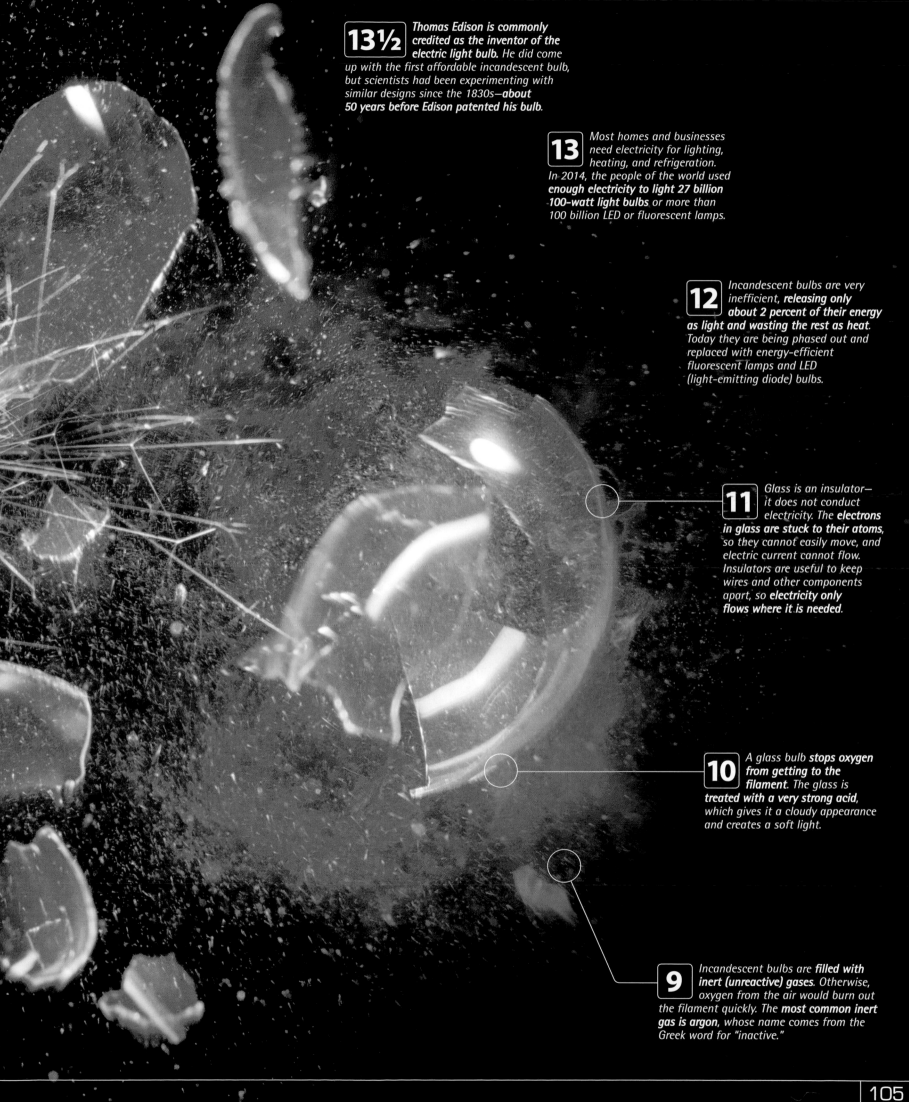

13½ **Thomas Edison is commonly credited as the inventor of the electric light bulb.** He did come up with the first affordable incandescent bulb, but scientists had been experimenting with similar designs since the 1830s—*about 50 years before Edison patented his bulb.*

13 Most homes and businesses need electricity for lighting, heating, and refrigeration. In 2014, the people of the world used **enough electricity to light 27 billion 100-watt light bulbs** or more than 100 billion LED or fluorescent lamps.

12 Incandescent bulbs are very inefficient, **releasing only about 2 percent of their energy as light and wasting the rest as heat.** Today they are being phased out and replaced with energy-efficient fluorescent lamps and LED (light-emitting diode) bulbs.

11 Glass is an insulator— it does not conduct electricity. The **electrons in glass are stuck to their atoms,** so they cannot easily move, and electric current cannot flow. Insulators are useful to keep wires and other components apart, so **electricity only flows where it is needed.**

10 A glass bulb **stops oxygen from getting to the filament.** The glass is **treated with a very strong acid,** which gives it a cloudy appearance and creates a soft light.

9 Incandescent bulbs are **filled with inert (unreactive) gases.** Otherwise, oxygen from the air would burn out the filament quickly. The **most common inert gas is argon,** whose name comes from the Greek word for "inactive."

WHALE TALE

Among the mightiest mammals of the sea, orcas are also known as killer whales due to their hunting prowess. Their big, bulky bodies allow them to tackle fearsome prey—including other top predators like the great white shark.

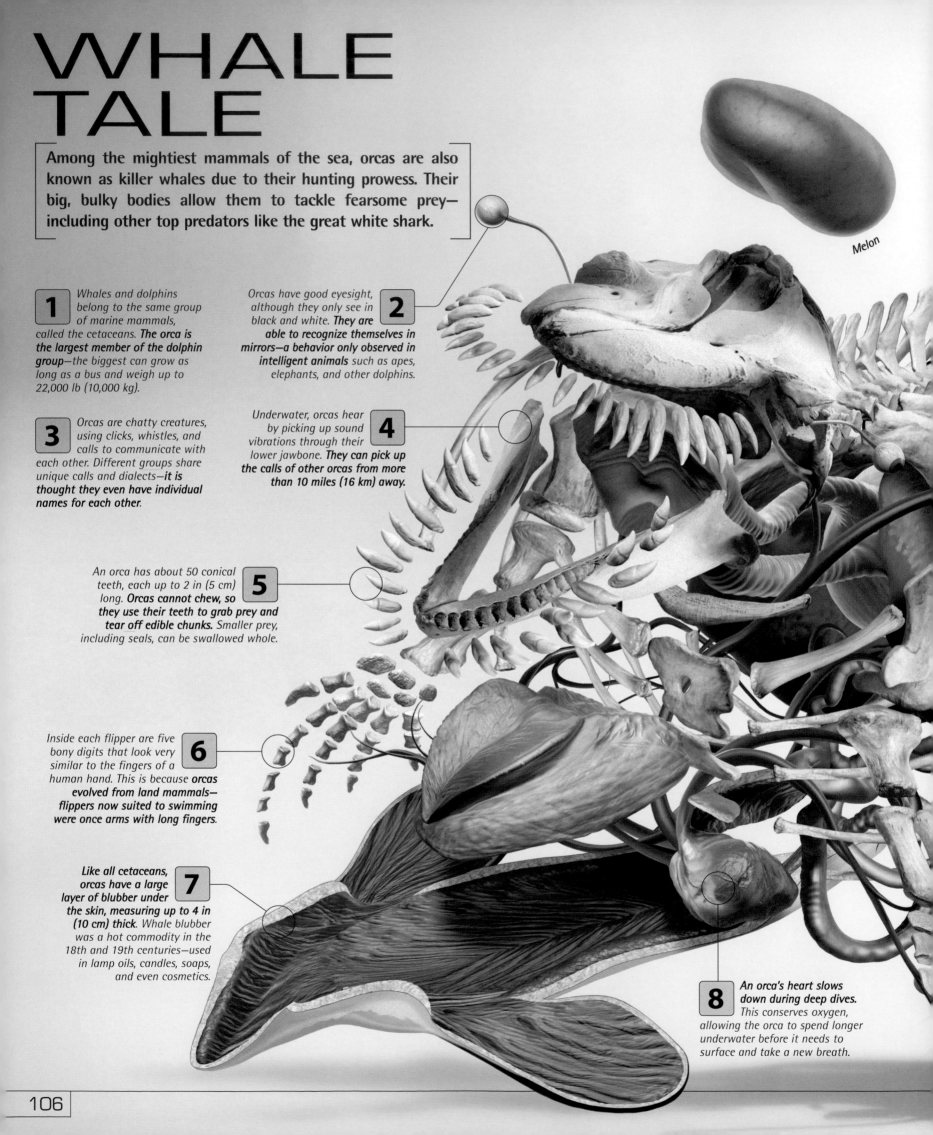

Melon

1 Whales and dolphins belong to the same group of marine mammals, called the cetaceans. *The orca is the largest member of the dolphin group*—the biggest can grow as long as a bus and weigh up to 22,000 lb (10,000 kg).

2 Orcas have good eyesight, although they only see in black and white. *They are able to recognize themselves in mirrors—a behavior only observed in intelligent animals* such as apes, elephants, and other dolphins.

3 Orcas are chatty creatures, using clicks, whistles, and calls to communicate with each other. Different groups share unique calls and dialects—*it is thought they even have individual names for each other.*

4 Underwater, orcas hear by picking up sound vibrations through their lower jawbone. *They can pick up the calls of other orcas from more than 10 miles (16 km) away.*

5 An orca has about 50 conical teeth, each up to 2 in (5 cm) long. *Orcas cannot chew, so they use their teeth to grab prey and tear off edible chunks.* Smaller prey, including seals, can be swallowed whole.

6 Inside each flipper are five bony digits that look very similar to the fingers of a human hand. This is because **orcas evolved from land mammals**—flippers now suited to swimming were once arms with long fingers.

7 Like all cetaceans, orcas have a large layer of blubber under the skin, measuring up to 4 in (10 cm) thick. Whale blubber was a hot commodity in the 18th and 19th centuries—used in lamp oils, candles, soaps, and even cosmetics.

8 *An orca's heart slows down during deep dives.* This conserves oxygen, allowing the orca to spend longer underwater before it needs to surface and take a new breath.

106

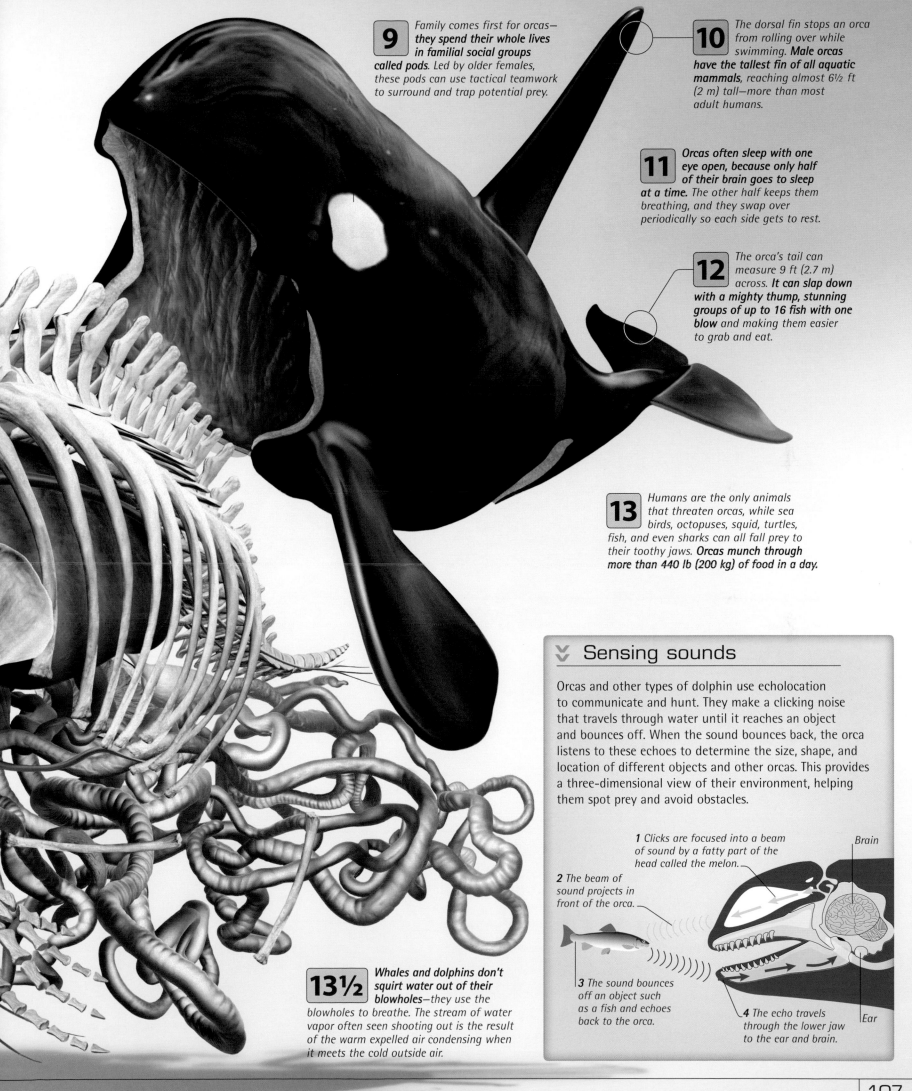

9 Family comes first for orcas—**they spend their whole lives in familial social groups called pods.** Led by older females, these pods can use tactical teamwork to surround and trap potential prey.

10 The dorsal fin stops an orca from rolling over while swimming. **Male orcas have the tallest fin of all aquatic mammals,** reaching almost 6½ ft (2 m) tall—more than most adult humans.

11 **Orcas often sleep with one eye open, because only half of their brain goes to sleep at a time.** The other half keeps them breathing, and they swap over periodically so each side gets to rest.

12 The orca's tail can measure 9 ft (2.7 m) across. **It can slap down with a mighty thump, stunning groups of up to 16 fish with one blow** and making them easier to grab and eat.

13 Humans are the only animals that threaten orcas, while sea birds, octopuses, squid, turtles, fish, and even sharks can all fall prey to their toothy jaws. **Orcas munch through more than 440 lb (200 kg) of food in a day.**

13½ Whales and dolphins don't **squirt water out of their blowholes**—they use the blowholes to breathe. The stream of water vapor often seen shooting out is the result of the warm expelled air condensing when it meets the cold outside air.

⌄⌄ Sensing sounds

Orcas and other types of dolphin use echolocation to communicate and hunt. They make a clicking noise that travels through water until it reaches an object and bounces off. When the sound bounces back, the orca listens to these echoes to determine the size, shape, and location of different objects and other orcas. This provides a three-dimensional view of their environment, helping them spot prey and avoid obstacles.

1 Clicks are focused into a beam of sound by a fatty part of the head called the melon.

2 The beam of sound projects in front of the orca.

3 The sound bounces off an object such as a fish and echoes back to the orca.

4 The echo travels through the lower jaw to the ear and brain.

Brain

Ear

1 Prehistoric people didn't have numbers, but we know that **they kept records of how many things they had by making marks in wood, bone, and stone.** Notched bones and antlers have been found dating back 30,000 years.

2 When people started counting they almost certainly used their hands. **The modern decimal system is based on the fact we have ten fingers.** If we had a total of eight fingers and thumbs, we would probably be counting in eights.

3 **Some numbers seem to have almost magical properties—three, for example.** If the individual numbers in any number add up to 3 or a multiple of 3, the entire number can be divided by 3. Take 5,394 and you'll find 5 + 3 + 9 + 4 = 21, which is a multiple of 3.

4 The **ancient Babylonians invented one of the first written number systems** about 5,000 years ago, and there have been many others through history. The numbers we use today are **based on the Hindu-Arabic system that was developed more than 1,000 years ago.**

5 Numbers can help us make sense of shapes, although circles are tricky. Greek geek Archimedes worked out that **the secret of a circle is "π",** pronounced pi. It represents a number that you can't calculate exactly but begins 3.14, and never ends. **Using pi you can calculate a circle's circumference** (outer edge) when you only know the diameter (width).

THINK OF A NUMBER

Numbers add up to a big part of our lives. Some are very odd, while others break even. One finds fortune, another brings bad luck. It's impossible to imagine life without them. You wouldn't know when your birthday was, or your age!

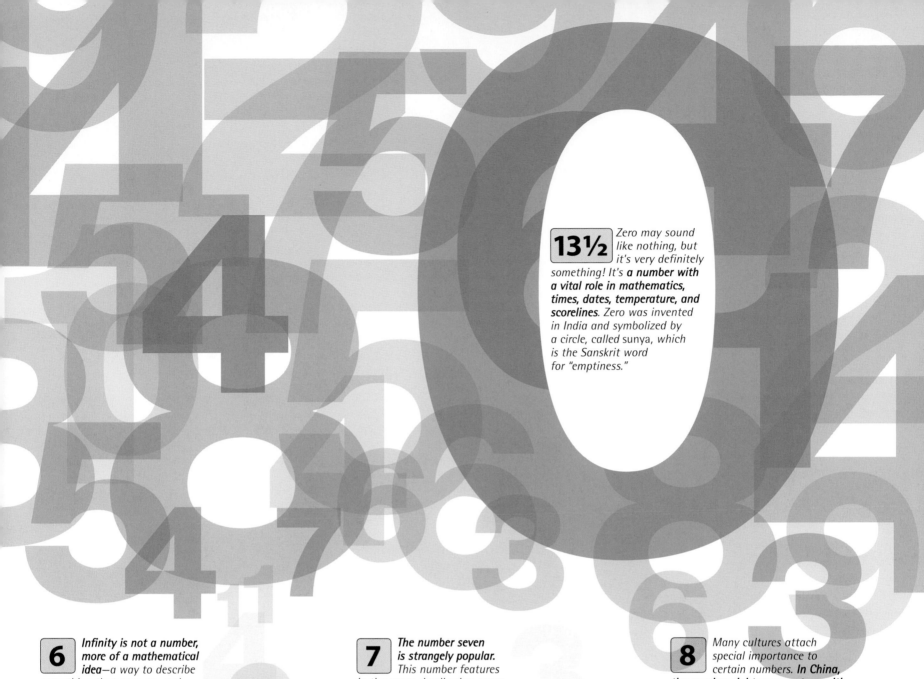

13½ Zero may sound like nothing, but it's very definitely something! It's **a number with a vital role in mathematics, times, dates, temperature, and scorelines**. Zero was invented in India and symbolized by a circle, called *sunya*, which is the Sanskrit word for "emptiness."

6 *Infinity is not a number, more of a mathematical idea*—a way to describe something that goes on, and on, and on, forever. So, despite what you may have heard, **it's impossible to reach infinity and there is no beyond.**

7 *The number seven is strangely popular.* This number features in the seven deadly sins, seven wonders of the world, seven colors of the rainbow, seven seas, seven days in a week, seven dwarves, and seven continents.

8 *Many cultures attach special importance to certain numbers.* **In China, the number eight represents wealth.** Houses, telephone numbers, and car registration plates featuring eights sell for large sums of money.

9 For tricky sums, an electronic calculator is handy. But **in some countries they still prefer an abacus**, a system thousands of years old that uses sliding beads on bars. In 1957, **when the Russians launched** Sputnik, **the first space satellite, it is said they used an abacus for some of the calculations.**

10 **When you've got numbers you can measure things**—not just length, height, and weight, but the severity of an earthquake, or the heat of a chili. **This fiery fruit is measured on the Scoville scale**, from 0 to 2,200,000—the record-breaking Carolina Reaper!

11 *A prime number is a number divisible only by itself and one,* such as 2 (the only even prime number), 3, 5, 7, and 11. This indivisible quality makes codes with prime numbers in them even harder to crack, so **primes are highly prized for use in data security coding.**

12 Numbers keep getting bigger. In 1920, US mathematician Edward Kasner asked his nephew what to call the **number 1 followed by 100 zeros.** He came up with the name **"googol."** The number 1 followed by a googol of zeros is a googolplex, and 1 followed by a googolplex of zeros is **a googolplexian, the biggest number to be given a name.**

13 In some countries the number 13 is considered unlucky. **Fear of 13 even has a name—triskaidekaphobia.** There are all sorts of different reasons why. The Romans, for example, believed it symbolized destruction, while Christians associate it with Judas, the 13th apostle who betrayed Jesus. **Many large hotels do not have a 13th floor, while some aircraft do not have a 13th row.**

3 A bee's buzz comes from the sound of its wings beating *rapidly*—*more than 200 times every second, or 12,000 times a minute. Honey bees have two pairs of wings, joined by hooks called hamuli.*

⌄ Bee colony

Within a bee colony there are three main roles: the workers, the drones, and the queen. The main job of the male drones is to mate with the queen, who lays up to 2,000 eggs per day. The female worker bees collect pollen and nectar, produce honey, keep the hive clean, and tend to the eggs and growing larvae. A typical colony will contain around 60,000 workers, 300 drones, a single queen, and up to 30,000 larvae and pupae.

Drone   Queen   Worker

The drones are larger than the workers, with bigger wings but no stingers. The queen has a long abdomen containing special egg-laying organs. Workers are half the weight of drones, with a longer proboscis and a barbed stinger.

1 *Flowers provide pollen, a protein-rich food source, and the nectar the bees use to make honey to feed the colony. Honey bees* **visit 2 million flowers and fly 50,000 miles (80,000 km)** *to make just 1 lb (500 g) of honey.*

2 *The bee pictured here is a female worker bee—as are all the bees that collect honey and pollen. The* **average lifespan of a worker is 5–6 weeks**, *during which time she'll make* **only one-twelfth of a teaspoon of honey.**

BUSY BEES

The honey bee is the best known of almost 20,000 species of bees. Armed with super senses and a sharp sting, these industrious insects buzz from flower to flower, pollinating the plants as they go.

4 A bee's **supersensitive antenna has thousands of scent receptors**. The bee can distinguish between different types of flowers and detect whether a flower has any pollen or nectar from 10 feet away.

5 The bee sucks up nectar using its strawlike tongue, or proboscis. **Back at the hive, it regurgitates the nectar**. Other workers **fan the liquid with their wings**, reducing the water content and turning it into thick, sticky honey.

6 Humans were collecting wild honey **as far back as 15,000** BCE. The ancient Egyptians kept bees in hives, and honey has been found in the tombs of pharaohs. Even after 3,000 years it was still edible, because **honey never goes off**.

7 Compound eyes on either side of the bee's head are made of **hundreds of tiny lenses**. Bees **are able to detect movement that happens in one-300th of a second**. On a movie screen we see a smooth projection but a honey bee would be able to distinguish each individual frame.

8 **Scientists in the US and Europe are training bees to detect bombs** by exposing them to the smell of explosives and sugar at the same time. Soon, **if the bees smell explosives, they extend their proboscis** in anticipation. In laboratory tests the bees performed well, but using them in real scenarios has proved challenging.

9 **Honey bees dance** to let the rest of the colony know about good food sources. The bee runs in a figure-eight shape while **waggling its body from side to side**. The angle of the dance indicates the direction of the food source, while the speed of the waggle reveals the distance.

10 The bee pollinates plants by **picking up pollen on its body and transferring it from one flower to the next**. Honey bees are one of the most important pollinators—they pollinate up to **one-third of all our food crops**. Without bees we'd lose many of our favorite fruit and vegetables.

11 Pads of bristles on the bee's back legs serve as **pollen baskets**: the bee packs pollen onto them to carry back to the hive. **One bee can carry half her body weight in pollen.**

12 They've been around for tens of millions of years, but today honey bees are **declining at record rates**. Across the US and Europe, **almost half of all hives have been wiped out by colony collapse disorder**—a mysterious phenomenon where all the workers suddenly abandon their hive.

13 Swarms of robotic bees sounds like something from science fiction but **RoboBees really are in development in the US**. Half the size of a paperclip and with wings controlled by artificial muscles, these micro machines could one day be used to help pollination.

13½ Everyone knows that **a bee dies after it stings**. But it only dies if it stings a mammal, because the stinger becomes embedded in the mammal's flesh and is ripped off as the bee flies away. **A bee can sting another insect and live to sting another day.**

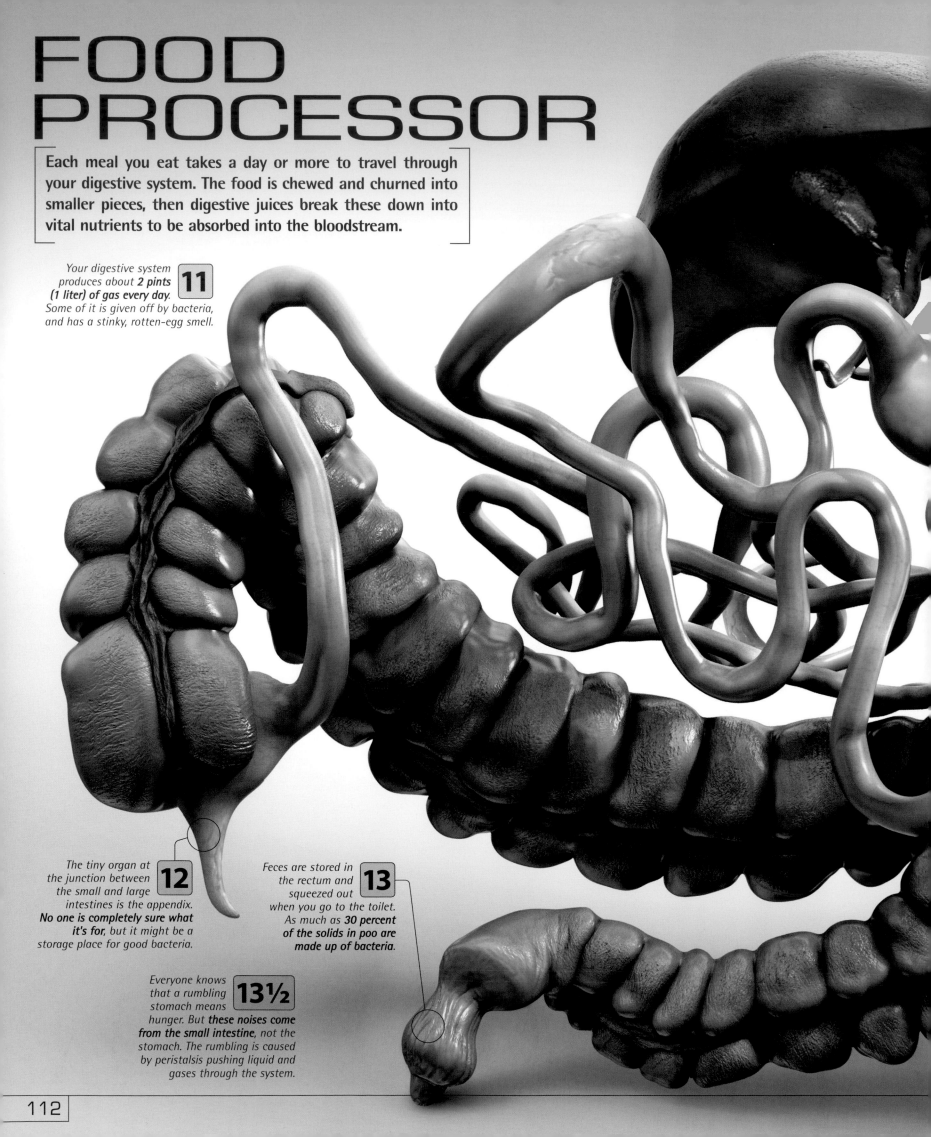

FOOD PROCESSOR

Each meal you eat takes a day or more to travel through your digestive system. The food is chewed and churned into smaller pieces, then digestive juices break these down into vital nutrients to be absorbed into the bloodstream.

*Your digestive system produces about **2 pints (1 liter) of gas every day.** Some of it is given off by bacteria, and has a stinky, rotten-egg smell.* **11**

*The tiny organ at the junction between the small and large intestines is the appendix. **No one is completely sure what it's for,** but it might be a storage place for good bacteria.* **12**

*Feces are stored in the rectum and squeezed out when you go to the toilet. As much as **30 percent of the solids in poo are made up of bacteria.*** **13**

*Everyone knows that a rumbling stomach means hunger. But **these noises come from the small intestine,** not the stomach. The rumbling is caused by peristalsis pushing liquid and gases through the system.* **13½**

6 The liver is the largest and heaviest internal organ, weighing up to 6 lb 10 oz (3 kg). It processes nutrients and it produces a green liquid called bile that helps break down fats.

2 Muscles in the esophagus **tighten and relax in rippling waves called peristalsis** to push chewed food into the stomach. Even if you did a headstand while eating, these muscles would still push the food in the right direction.

1 Digestion starts in the mouth. Teeth mash up the food, and **saliva makes it soft and easy to swallow.** Your salivary glands produce **up to 4 pints (2 liters) of saliva a day.**

5 The pancreas secretes digestive juices into the small intestine, and releases insulin into the blood to control blood sugar levels. **The pancreas has "taste receptors," like those on the tongue,** to detect sugary food so that it can produce the right amount of insulin.

3 An adult's stomach can **expand to the size of a soccer ball** to hold a big meal. In the stomach, chewed up food is mixed with digestive juices and churned up to turn it into a mixture called chyme.

4 The inner wall of the stomach is coated with a thick layer of mucus. **Without this, the stomach would digest itself.** The hydrochloric acid secreted by the stomach wall to kill harmful bacteria is powerful enough to dissolve metal.

7 In the small intestine, the chyme is broken down into nutrients. **The surface area inside the small intestine is about the size of a tennis court.** This is because it is covered with millions of tiny fingerlike projections called villi, which transfer nutrients into the bloodstream.

8 **You could survive without a stomach.** Some people with certain illnesses **have their stomachs removed.** They have to eat smaller portions, but the body gradually adapts.

9 Doctors use a tool called an endoscope to see inside the digestive tract. The first endoscope—a 18¹/₂-in (47-cm) tube—was not flexible like today's instruments. **A sword-swallower had to be employed to test it out.**

10 There are more than **100 trillion bacteria in the digestive tract, most of them in the large intestine.** Here they break down and absorb any nutrients still present. The remaining lumps are called feces (poo).

⋙ Digesting a meal

The digestive tract is a long tube that stretches from mouth to anus. It measures 30 ft (9 m) but fits, neatly coiled up, inside the abdomen. The small intestine itself is 20 ft (6 m) long—twice the length of the large intestine. A big meal takes around 24 hours to travel through the digestive system. In the stomach it is churned into a soupy mixture called chyme, which is then squeezed through the intestines. Nutrients are absorbed into the bloodstream and waste exits the body via the anus.

10 seconds
Food is chewed and travels down the esophagus, arriving in the stomach within seconds.

4 hours
Food spends roughly four hours in the stomach.

6 hours
As the mixture passes through the small intestine nutrients are absorbed.

12 hours
It takes between 12 and 24 hours for undigested waste to pass through the large intestine and out of the body.

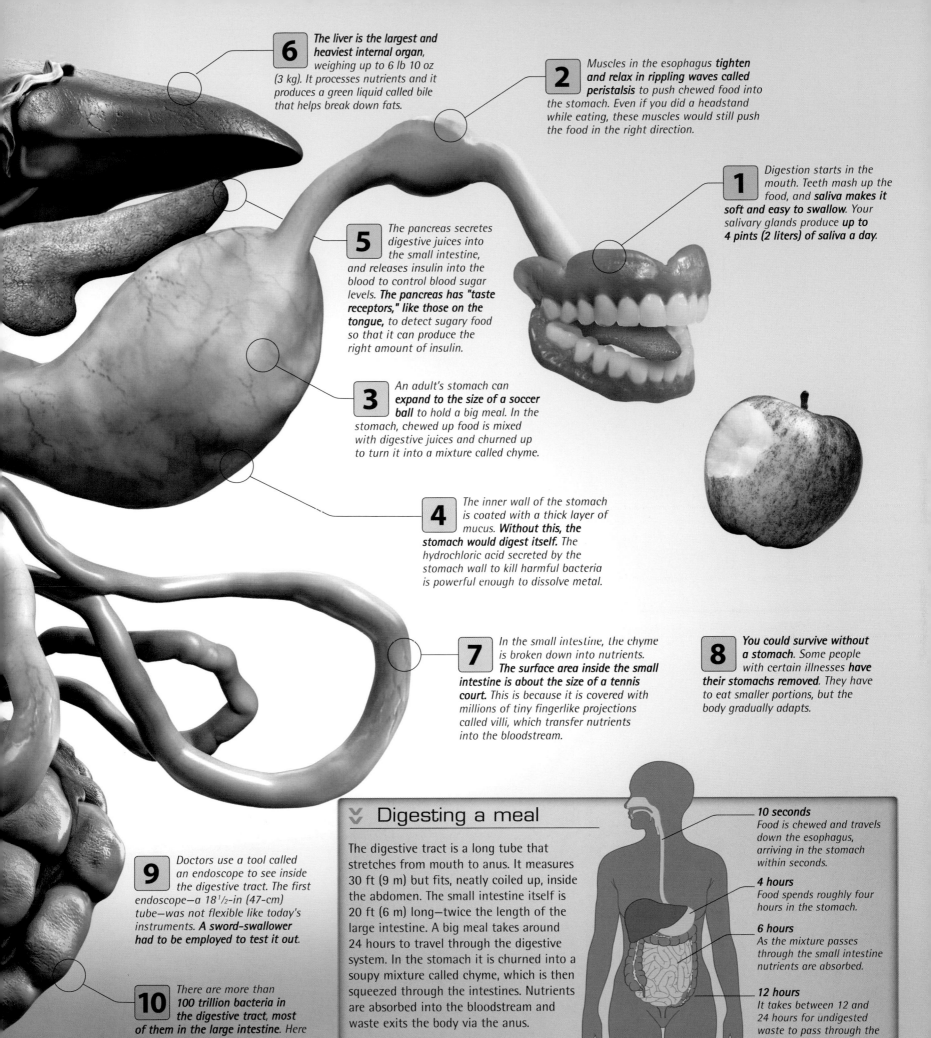

STUNNING SATURN

This giant ball of gas is the sixth planet from the Sun and the second largest in the Solar System. It is most famous for its spectacular ring system—billions of icy particles suspended in space that sparkle in the light of the distant Sun.

1 Saturn is a giant planet —the **second biggest in our Solar System** after Jupiter, and **big enough to fit 764 Earths inside**. It's the farthest planet from Earth easily visible to the naked eye.

2 The planet is made up of hydrogen and helium. In the stormy upper atmosphere, where **winds blow at speeds of up to 1,118 mph (1,800 km/h)**, these are in gas form. Deep inside the planet the intense pressure squeezes them into a liquid.

3 Saturn's rings are made of **chunks of water ice, some as big as buildings and some as small as dust specks**. The main rings are thought to have formed at the same time as Saturn itself, around 4.6 billion years ago.

4 Saturn is the name of the Roman god of agriculture. The Romans held a festival in honor of Saturn in December, with feasting, games, and gift-giving. It may have **influenced the Christian festival of Christmas.**

5 Saturn spins faster than any other planet except Jupiter—a full day on Saturn lasts only 10 hours and 33 minutes. This rapid spinning causes the planet to **bulge out at its equator** and flatten at the poles.

6 The days on Saturn may be short, but the years are long. At a distance of roughly **900 million miles (1.5 billion km)** from the Sun, Saturn takes more than 29 Earth years to complete one orbit.

7 At its closest, Saturn is 1.2 billion km (746 million miles) from Earth. At a steady speed of 110 km/h (68 mph), which is the typical speed of a car, it would take you 1,245 years to get there.

8 Saturn has at least 62 moons. Titan, its largest, is **the only moon with clouds** and a dense, planetlike atmosphere. It has lakes and seas, and rains liquid methane and ethane.

9 Italian astronomer Galileo Galilei discovered Saturn's rings in 1610, but **he didn't know what they were and described them as "ears."** In the 1650s, Dutch astronomer Christiaan Huygens realized the ears were actually rings.

⩔ Inside Saturn

Saturn is mostly hydrogen and helium with a small rocky core at the middle. The stormy atmosphere tops a layer of gas. Further down, the weight of the gas compresses the hydrogen and helium into a liquid. At great depths, the liquid is squeezed so hard it becomes like a metal with magnetic properties.

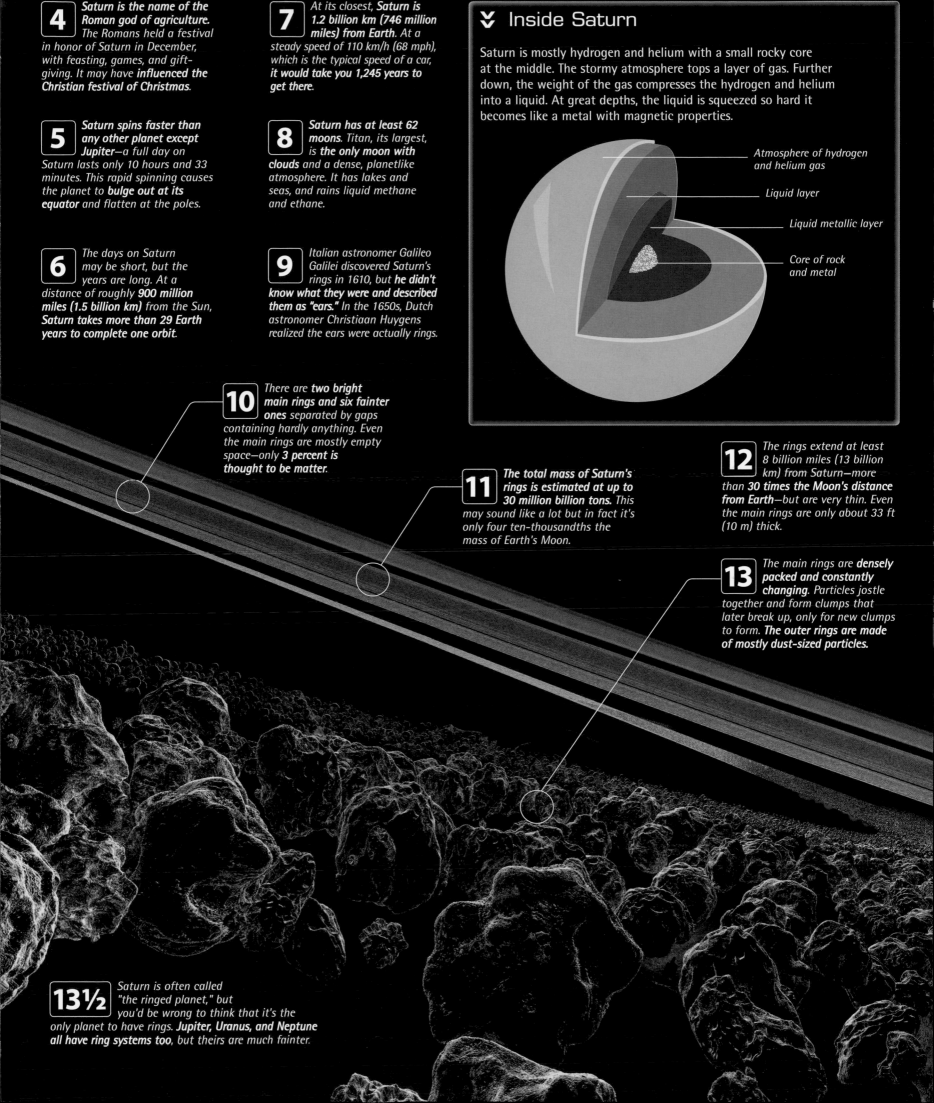

Atmosphere of hydrogen and helium gas

Liquid layer

Liquid metallic layer

Core of rock and metal

10 There are **two bright main rings and six fainter ones** separated by gaps containing hardly anything. Even the main rings are mostly empty space—only **3 percent is thought to be matter.**

11 The total mass of Saturn's rings is estimated at up to **30 million billion tons.** This may sound like a lot but in fact it's only four ten-thousandths the mass of Earth's Moon.

12 The rings extend at least 8 billion miles (13 billion km) from Saturn—more than **30 times the Moon's distance from Earth**—but are very thin. Even the main rings are only about 33 ft (10 m) thick.

13 The main rings are **densely packed and constantly changing.** Particles jostle together and form clumps that later break up, only for new clumps to form. **The outer rings are made of mostly dust-sized particles.**

13½ Saturn is often called "the ringed planet," but you'd be wrong to think that it's the only planet to have rings. **Jupiter, Uranus, and Neptune all have ring systems too,** but theirs are much fainter.

1 Harpy eagles are the **Amazon rain forest's largest flying predators,** snatching monkeys from treetops in **talons 4 in (10 cm) long**—as large as a grizzly bear's claws.

2 The ostrich is the **fastest animal on two legs,** escaping predators by running at 43 mph (70 km/h). At up to 9 ft (2.8 m) tall, the **world's biggest bird is too large to fly.**

3 Native to Europe, **all the starlings in North America are descended from just 60 birds** released in 1890 by a Shakespeare enthusiast, who tried to introduce birds from all the English playwright's works.

4 Parrots are intelligent— **hyacinth macaws use wood as a wedge to crack open nuts.** Some species are as bright as a three-year-old child: Alex, a pet African gray, **could count to six and knew more than 100 words.**

5 The **fulmar gets its name from the Icelandic for "foul gull"**—a reference to the disgusting smell of its stomach oil, which it **projectile-vomits over intruders** who come too close.

7 A peacock's 5-ft- (1.6-m-) **long train grows above its tail.** When fanned out, it makes a **low rustling noise that attracts females,** but is too low for humans to hear.

8 With the **longest bill of any bird,** the Australian pelican can scoop up dozens of fish— and even the odd gull or duck. Up to **24 pints (14 liters) of water are drained** before the catch is swallowed.

6 A contender for the **loudest bird call, a male kakapo's boom carries for 3 miles (5 km).** They call nonstop, eight hours a night for up to five months to attract mates.

BIRDS OF A FEATHER

There are more than 10,000 bird species on Earth. These warm-blooded descendants of the dinosaurs can be found on every continent and are so skillful on the wing that few other flying animals can match their mastery of the skies.

13 The **male weaver builds an extravagant nest** out of 3-ft- (1-m-) long strips of palm and blades of grass, using just its bill. It will **only complete the nest if the female moves in.**

13½ "Bird brained" is an insult, but **birds have as many brain cells as a primate,** just packed into a smaller space. Many **birds can solve problems to get food** and a few use tools—some **crows use sticks to skewer insects.**

12 A puffin can **fly 60 miles (100 km) to find fish** for its chicks. To save on trips, it catches lots of fish during a dive and **stacks them all crosswise in its bill.** The record haul is **62 fish at once.**

10 Birds have an **internal compass that can sense Earth's magnetic field.** This helps them **navigate during migrations** between their nesting and wintering areas—essential when you're an **Arctic tern** migrating a record-breaking 59,650 miles (96,000 km).

11 Hummingbird **wings beat up to 200 times a second**—fueled by **drinking their body weight in nectar** in just hours. You would need to chug **500 cans of soda** for the same sugar intake—but don't try this yourself!

Humboldt penguin

King penguin

⌄⌄ Feather structure

Birds are the only living creatures to have feathers—a multitasking body covering that is used for flight, insulation, camouflage, and courtship displays. A feather is made up of a vane of barbs attached to a shaft. The barbs hook together to form a smooth surface. Birds preen to keep the barbs in order and clean, and also to spread oil from their preen gland, which waterproofs the feathers.

Vane, made up of barbs

Barb

Barbules

Tiny branches called barbules attach to each barb. They hook together, forming a smooth surface.

Shaft

9 Penguins can't fly and waddle awkwardly on land, but they glide through water with ease, using their **rigid wings as flippers for swimming.** One species can **dive to 1,920 ft (585 m)** and stay under water for **up to 20 minutes** on a single breath.

1 The Vikings built different boats for inland waters and open sea, cargo, and warfare. **Only the longest and fastest like this one were used for raiding.** These slender vessels could be dragged onto a beach to launch lightning-swift attacks and quick escapes.

2 The Vikings journeyed far and wide. They **were the first Europeans to reach North America,** around 1000 CE—about 500 years before Christopher Columbus.

VIKING VOYAGES

Aside from their bloodthirsty reputation, the Vikings of Scandinavia were brilliant boatbuilders and seafarers. From the late 700s for nearly 300 years, they navigated, explored, traded, and raided their way along the coasts of Europe.

3 When sailing closer to home, Vikings hugged the coast, looking for landmarks. With no charts or compasses, **navigators relied on the Sun, Moon, and stars,** and learned to recognize seabirds and sea life to help find their way.

4 Ships had one big square sail made from wool. It could be lowered and **used like a tarpaulin to protect** the crew from bad weather.

5 Life on board was basic. **There were no toilets.** The sailors slept in fur-lined sleeping bags and **for fire they used fungus soaked in urine,** which would smoulder rather than burn.

6 Excavations of Viking settlements have uncovered razors, combs, and even **ear cleaners made from animal bones.** Some men bleached their hair. It seems these ax-flinging warriors cared about their appearance, or maybe they were trying to get rid of headlice.

7 The ships were constructed from overlapping planks, which made them strong. Any gaps were filled with **animal hair soaked in pitch to make the ship watertight.** In rough weather, a bailer had to scoop out water that splashed in.

8 Each Viking had a round wooden shield, which slotted into a rack along the side of the ship or hung from cords when not in use. The iron boss in the center protected the warrior's hand gripping it on the other side.

9 If there was no wind, the crew of up to **60 men uncovered the oar holes and rowed.** They sat on chests containing their belongings. A rudder, or steer board, was on the right of the ship. **Today, sailors still say "starboard" for right.**

10 When not raiding, **most Vikings spent their time farming**. In the far north, their animals included reindeer, for milk, meat, and hides. They got around on **skis, sleighs, and skates**, which they called "ice-legs."

11 Vessels were often mounted with **a menacing dragon or serpent's head on the prow**. This was intended to frighten enemies, as well as ward off sea monsters and spirits. In particular, thoughts of the **Midgard Serpent** struck fear into the toughest of Vikings.

12 It wasn't just men who sailed the seas. **Significant numbers of Viking women went on expeditions** to settle places including Ireland, Scotland, Iceland, and Greenland.

13 Most Viking ships have rotted away. In one of the few surviving ships, the **keel** (central timber) is a **single piece of oak, cut from a tree that was at least 82 ft (25 m) tall**, the length of a blue whale.

13½ It's a common myth that **Vikings wore horned helmets**. Although these have been included in depictions of Vikings since the 19th century, **horns would have made a helmet too heavy in battle**.

BLOWING UP A STORM

When a storm cloud unleashes rain, wind, thunder, and lightning, the result is spectacular. The most dangerous type of thunderstorm is a supercell, which can produce even more extremes: monster hailstones, raging winds, and tornadoes.

1 *Thunderstorms are born inside towering cumulonimbus clouds.* These rapidly grow in hot, humid weather, when warm air rises from Earth's surface. **As this air cools, water droplets and ice crystals form.**

2 **A cumulonimbus can extend up into the atmosphere as far as 7¹/₂ miles (12 km).** Strong air currents move up and down through the cloud at up to 100 mph (160 km/h), making the cloud grow taller and taller.

3 **A storm like this one in West Point, Nebraska, in the US's notorious Tornado Alley is called a supercell.** It forms when rising warm air is set spinning by strong winds blowing in different directions at different heights. It contains a huge volume of water and can last for several hours.

4 At any given moment, there are around **2,000 thunderstorms in progress on Earth,** totaling about 16 million a year.

5 Supercells are the rarest type of thunderstorm but produce the most violent weather, including giant hail. The **heaviest hailstone ever recorded** fell in South Dakota, US, in 2010. Weighing a staggering 2 lb (1 kg), it was **three times the size of a tennis ball.**

6 **A tornado is an extremely powerful updraft within a rotating funnel-shaped cloud** that extends to the ground beneath a supercell. The updraft can achieve speeds of up to 150 mph (240 km/h)— acting like a giant vacuum cleaner— **ripping roofs off houses and even plucking the feathers off chickens.**

7 The 1999 outbreak of tornadoes in Oklahoma, US, produced the **highest wind speed ever recorded** on Earth—301 mph (484 km/h). The most deadly tornado in US history **killed more than 700 people** in Missouri, Illinois, and Indiana in 1925.

13½ Lightning never strikes the same place twice, according—wrongly—to the saying. Lightning can strike repeatedly, particularly tall, isolated objects. The **Statue of Liberty in New York City has been struck more than 600 times** since it was put in place in 1886.

13 A hailstorm set the stage for the French Revolution. In 1788, the country was in economic crisis caused by war. Spring drought had put the price of food out of most people's reach, and **when a hailstorm destroyed crops and farms, the starving French populace revolted.**

12 Men are struck by lightning five times more often than women, possibly because more men than women work outdoors. One particularly unlucky man, US park ranger Roy Sullivan, was **struck a record seven times in his life and survived.**

11 If your hair stands up on end during a storm, it's bad news. A positive charge in you is rising to meet a negative charge above. Get indoors fast.

10 Lightning can heat the air to about 54,000°F (30,000°C)—**five times hotter than the surface of the Sun.** This air expands at supersonic speed, creating the boom of thunder.

Lightning can leap from the base of a cloud to the ground, but it can also occur within a cloud, or from one cloud to another cloud. **Some supercells can produce lightning at a rate of 15,000 strikes per hour.** **9**

In the cloud, **water droplets and ice crystals smash into each other,** generating static electricity. This charges the cloud like a giant battery, with a positive electrical charge at the top, and a negative charge at the bottom. **Eventually the charge can reach 100 million volts or more—and flash as a bolt of lightning.** **8**

Cephalopods (octopuses, squid, and cuttlefish) are the most intelligent invertebrates. One quick-witted octopus was smart enough to stage a daring escape from a New Zealand aquarium, slipping out of his tank and through a drainpipe.

3

Opalescent inshore squid

1 Snails and slugs make up more than **three-quarters of the 100,000 known mollusk species.** The queen conch is one of many aquatic snails that glide over the seabed on a single muscular "foot."

2 The giant Pacific octopus can grow up to 10 ft (3 m)—more than one and a half times the height of a man. Octopuses are expert contortionists, **able to squeeze their entire bodies through a hole the size of a coin.**

MIGHTY MOLLUSKS

The snails at the bottom of your garden are a type of mollusk, a diverse group of animals that includes tiny clams and giant squids. Most species found in water; these soft-bodied invertebrates often hide away inside sturdy shells.

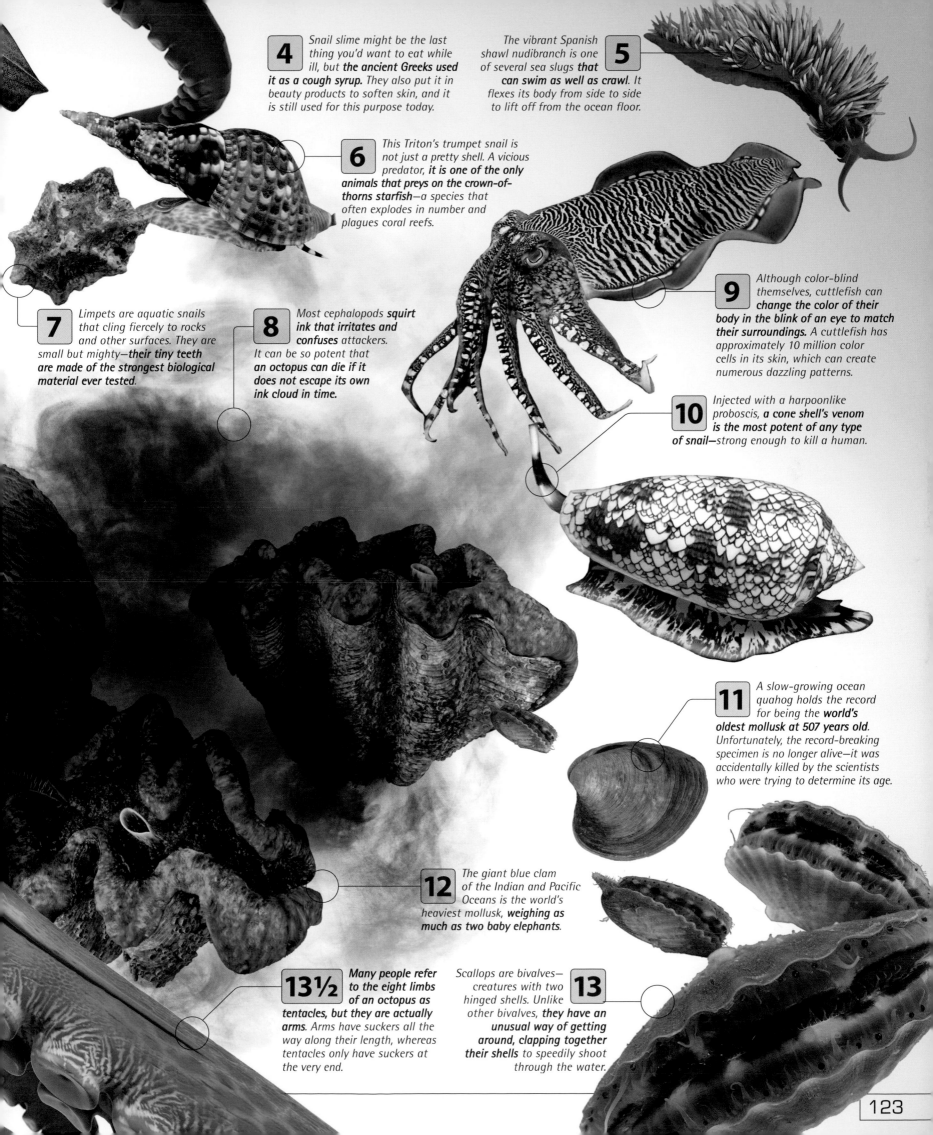

4 Snail slime might be the last thing you'd want to eat while ill, but **the ancient Greeks used it as a cough syrup.** They also put it in beauty products to soften skin, and it is still used for this purpose today.

The vibrant Spanish shawl nudibranch is one of several sea slugs **that can swim as well as crawl.** It flexes its body from side to side to lift off from the ocean floor. **5**

6 This Triton's trumpet snail is not just a pretty shell. A vicious predator, **it is one of the only animals that preys on the crown-of-thorns starfish**—a species that often explodes in number and plagues coral reefs.

7 Limpets are aquatic snails that cling fiercely to rocks and other surfaces. They are small but mighty—**their tiny teeth are made of the strongest biological material ever tested.**

8 Most cephalopods **squirt ink that irritates and confuses** attackers. It can be so potent that **an octopus can die if it does not escape its own ink cloud in time.**

9 Although color-blind themselves, cuttlefish can **change the color of their body in the blink of an eye to match their surroundings.** A cuttlefish has approximately 10 million color cells in its skin, which can create numerous dazzling patterns.

10 Injected with a harpoonlike proboscis, **a cone shell's venom is the most potent of any type of snail**—strong enough to kill a human.

11 A slow-growing ocean quahog holds the record for being the **world's oldest mollusk at 507 years old.** Unfortunately, the record-breaking specimen is no longer alive—it was accidentally killed by the scientists who were trying to determine its age.

12 The giant blue clam of the Indian and Pacific Oceans is the world's heaviest mollusk, **weighing as much as two baby elephants.**

13½ Many people refer to the eight limbs of an octopus as tentacles, but they are actually **arms.** Arms have suckers all the way along their length, whereas tentacles only have suckers at the very end.

Scallops are bivalves—creatures with two hinged shells. Unlike other bivalves, **they have an unusual way of getting around, clapping together their shells** to speedily shoot through the water. **13**

EARTH MATTERS

We need to talk about our planet. But more importantly, we need to act. Changes have occurred in our precious world, and we need to turn things around so Earth can keep spinning and the cycle of life can continue.

1 Humans have taken over the planet. *Just 90 years ago the world population stood at 2 billion people. It now tops 7 billion,* having more than doubled since 1960. Half of these people live in cities, but they all need food, water, and energy.

2 As populations have grown, humanity has taken over more and more land. *We now use around one-third of the world's land to grow crops and rear animals,* as well as even more to live on, and supply us with other resources.

3 Earth supports at least *8 million species of animals and plants.* But many exist in very small numbers, and may soon be extinct. Due to deforestation of the bamboo forests where they live, there are only around 1,800 giant pandas left in the world. As humans work to conserve their habitat, their numbers are gradually improving.

4 Life on Earth depends on the energy of the Sun. *Carbon dioxide and other gases act like greenhouse glass and trap the Sun's warmth in the atmosphere—the so-called greenhouse effect.* As we release more carbon dioxide into the atmosphere, it traps more heat, meaning the planet is heating up.

5 Global temperatures have risen by 0.9°F (0.5°C) since 1970. It doesn't sound like much, but it's enough to melt vast amounts of ice in the Arctic and Antarctic. The rise is due to an *increased greenhouse effect,* partly caused by carbon dioxide released by burning coal, oil, and gas. In 2016, 194 countries plus the European Union signed a treaty to *reduce these gas emissions.*

6 Climate change could cause mass extinction, threatening all life on Earth. However, we can tackle it by using *renewable energy— turning the energy of the Sun or wind into electricity,* instead of burning carbon-rich fuels. Sweden already gets half of its power from renewable sources, and is aiming to be completely renewable by 2050.

7 We can all help prevent climate change by reducing our carbon footprint—the amount of carbon dioxide released into the air as a result of our daily activities. *On average, every person generates around 10 tons of emissions per year.* Even something as simple as using energy-saving lightbulbs can help reduce your carbon footprint.

8 One of the world's biggest problems is the destruction of forests, threatening some of Earth's richest wildlife habitats. Trees also soak up carbon that would otherwise add to the greenhouse effect. Some countries such as Costa Rica have found a great way to protect their rain forests—by promoting them as exciting tourist destinations.

9 The oceans are in trouble. **Overfishing has reduced fish stocks to an all-time low,** and animals such as whales, turtles, and seabirds are dying because of the vast amounts of plastic and other waste in the water, which can take hundreds of years to decompose. **By 2050, it is estimated that there will be more waste plastic in the sea than fish.**

10 Pollution by chemicals, sewage, and garbage is a major problem on land as well as in the oceans. Many materials such as plastics and glass can be recycled—a process that saves energy as well as reducing pollution. **It takes 70 percent less energy to produce recycled paper than making it from scratch.**

11 Much of the land opened up by cutting down forests is used for grazing cattle. **If we all ate less meat, we could leave a lot more forest standing.** Cows are also big climate change culprits—the large quantity of methane gas that cows give off as gas is a significant factor in the increase of greenhouse gases.

12 We would not need to produce so much food from the land if we stopped wasting it. **One-third of all food worldwide is not eaten, but thrown away.** If just a quarter of that food were saved, it would feed 870 million hungry people.

13 The most vital resource is water, yet more than a billion people worldwide live in places where it is scarce. Climate change is making the problem worse, forcing people to leave areas that are turning to desert. However, saving water can be simple. Having a quick shower uses around a third less water than having a bath.

13½ Some people don't believe that climate change is real, but **97 percent of scientists think global warming is happening now.** Whatever the truth, there are many ways we can act to stop the pollution of our planet.

1 Armstrong and Aldrin's mission was called Apollo 11. Along with Michael Collins, who stayed in orbit around the Moon while the two others touched down, **they traveled 953,054 miles (1,533,792 km) in just over eight days.**

2 About 600 million people—**one-sixth of the world's population**—watched on television as Neil Armstrong made the first ever moonwalk. **The astronauts spent 21 hours on the Moon.** They planted the US flag, took photographs, set up experiments, collected rock samples, and had some well-earned sleep.

3 The crew wore their space suits for takeoff, the lunar landing, and reentry to Earth's atmosphere. They put on the bulky gear inside the spacecraft, **a space about the size of a station wagon.**

6 A large, clear plastic pressure helmet was worn as part of the basic suit. A **visor assembly**, worn on top while walking on the Moon, had a set of gold-plated visors to **protect against the Sun's intense rays.**

Plastic pressure helmet

5 The suit included a pressurized layer that was **inflated with air and sealed,** to keep the wearer's body under similar pressure to that on Earth. Without a pressurized suit, **human body fluids would boil** in the vacuum of space.

High-performance watch

4 The outer part of the suit was made from material consisting of **14 different layers.** The company that made the suit, International Latex Corporation, is more famous as **an underwear manufacturer.**

Cine camera and handle

MOON SUIT

On July 20, 1969, US astronauts Neil Armstrong and Edwin "Buzz" Aldrin made history as the first people to set foot on the Moon. Their space suits were their life-support systems and their only protection on this alien world.

13½ It is a myth that US space agency NASA invented Teflon and Velcro for the Apollo program, although they did **use these materials extensively.** The space program did **lead to many other spinoffs,** including baby milk formula, air-cushioned soles, and chips used in digital cameras.

7 A **communications cap** carried earphones and microphones, **allowing the astronauts to talk to one another**, and to ground control. It was nicknamed the **"Snoopy Cap"** because it made the wearer look like the cartoon dog Snoopy.

8 A backpack contained oxygen, carbon-dioxide removal equipment, and cooling water. Together, the suit and backpack had a **combined weight of 180 lb (82 kg)**—about the weight of an average man— but in the Moon's low gravity this would have **felt a lot lighter**.

9 Temperatures on the Moon can reach 250°F (121°C) in direct sunlight, so a "cool suit" was worn next to the skin. This contained tubes through which a coolant was circulated.

10 Flexible metal joints at the arms and legs allowed the astronauts to move their limbs. The pressurized suit would otherwise have been **completely rigid**, like a fully inflated tire.

13 Arriving back on Earth, the astronauts **splashed down in the Pacific Ocean**. On entering the United States **they filled out customs forms** like any other travelers. Under "departure from" they wrote "Moon," and as cargo they declared Moon dust and rocks.

12 In the spacecraft the astronauts used **tubes and plastic bags to collect their body waste**. But on the lunar surface, they had **special underpants**. Aldrin was the second man to walk on the Moon, but **claimed he was the first to wee in his pants**.

11 The astronauts wore special overboots on the Moon. When they removed their helmets after being on the lunar surface, they described **a strong smell like "wet ashes" and "spent gunpowder."** This was the smell of four-billion-year-old Moon dust carried into the spacecraft on their boots.

127

FEEL THE FORCE

Snowboarding is an all-action mountain sport taken up by thousands of thrill-seekers around the world. With a board attached to the feet, the rider slides down steep slopes at high speed, as different forces impact on the body.

4 A force is a push or a pull that acts on an object, making it speed up, slow down, or change direction. **The force of gravity pulls everything toward the center of Earth.** The greater the distance between the top and bottom of the slope, the faster the snowboarder will be moving when he reaches the bottom.

3 The snowboarder needs to be moving at high speed in order to complete the trick. **The force of gravity accelerates him downhill at ever faster speeds—** and the force of friction that would normally slow him down is almost completely absent on the slippery slope.

1 *Snowboarding evolved from existing extreme sports*, such as skiing, skateboarding, and surfing. In the 1960s, American Sherman Poppen built the first snowboard as a toy for his daughter. It was called the Snurfer (from "snow" and "surfer").

2 *Snowboarders perform spectacular tricks to win competitions.* This complex trick begins with a jump from a ramp (far right), with the snowboarder turning the board through three full rotations while airborne.

13 When the snowboarder meets the ground again, the force between the ground and the board **quickly changes his downward speed to almost zero.** However, his horizontal movement is still high and friction is low, so he continues moving downhill.

12 As he comes out of the final spin, the snowboarder **straightens his body and puts his arms out** to slow down. When touching down, he leans backward into the slope. The farther back the body goes, the faster the stop.

13½ You may think snowboarding is more dangerous than most sports. However, **people are much more likely to get hurt playing football, basketball, or hockey.**

5 The **fastest snowboarder is Frenchman Edmond Plawczyk,** who set the record at 126 mph (203 km/h) in 2015. The average snowboarder cruises at roughly 30 mph (48 km/h), with short bursts at about 40 mph (64 km/h).

6 Snowboarders wax their boards to reduce friction, allowing them to reach higher speeds. **Friction is a force that acts between any two surfaces that are in contact.** It is caused by trillions of tiny forces between the atoms of the two surfaces as they catch and snag on one another.

7 A moving object **continues at the same speed in the same direction** unless and until a force acts on it. **This is called inertia.** Snowboarders alter their direction by shifting their weight, to increase friction on one side of the board.

11 Gravity is always pulling the snowboarder downward. So the moment he launches from the ramp, his upward speed begins to slow. For a **split second at the top of the jump, he is moving neither upward nor downward**—and then his downward speed begins to increase again.

10 Round objects require less energy to spin than long ones. The snowboarder **spins much faster when he rolls himself up into a tight ball** by hugging his board—giving him more time to complete the trick.

9 The best kind of snow for snowboarding is freshly laid, dry "powder." The snow melts under the pressure of the board, creating a film of water over which the board easily glides.

8 To start the jump, the snowboarder accelerates **down a steep slope and onto a ramp.** When he hits the ramp, **forces between the ramp and the board change his direction of motion**—up into the air!

Laws of motion

Scientist Isaac Newton published his laws of motion in 1687 to explain how forces make objects move. When the forces acting on an object are balanced, there is no change in how an object moves. When unbalanced, the overall force alters the speed or direction of a moving object. Newton's first law states that an object remains still or moves in a straight line at one speed, unless a force acts on it.

Rider is stationary

Rider applies force with leading foot and board moves

Rider applies force with heels, snow pushes back, and board stops

Motion

At the top of a slope, the ground exerts an upward force that balances the downward force of gravity.

When weight is pushed down on the toes of the lead (front) foot, the force moves the board forward.

To stop, the rider transfers weight to his heels, the board tilts back and friction gradually brings it to a stop.

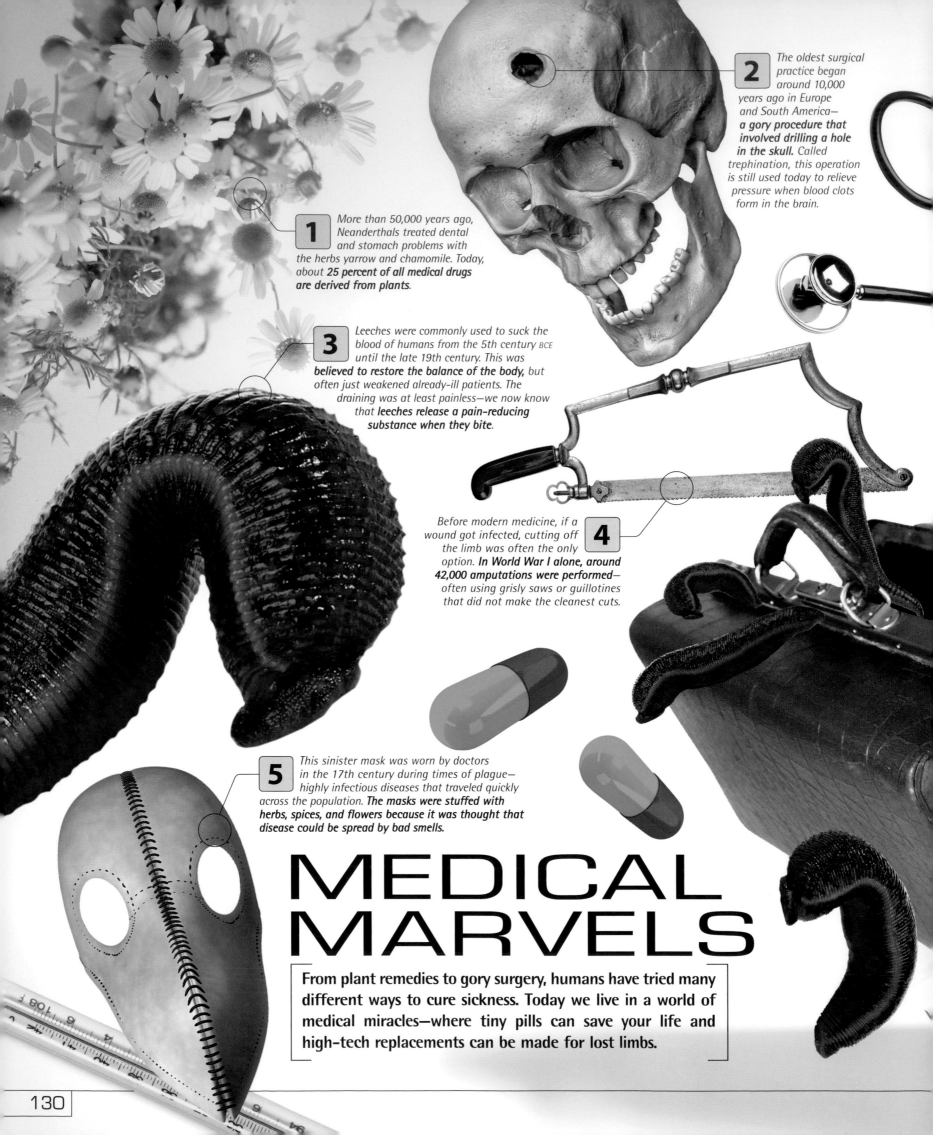

1 More than 50,000 years ago, Neanderthals treated dental and stomach problems with the herbs yarrow and chamomile. Today, about **25 percent of all medical drugs are derived from plants**.

2 The oldest surgical practice began around 10,000 years ago in Europe and South America— **a gory procedure that involved drilling a hole in the skull.** Called trephination, this operation is still used today to relieve pressure when blood clots form in the brain.

3 Leeches were commonly used to suck the blood of humans from the 5th century BCE until the late 19th century. This was **believed to restore the balance of the body,** but often just weakened already-ill patients. The draining was at least painless—we now know that **leeches release a pain-reducing substance when they bite.**

4 Before modern medicine, if a wound got infected, cutting off the limb was often the only option. **In World War I alone, around 42,000 amputations were performed**— often using grisly saws or guillotines that did not make the cleanest cuts.

5 This sinister mask was worn by doctors in the 17th century during times of plague— highly infectious diseases that traveled quickly across the population. **The masks were stuffed with herbs, spices, and flowers because it was thought that disease could be spread by bad smells.**

MEDICAL MARVELS

From plant remedies to gory surgery, humans have tried many different ways to cure sickness. Today we live in a world of medical miracles—where tiny pills can save your life and high-tech replacements can be made for lost limbs.

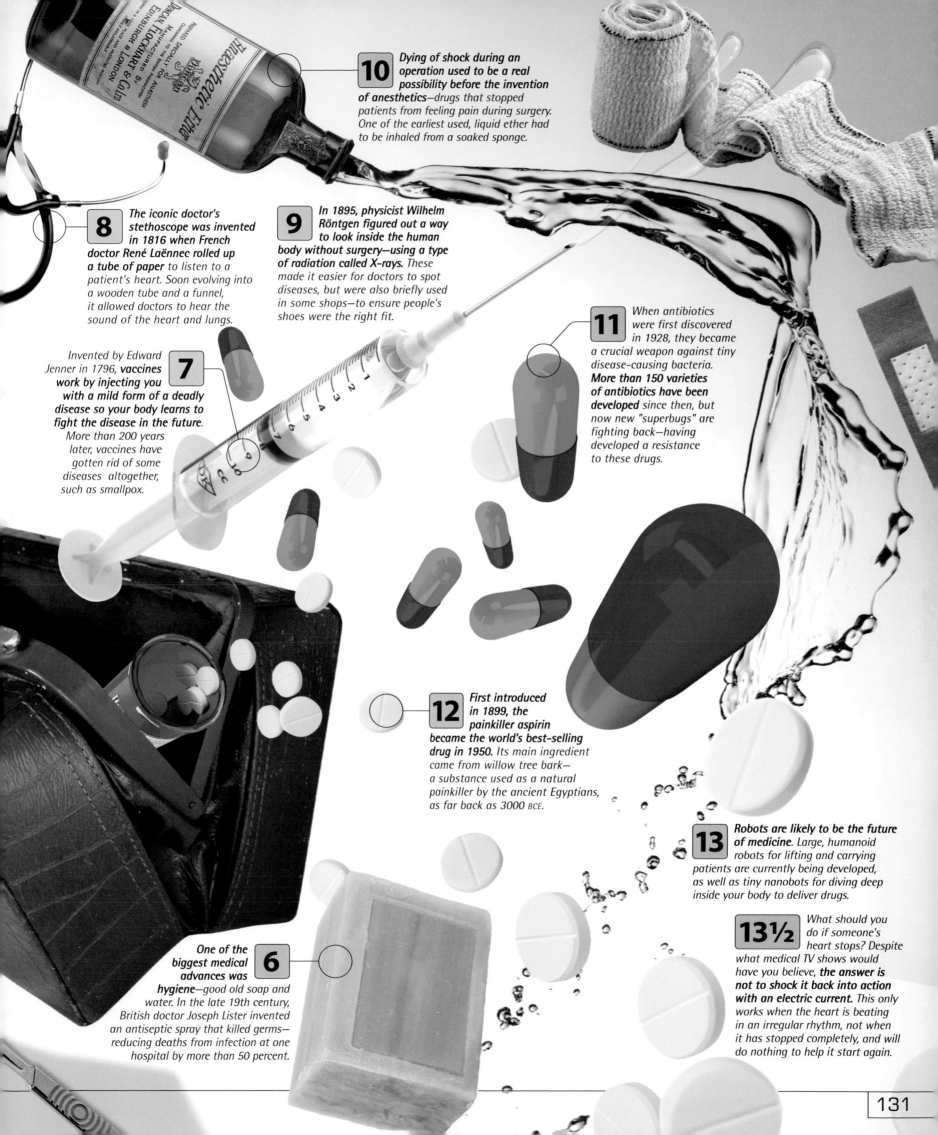

10 Dying of shock during an operation used to be a real possibility before the invention of anesthetics—drugs that stopped patients from feeling pain during surgery. One of the earliest used, liquid ether had to be inhaled from a soaked sponge.

8 The iconic doctor's stethoscope was invented in 1816 when French doctor René Laënnec rolled up a tube of paper to listen to a patient's heart. Soon evolving into a wooden tube and a funnel, it allowed doctors to hear the sound of the heart and lungs.

9 In 1895, physicist Wilhelm Röntgen figured out a way to look inside the human body without surgery—using a type of radiation called X-rays. These made it easier for doctors to spot diseases, but were also briefly used in some shops—to ensure people's shoes were the right fit.

7 Invented by Edward Jenner in 1796, vaccines work by injecting you with a mild form of a deadly disease so your body learns to fight the disease in the future. More than 200 years later, vaccines have gotten rid of some diseases altogether, such as smallpox.

11 When antibiotics were first discovered in 1928, they became a crucial weapon against tiny disease-causing bacteria. More than 150 varieties of antibiotics have been developed since then, but now new "superbugs" are fighting back—having developed a resistance to these drugs.

12 First introduced in 1899, the painkiller aspirin became the world's best-selling drug in 1950. Its main ingredient came from willow tree bark—a substance used as a natural painkiller by the ancient Egyptians, as far back as 3000 BCE.

13 Robots are likely to be the future of medicine. Large, humanoid robots for lifting and carrying patients are currently being developed, as well as tiny nanobots for diving deep inside your body to deliver drugs.

13½ What should you do if someone's heart stops? Despite what medical TV shows would have you believe, the answer is not to shock it back into action with an electric current. This only works when the heart is beating in an irregular rhythm, not when it has stopped completely, and will do nothing to help it start again.

6 One of the biggest medical advances was hygiene—good old soap and water. In the late 19th century, British doctor Joseph Lister invented an antiseptic spray that killed germs—reducing deaths from infection at one hospital by more than 50 percent.

SKY

This sparkling starscape, photographed in a cold desert high in the Chilean Andes, captures the night sky in all its beauty. The dusty band of stars that stretches from one side to the other is the Milky Way, our home galaxy.

1 Ancient people were **fascinated by the night sky** and tracked the movement of the Moon and stars. The invention of the telescope in the 17th century **revealed new sights and more detail than ever before.**

2 For a good view you need a **clear, moonless night**, away from the glare of city lights. Observatories are usually set up in mountaintop locations, where the air is clear, dry, and cloudless.

3 The observatory pictured here is the **Atacama Large Millimeter Array (ALMA)** in the Atacama Desert, Chile. This is **one of the driest places on Earth**, with areas where no rainfall has ever been recorded.

4 ALMA has 66 antennas, which collect invisible radio waves. **Objects that are dark in terms of visible light may emit lots of radio waves**, so ALMA can picture some of the coldest, most distant parts of space.

5 The closest large galaxy to us is the Andromeda Galaxy, 2.5 million light-years away. **It is set to collide with the Milky Way— but not for another 4 billion years.**

6 We can't see all of the Milky Way since we're inside it, but **we know it is a spiral galaxy.** Our Solar System lies in one of the spiral arms, about 26,000 light-years from the center.

7 We are orbiting the center of the Milky Way at around 515,000 mph (828,000 km/h). **One complete orbit takes around 225 million years.** The last time we were in the same place in space, dinosaurs ruled the Earth.

8 All the individual stars you **can see without a telescope are part of the Milky Way.** In a very dark sky, there are about 9,000 stars visible to the naked eye, but the total number of stars in the galaxy is in the billions.

9 At the center of the galaxy is **a supermassive black hole called Sagittarius A*.** This region of space, so dense that light itself cannot escape, is thought to have the mass of around 4 million Suns.

10 Although the galaxy has a black hole at its heart, the central region appears bright. **This is because billions of stars gather around this massive object in dense clusters.**

11 Astronomers now know **there are billions of galaxies but they used to think the Milky Way was all there was.** In the 1920s they realized that Andromeda—thought to be a cloud of gas and dust inside the Milky Way— was in fact a galaxy in its own right.

12 The brightest object in the night sky after the Moon is Venus, the nearest planet to Earth. **Planets shine with a steady light, while stars appear to twinkle.** This is because stars are so much farther away.

13½ You may have heard the phrase **"the vacuum of space,"** which makes it sound as though space is an empty void. **But space is not totally empty.** Galaxies contain gas and dust between the stars and even between galaxies there are a few atoms in every cubic yard.

13 This smudge of light is the **Small Magellanic Cloud**, a dwarf galaxy 200,000 light-years away. It is one of the Milky Way's **nearest neighbors in space.**

COLOR CLASH

Roses are red, violets are blue... except they're not, because color is an optical illusion. Objects aren't actually colored, but appear colorful because they reflect different amounts of light. It's your eyes and brain that see this light as color.

1 *Pigments are natural colorings* found in animals and plants. *Flamingos are born with gray feathers,* but they feed on algae that are loaded with pigments called carotenoids. These cause the birds' feathers to turn bright pink or orange.

2 Leaves look green because *they contain chlorophyll,* a pigment plants use to absorb sunlight so they can make food. *Chlorophyll absorbs red and blue light, but it reflects green,* so that is the color the leaf appears.

3 Many of the *pigments that give plants their colors are vitamins* or other important nutrients. Eating *fruit and vegetables with a variety of colors* is a good way to a healthy diet.

4 *Colors can be nature's warning signs. The golden poison dart frog is one of the world's most toxic animals.* It's just 2 in (5 cm) long, but has *enough venom to kill 10 adult humans.*

5 *Color can influence the taste of food.* In tests, people thought that *yellow and green foods tasted more sour* than they are; *red- and orange-colored foods tasted sweeter;* and coffee tasted less bitter drunk from an orange cup than a white one.

6 *Babies are born able to see only shades of gray.* At around two weeks, they start to distinguish high-contrast colors such as red and green.

7 *Some people can hear colors,* see letters or numbers in color, or even taste colors. These are all *forms of synesthesia*—a condition in which a person's senses blend together.

8 Many *animals can see colors that are beyond the range of human vision.* Goldfish can see ultraviolet (UV) light, which they use to find food, and to tell males and females apart.

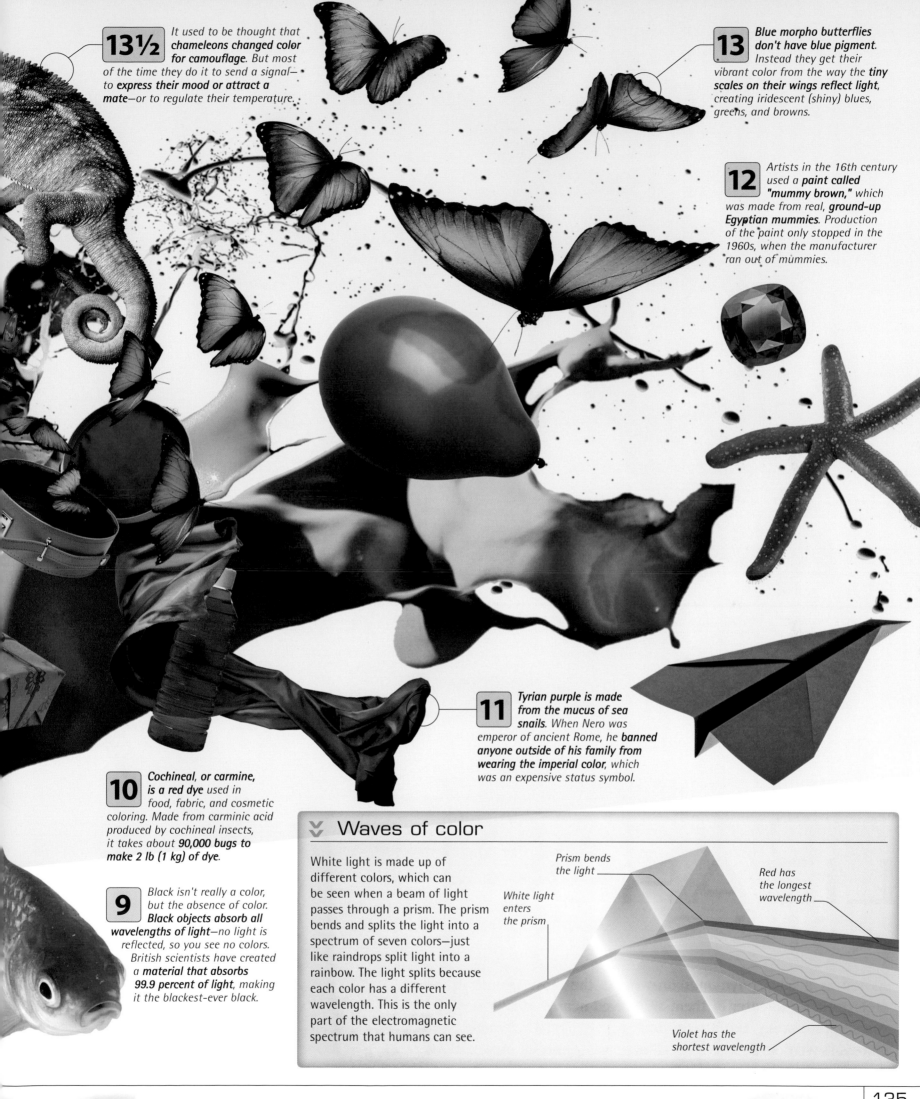

13½ It used to be thought that chameleons changed color for camouflage. But most of the time they do it to send a signal—to *express their mood or attract a mate*—or to regulate their temperature.

13 *Blue morpho butterflies don't have blue pigment.* Instead they get their vibrant color from the way the **tiny scales on their wings reflect light**, creating iridescent (shiny) blues, greens, and browns.

12 Artists in the 16th century used a *paint called "mummy brown,"* which was made from real, **ground-up Egyptian mummies**. Production of the paint only stopped in the 1960s, when the manufacturer ran out of mummies.

11 *Tyrian purple is made from the mucus of sea snails.* When Nero was emperor of ancient Rome, he **banned anyone outside of his family from wearing the imperial color**, which was an expensive status symbol.

10 Cochineal, or carmine, is a *red dye* used in food, fabric, and cosmetic coloring. Made from carminic acid produced by cochineal insects, it takes about **90,000 bugs to make 2 lb (1 kg) of dye**.

9 Black isn't really a color, but the absence of color. *Black objects absorb all wavelengths of light*—no light is reflected, so you see no colors. British scientists have created a *material that absorbs 99.9 percent of light*, making it the blackest-ever black.

⌄ Waves of color

White light is made up of different colors, which can be seen when a beam of light passes through a prism. The prism bends and splits the light into a spectrum of seven colors—just like raindrops split light into a rainbow. The light splits because each color has a different wavelength. This is the only part of the electromagnetic spectrum that humans can see.

Prism bends the light

White light enters the prism

Red has the longest wavelength

Violet has the shortest wavelength

The **first** **T. rex** **fossils were** **discovered in 1902** *and since then more than 30 skeletons have been found.* **T. rex** *lived on Earth for around 3 million years*—15 times longer than modern humans have been around.

1

Many experts now think that **T. rex** **was covered in a downy featherlike fuzz** *instead of scaly skin. This may have helped the giant predator keep warm.*

2

Bones are often all that remains of dinosaurs today. The **largest T. rex** **skeleton ever found stretched to 40 ft (12.2 m) long** *and was named "Sue" after its discoverer. It was sold to a US museum in 1997 for $8.3 million.*

3

T. rex's **tail was as long as a bus.** *Huge muscles running through the side of the tail controlled the animal's movement. The weight of the tail also* **helped counter-balance T. rex's enormous head.**

4

The **upper leg muscles were bigger** *in relation to* T. rex's *body size* **than those of any animal alive today.** *They helped* T. rex *reach an estimated running speed of 18 mph (29 km/h) or more.*

5

Soft tissues don't survive, so no one is completely sure what T. rex's *insides looked like. However, skeletons show spaces where* **T. rex** **may have had air sacs** **like modern birds.** *Birds use these sacs like bellows to* **flush fresh air through their lungs.**

6

Lungs

Large intestine

Small intestine

LIZARD KING

As tall as a house, *Tyrannosaurus rex* is the most famous prehistoric meat-eater of them all. It lived nearly 70 million years ago during the Cretaceous period, a time when dinosaurs were at their peak and there was plenty of prey.

Air sacs

A T. rex's brain may not look big, but it was **one of the largest brains relative to body size** of all the dinosaurs. Many **giant herbivores had comparatively tiny brains**—around the size of tennis balls.

7

10 T. rex *probably had the **most powerful bite of any land animal ever**—capable of killing giant armored herbivores, such as Triceratops. It was **three and a half times stronger than that of a saltwater crocodile**—the animal with the strongest bite alive today.*

11 *The teeth were up to 12 in (30 cm) **long** and sliced through tough skin and flesh. Serrated like a steak knife, they are currently thought to be the **biggest teeth of any meat-eating dinosaur.***

Heart

12 *Although they look tiny, T. rex's arms were actually very muscular. Its **biceps were more than three times stronger than those of a human.** It may seem strange that the arms could not reach up to its mouth, but they were likely **used to grasp struggling prey.***

8 *T. rex probably digested most of its meaty food in its stomach—just like modern birds of prey. Its **stomach lining would have released acidic juices** that helped **break down the muscle fibers** in meat.*

13 **T. rex's feet had three toes**—just like modern birds. These long toes helped T. rex build up speed when moving over land. **Big, fearsome claws**—up to 8 in (20 cm) long—added to the predator's weaponry and helped it grip the ground.

13½ *Could we really clone a T. rex? Dinosaurs lived so long ago that **it is not possible to extract their DNA** from what survives today. But while a Jurassic Park isn't possible, a Neolithic Park could be. **Small fragments of mammoth DNA still survive**, meaning cloning one of these creatures could be a possibility in the future.*

9 *Fossilized dinosaur droppings are called **coprolites.** The largest piece of prehistoric poo found so far was from a T. rex. About **half of it was made of bone shards**—showing that T. rex wolfed down its prey whole.*

READ ALL ABOUT IT

Books are brilliant! They amuse, amaze, and inform, and take us on extraordinary adventures of the imagination. Books are also windows into the worlds of our ancestors, and can introduce us to new ways of understanding our own world.

3 The Romans wrote on sheets of papyrus or vellum (treated animal skin), joined together to form long scrolls. These were awkward to handle, however, so **they began stacking the sheets and putting them between wooden boards—** the first very hardback books.

1 It seems that the world just can't get enough books! **It's estimated that 134 million books have been published to date,** with this number rising by millions every year. **In the US alone, a million new titles are published each year.**

2 The **oldest multi-page book discovered was found in modern-day** Bulgaria and dates back to 660 BCE. Made up of six sheets of 24-carat gold, this expensive edition is written in the lost Etruscan language— a script still indecipherable to modern historians.

6 The largest library in the world is the Library of Congress in Washington D.C., which contains more than **164 million items,** including books, recordings, photographs, maps, and sheet music that cover **approximately 838 miles (1,349 km) of shelves.** Half of the collection is not in English, but in one of 470 other languages.

4 It was the invention of the printing press by German Johannes Gutenberg that first made books cheaper and easier to produce. **The Gutenberg Bible, published in 1455, was the first mass-produced book in Europe** and 48 copies of it still survive. The greater availability of books led to a steep rise in the sales of reading glasses.

5 *The priciest book ever sold is the* Codex Leicester *by Italian artist Leonardo da Vinci.* This handwritten manuscript dates from the early 16th century, and details many of da Vinci's scientific theories, accompanied by sketches and notes. **It was bought at auction in 1994 for a staggering $30.8 million,** by US billionaire Bill Gates, but is valued today at $49.5 million.

7 The largest book in the world won't fit on a shelf. **The Tripitaka, a "book" of Buddhist teachings, is printed on 730 huge marble tablets** surrounding the Kuthdaw Pagoda in Myanmar. Made in the 1860s, the stones are each 5 ft (1.5 m) tall.

8 Until 1100, books **were rare** and usually only found in monastery libraries. All books were written out by hand, using goose-feather pens. **A long book such as the Bible might take one monk a year to copy out.** These richly detailed books were called illuminated manuscripts because they often glowed with gold- or silver-leaf decoration.

9 Although we no longer rely on hefty tomes of knowledge, **the books we read for fun are getting longer.** A 2015 study found that the average length of a bestselling book increased **from 320 pages in 1999 to 407 pages in 2014.**

10 India tops the list of nations that read **the most**, with the average person devoting 10 hours a week to reading. Today, around 85 percent of the world's population can read, compared to just 32 percent 100 years ago.

11 In some languages, **a person who can't get enough of books is called a bookworm;** in others, a book-lover is known as a library mouse or rat. These names **originate from when musty library collections attracted pests**—tiny insects and rodents—that devoured books more literally than we do.

12 Soon we may be able to read books without even opening them. **A camera is being developed that uses a type of low-frequency radiation to scan through layers of paper and** read the text inside. This technology could help us see inside old books that are too fragile to open.

13 Some people can't resist buying new **books, which then gather on shelves, unread.** This must be a common condition in Japan, because they actually have a name for it—tsundoku—which means "piling up books without reading them." It seems lots of people just like having books around!

13½ J.K. Rowling's Harry Potter series is a **global phenomenon,** with more than 450 million copies in print. However, **they are not the best-selling work of fiction**—even if you count all the books in the series together. That title goes to the classic Spanish novel of 1612, Don Quixote, by Miguel de Cervantes, which has sold around 500 million copies.

2 Samurai were the only people allowed to carry swords. *The katana sword had a steel blade up to 31 in (80 cm) long* and a hilt large enough for **two hands to swing the sword.** *The hilt was made of shark or ray skin to provide grip.*

3 *Made at temperatures of 2,370°F (1,300°C), **a sword's blade was razor-sharp and very strong** and it was used to deliver deadly slashing blows in battle. **Sharpness was tested by slicing through dead bodies.** Wielding such a sword required great skill and training.*

Samurai armor looks ornate, but the **layers of varnished metal linked with silk** *were very practical, **allowing the wearer to move easily** (unlike a European suit of armor). It is said that the US army based their WWII flak jacket on samurai armor.* **4**

1 *Samurai were originally bodyguards for the emperor of Japan. By the 12th century, they had become the **ruling class of society.** There was an era of peace from 1600, so the warriors found jobs in government. **By the late 1870s, the samurai class had been abolished.***

WAY OF THE WARRIOR

The samurai of medieval Japan were no ordinary knights: they were a powerful class of warriors. Samurai clans fought for their daimyo (lord) to become shogun—the military leader of the country who wielded more power than the emperor.

5 Samurai were instructed to live by *a code of honor called* **bushido (meaning "the way of the warrior").** *This told them to fight bravely, tell the truth, behave with honor, show compassion to others, and respect all life. They did not always manage to achieve all this.*

6 **When not fighting, samurai wrote poetry** *and enjoyed other Japanese traditions: painting and block-printing, calligraphy, rock gardening, flower arranging, and tea ceremonies.*

7 *The modern Japanese martial art of kendo—fighting with wooden sticks—comes from the kenjutsu schools in which samurai practiced their sword skills.* **Samurai were also expert archers and horseback-riders.**

8 Traditional **straw-soled waraji (sandals) were worn by everyone in Japan,** *from samurai to commoners. Split-toed socks, called tabi, were worn with them to accommodate the rope between the first and second toes.*

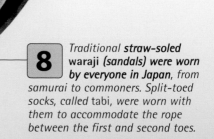

9 This **metal crest at the front of the kabuto (helmet) represented animal horns**—a show of strength to intimidate enemies. To make the helmet more comfortable to wear, **samurai wore their hair in a top-knot and shaved their foreheads,** which became a sign of their status.

10 An ugly **mengu (mask) with threatening eyes was designed to scare the enemy.** The face-armor usually had a hole under the chin so sweat could escape, and it also helped keep the helmet in place.

The **wakizashi was a samurai's "little sword," used for indoor fighting or close combat**—and also for committing seppuku (ritual suicide, also called hara-kiri) if caught by the enemy. This generally involved the **dishonored warrior stabbing himself in the stomach,** then having a friend chop off his head with his katana sword. **11**

12 The wooden, lacquered **scabbard for the katana was worn on the left,** tucked into his belt. This allowed the samurai to quickly whip out the sword with his stronger right hand.

13 Ninjas were soldiers who were not **born in the samurai class.** They often acted as **spies and assassins**—roles thought of as too dishonorable for samurai. Legends were told about ninjas, such as their ability to make themselves invisible.

13½ Most people imagine Japanese warriors were all men, but there were female fighters too. **Onna-bugeisha were women from the samurai class.** Instead of brandishing heavy swords, they tended to use naginata—polearms with a curved blade at the end.

1 The piano has a *unique position in the orchestra*, between the string section and the percussion (striking) instruments. Although a piano has strings, the sound is made by hammers that strike those strings.

2 The first true piano was constructed in Italy by Bartolomeo Cristofori around 1700. Before that keyboard players used a harpsichord, but that *only had one unvarying volume*. The piano, by contrast, can make notes louder or softer.

3 *A standard grand piano has 88 white and black keys*, each connected to a hammer. When a key is pressed, it moves its hammer upward to strike a string or strings. The mechanism that makes this work is called the "action."

4 *"Tickling the ivories"* is an expression for playing the piano dating from when **the white keys were made of ivory—** elephants' tusks. Ivory was banned in the mid-1900s; **now the keys are made of plastic.**

5 A concert-sized grand piano can be up to 10 ft (3 m) long and weigh more than 990 lb (450 kg). A typical piano **contains several thousand moving parts** in the action that moves the keys.

6 The hammers are **made of wood tightly covered with felt**. After striking a string, a hammer instantly drops away so as not to stop the string's vibration.

PIANO PIECES

Beneath its sleek exterior, a grand piano is an extraordinarily complex instrument, with the widest range of notes of any instrument in the orchestra. Thousands of moving parts work together to deliver just the right touch and tone.

7 *Playing the piano makes you cleverer.* According to recent research, regular practice can improve the brain's ability to process information, solve problems, and retain memories. It may even increase IQ.

8 Some professional piano players can play notes *faster than the ear can hear them*. Hungarian Peter Bence holds the world record for fastest fingers—*he played 765 key strokes in just one minute.*

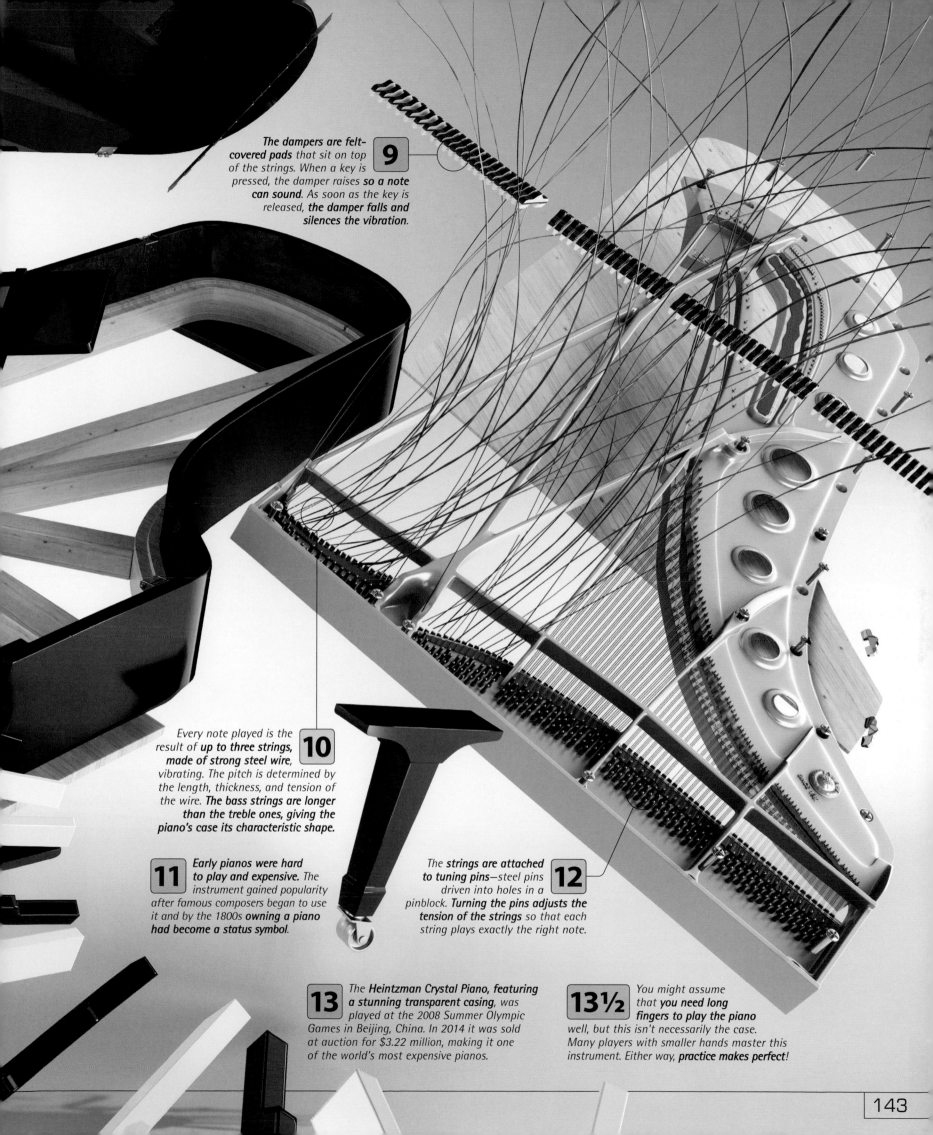

The dampers are felt-covered pads that sit on top of the strings. When a key is pressed, the damper raises **so a note can sound**. As soon as the key is released, **the damper falls and silences the vibration.**

9

Every note played is the result of **up to three strings, made of strong steel wire**, vibrating. The pitch is determined by the length, thickness, and tension of the wire. **The bass strings are longer than the treble ones, giving the piano's case its characteristic shape.**

10

11 Early pianos were hard to play and expensive. The instrument gained popularity after famous composers began to use it and by the 1800s **owning a piano had become a status symbol.**

The strings are attached to tuning pins—steel pins driven into holes in a pinblock. **Turning the pins adjusts the tension of the strings** so that each string plays exactly the right note.

12

13 The *Heintzman Crystal Piano, featuring a stunning transparent casing*, was played at the 2008 Summer Olympic Games in Beijing, China. In 2014 it was sold at auction for $3.22 million, making it one of the world's most expensive pianos.

13½ You might assume that **you need long fingers to play the piano** well, but this isn't necessarily the case. Many players with smaller hands master this instrument. Either way, **practice makes perfect!**

STEALTHY STINGER

It glows with eerie beauty, but the long-tentacled Portuguese man o' war has a seriously painful sting. Belonging to an ancient group that also includes jellyfish, corals, and sea anemones, this extraordinary animal is not what it seems.

1 Although the Portuguese man o' war looks like a jellyfish, it's actually a colony of hundreds of cooperating organisms specializing in feeding, stinging, or reproduction.

2 The float is one organism and shows above the water. It can't propel itself but drifts at an angle of 45 degrees to the wind. It can be left-sided or right-sided. Half are blown one way and half the other around the warm oceans of the world.

3 The float is filled with gas, which it can release to sink if threatened. Physalia physalis, the scientific name for the Portuguese man o' war, means "bladder" to describe its expanded float.

4 The feeding parts of the colony have tiny dangling mouths waiting for food, which swallow any prey caught by the tentacles. It takes just a couple of hours to digest tiny shrimps, but up to 18 hours to break down big fishes.

5

Long strings of beadlike stingers are lined with **poisonous stinging cells that paralyze anything they touch** and can extend to form a **deadly net for trapping animals** up to the size of mackerel and flying fishes. An entire colony could trap 120 tiny fish larvae each day.

6

The creature is found in all warm seas, not just around Portugal. It gets its common name from a **type of ship whose triangular sails resembled the gas-filled float.** The Portuguese man o' war ship was a naval vessel that carried armed men—men of war.

7

Like jellyfish, **Portuguese men o' war are 95 percent water.** They have no brains, blood, bones, teeth, hearts, or fins. The ancient Greeks called them sea nettles for their resemblance to stinging plants.

❯ Stinging cells

Triggered by touch, the microscopic stinging cells fire within thousandths of a second, injecting a cocktail of harmful substances similar to certain kinds of snake venom. These interfere with nerves and muscles, quickly paralyzing prey.

Before firing

Each stinging cell contains a coiled-up harpoon.

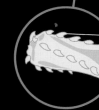

After firing

Stinging cell is empty.

Venomous harpoon shoots out.

Sharp barbs on the harpoon stick in the flesh of the victim.

8

Some kinds of fish live within the colony. The **man-of-war fish has some resistance to the poison** but is also super-agile so it can avoid the longer tentacles. It eats food scraps and even nibbles on the colony—but also might help lure other fish into the deadly net.

9

Some of the Portuguese man o' war's deep-sea relatives are **bioluminescent—they produce light to lure prey.** The Portuguese man o' war is a surface-floating animal, and does not need to be bioluminescent, but its **blue-purple color glows under certain light.** The pigments may act as a kind of UV sunscreen.

10

Muscular stinging tentacles "fish" for prey and can be as long as 165 ft (50 m)—the length of five buses—making the Portuguese man o' war one of the longest species on the planet. If you see the distinctive float when you're swimming, it's probably too late to avoid its tentacles.

11

Hardly any animals except sea turtles and sea slugs eat Portuguese men o' war, but **some of their jellyfish cousins are considered a delicacy by humans.** Malaysians call jellyfish "music to the teeth" and specimens made edible by a drying process often appear on the menu in Asian restaurants.

12

While rarely fatal, Portuguese man o' war stings are extremely painful and can last for days. **Some of their relatives are deadly to humans**—box jellyfish are the most poisonous. Their sting kills and is also so painful that affected swimmers have been known to die of shock before they even reach the shore.

13

Each summer, **Portuguese men o' war sting up to 10,000 humans in Australia alone.** The numbers are so high because the creatures often **swarm in their hundreds,** either pushed together by ocean currents or because they have mated and reproduced in large numbers.

13½

It's a common misconception that **urine can soothe the sting of a jellyfish or Portuguese man o' war.** Recent research suggests that urine, and even freshwater, may make matters worse by spreading the stinging cells. It is best to **wash the skin with saltwater,** which deactivates the cells.

OIL BOOM

Crude oil (or petroleum) is a thick liquid found underground. Without it, modern life would be very different. Oil gives us fuels to work machines, and it is used to make everything seen on these two pages—even the words you are reading.

1 Oil is a fossil fuel—it *formed from the remains of ancient living things deep underground.* Three-quarters of the oil we use is burned as fuel (including gasoline, diesel, heating oil, and jet fuel); the rest is used as a raw material to make all kinds of goods.

3 It takes 100 tons of ancient, buried sea creatures to produce one *gallon (five liters) of gasoline.* Weight for weight, gasoline contains three times as much energy as wood and 100 times as much as a typical battery.

2 *The world's working oil fields contain about 1.3 trillion barrels of oil.* One barrel contains 35 gallons (159 liters). The world uses at least 30 billion barrels of oil in one year.

4 *As much oil goes into making plastic as is used to fuel planes: about 8 percent of all the oil we use.* Plastics are so useful because they can be formed into almost any shape.

5 *Before the invention of the car, gasoline was almost worthless.* When oil was first exploited, it was mainly for kerosene (used for lamp fuel)—gasoline was just a by-product. It was used to treat lice and to remove grease stains from clothing, or it was just dumped.

6 *Around 7 gallons (27 liters) of oil are needed to make a tire.* Some 5 gallons (19 liters) of oil are turned into the synthetic rubber tire, while 2 gallons (8 liters) are burned as fuel during the tire's production.

7 Processing oil produces a wide range of petrochemicals that can be used to make products as different as plastics and painkillers. *Many modern medicines, such as steroids and aspirin, are derived from crude oil.*

13 Nylon, polyester, and the rest of the polyamide family of *manmade fibers are a kind of plastic made from petrochemicals.* Clothes made from these fibers can be **water-resistant, fireproof, and even bullet-proof.**

13½ When you think of oil, you probably picture a black sludge. *Most oil is black, but it can be yellow, red, or even green.* The highest-quality oil looks amber or gold in color.

12 Soapless cleaning products contain petrochemicals that have been turned into "surfactants." These are chemical compounds that **cling to grease and dirt but also dissolve in water,** so the dirt will wash off.

11 Up to 80 percent of the ingredients in cosmetics come from crude oil. As well as wax and dyes, synthetic scent is oil-based.

10 Oil-based gloss paint contains solvent (a liquid that makes the paint thin enough to use). *A common solvent is naphtha, which comes from crude oil.* As the paint dries, the naphtha evaporates, which can cause a strong smell in the air.

9 *Colorful crayons are made from white paraffin wax,* which is distilled from crude oil. Dyes are added to crayons, but the undyed, **tasteless, odorless, water-repelling wax** has a variety of uses, from candles to lining the inside of milk cartons.

⌄⌄ Distilling crude oil

Crude oil is a mixture that can be separated into different parts (called fractions) by a process known as distillation. The oil is heated so that it becomes a mixture of gases. The gases pass into a distillation tower, which is hot at the bottom and cold at the top. Fractions condense (become liquid again) at different temperatures, so can be "drawn off" through pipes set at different levels.

−40°F (−40°C) **Natural gas**

↑104°F (40°C) **Gasoline**

356°F (180°C) **Kerosene**

Crude oil is heated before reaching the tower.

392°F (200°C) **Diesel**

572°F (300°C) **Wax**

977°F (525°C) **Bitumen**

8 Most artificial food dyes, *such as the blue lines in this toothpaste, come from oil.* Also used in medicines, cosmetics, and craft supplies such as colored paper and crayons, many artificial dyes are made from petrochemicals.

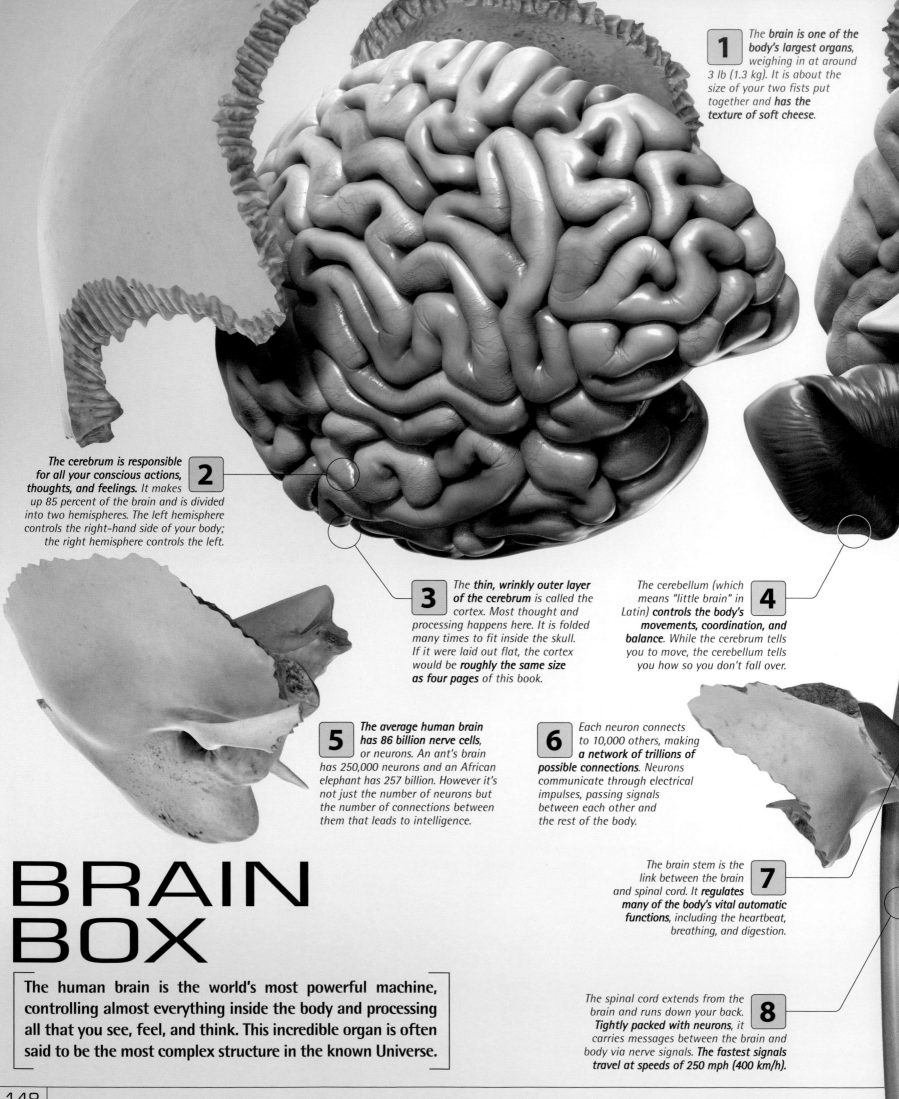

1 The **brain is one of the body's largest organs**, weighing in at around 3 lb (1.3 kg). It is about the size of your two fists put together and **has the texture of soft cheese**.

2 *The cerebrum is responsible for all your conscious actions, thoughts, and feelings. It makes up 85 percent of the brain and is divided into two hemispheres. The left hemisphere controls the right-hand side of your body; the right hemisphere controls the left.*

3 The **thin, wrinkly outer layer of the cerebrum** is called the cortex. Most thought and processing happens here. It is folded many times to fit inside the skull. If it were laid out flat, the cortex would be **roughly the same size as four pages** of this book.

4 The cerebellum (which means "little brain" in Latin) **controls the body's movements, coordination, and balance**. While the cerebrum tells you to move, the cerebellum tells you how so you don't fall over.

5 *The average human brain has 86 billion nerve cells*, or neurons. An ant's brain has 250,000 neurons and an African elephant has 257 billion. However it's not just the number of neurons but the number of connections between them that leads to intelligence.

6 Each neuron connects to 10,000 others, making **a network of trillions of possible connections**. Neurons communicate through electrical impulses, passing signals between each other and the rest of the body.

7 The brain stem is the link between the brain and spinal cord. It **regulates many of the body's vital automatic functions**, including the heartbeat, breathing, and digestion.

8 The spinal cord extends from the brain and runs down your back. **Tightly packed with neurons, it** carries messages between the brain and body via nerve signals. **The fastest signals travel at speeds of 250 mph (400 km/h).**

BRAIN BOX

The human brain is the world's most powerful machine, controlling almost everything inside the body and processing all that you see, feel, and think. This incredible organ is often said to be the most complex structure in the known Universe.

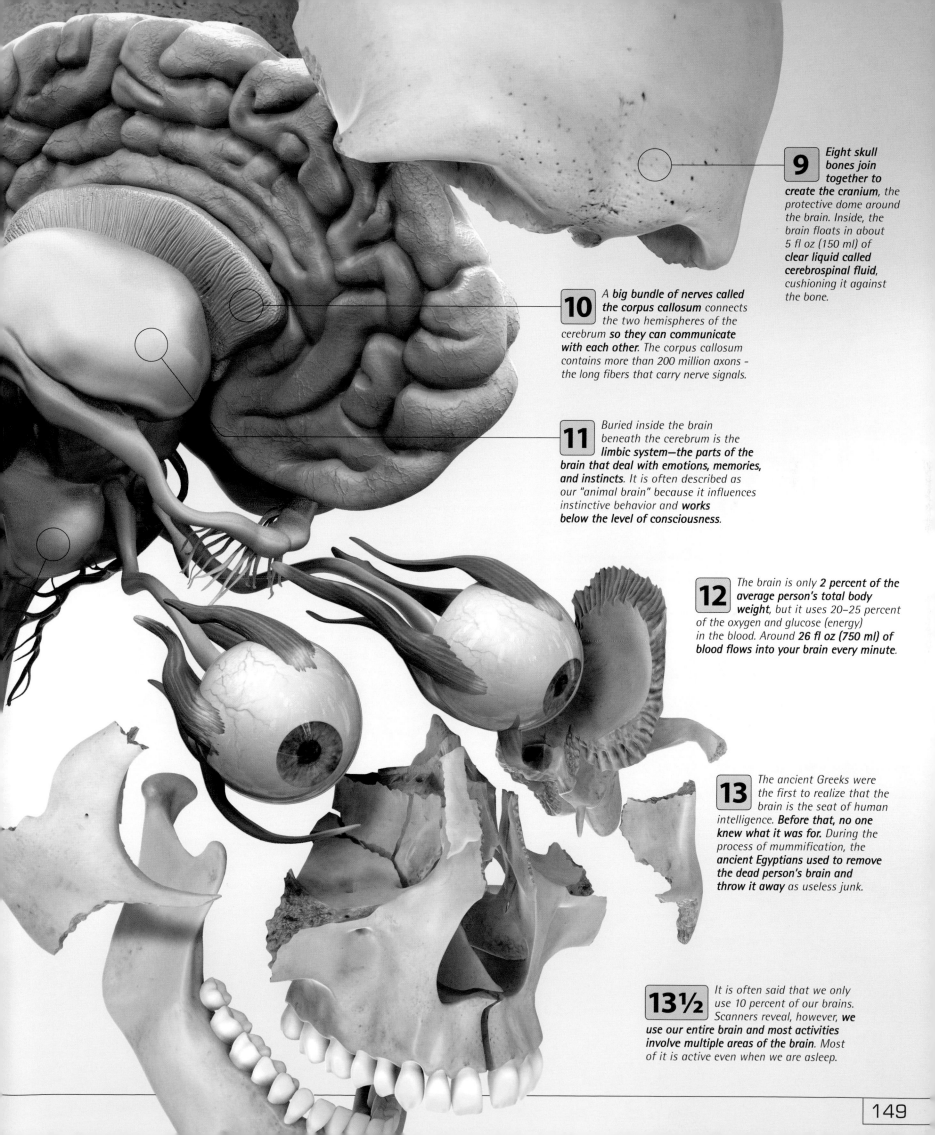

9 *Eight skull bones join together to create the cranium*, the protective dome around the brain. Inside, the brain floats in about 5 fl oz (150 ml) of *clear liquid called cerebrospinal fluid*, cushioning it against the bone.

10 *A big bundle of nerves called the corpus callosum* connects *the two hemispheres of the* cerebrum *so they can communicate with each other*. The corpus callosum contains more than 200 million axons - the long fibers that carry nerve signals.

11 Buried inside the brain beneath the cerebrum is the *limbic system—the parts of the brain that deal with emotions, memories, and instincts.* It is often described as our "animal brain" because it influences instinctive behavior and *works below the level of consciousness*.

12 The brain is only *2 percent of the average person's total body weight*, but it uses 20–25 percent of the oxygen and glucose (energy) in the blood. Around *26 fl oz (750 ml) of blood flows into your brain every minute.*

13 The ancient Greeks were the first to realize that the brain is the seat of human intelligence. *Before that, no one knew what it was for.* During the process of mummification, the *ancient Egyptians used to remove the dead person's brain and throw it away* as useless junk.

13½ It is often said that we only use 10 percent of our brains. Scanners reveal, however, *we use our entire brain and most activities involve multiple areas of the brain.* Most of it is active even when we are asleep.

1 The word "myth" comes from the Greek word mythos, meaning "word" or "story." Myths are **stories that helped people understand the world** around them or provide explanations for some of life's mysteries.

2 **Dragons appear in myths from all over the world.** They are thought to have **arisen independently and yet share striking similarities.** The creatures have four legs, lizard- or snakelike features, and the **ability to breathe fire.**

3 In China the dragon is a **national symbol of power and majesty.** Chinese emperors claimed they were descended from dragons, and today people still **hold dragon festivals and dances.**

4 Sun Wukong, or the **Monkey King,** dates back 1,000 years to Song-dynasty China. This mischievous monkey could **shape-shift into 72 different forms and had many adventures.** In Singapore, there are temples in his honor and his birthday is celebrated annually.

5 In the days before people knew about dinosaurs, **fossil finds were believed to be dragon bones.** The lack of real live dragons was explained by the success rate of legendary dragon-slayers.

6 The ancient Egyptian sphinx had **a lion's body with a human head.** Sphinx statues were built to guard temples and tombs. The **Great Sphinx at Giza in Egypt is one of the largest and oldest stone statues** in the world. It has stood for more than 4,500 years.

7 The **kappa is a water sprite** in medieval Japanese legend. With a shelled back, webbed hands and feet, and a beaky mouth, it was said to **lie in wait by lakes and rivers** to drown people who came to the water's edge.

8 **Medusa was a snake-haired woman** in ancient Greek mythology. One look at her terrible face could **turn a person to stone.** Today she gives her name to the adult form of jellyfish, whose flowing tentacles deliver a nasty sting.

MYTHICAL BEASTS

For thousands of years, different cultures around the world have immortalized mythical beasts in traditional tales passed down through the generations. Some are monstrous, bringing death and destruction, but others represent life itself.

9 *The **one-eyed Cyclops was a giant** in Greek and Roman mythology. The Cyclops had a fearsome appetite, and would **tear victims apart with his huge teeth.***

*Mermaids have the head and body of a beautiful woman, with the tail of a fish. In 1493, explorer **Christopher Columbus** mistook three manatees (also known as sea cows) for mermaids in the waters off Haiti.* **10**

*The **thunderbird—possibly an eagle—was worshipped by Native Americans**, who claimed it brought rainstorms, making thunder by flapping vast wings and lightning by blinking its big eyes.* **11**

12 *Dating back to the Indus Valley civilizations of 3300 BCE, the **unicorn** has morphed over time from being a goat to a horse—but **the horn has always had healing powers**.*

*The **feathered serpent Quetzalcoatl** could shape-shift into human form, wearing a bird-mask. As the Aztec and Maya god of rain, fertility, wind, and learning, he was **worshipped as the god of life**.* **13**

13½ *You might think that all mythical beasts are just that, but there is one exception. The **Kraken was a huge, tentacled sea monster** in Scandinavian myth. Many now think that the legends were **based on sightings of the giant squid**—a creature unknown to science before 1853.*

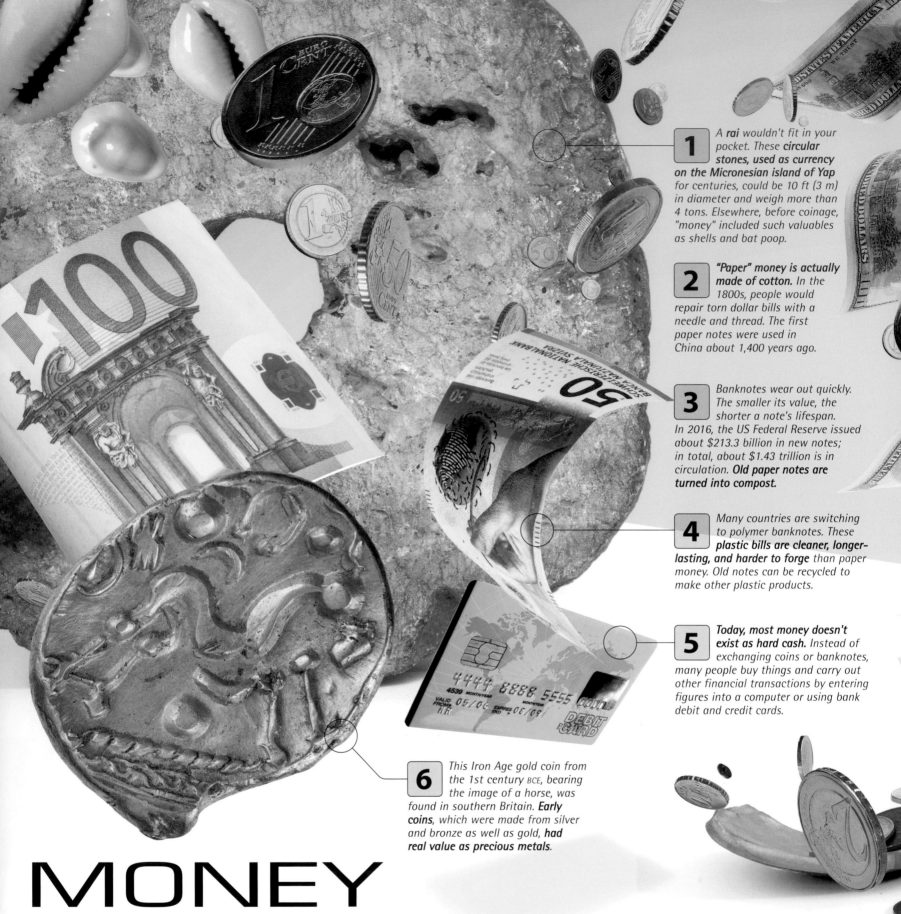

1 A **rai** wouldn't fit in your pocket. These **circular stones, used as currency on the Micronesian island of Yap** for centuries, could be 10 ft (3 m) in diameter and weigh more than 4 tons. Elsewhere, before coinage, "money" included such valuables as shells and bat poop.

2 **"Paper" money is actually made of cotton.** In the 1800s, people would repair torn dollar bills with a needle and thread. The first paper notes were used in China about 1,400 years ago.

3 Banknotes wear out quickly. The smaller its value, the shorter a note's lifespan. In 2016, the US Federal Reserve issued about $213.3 billion in new notes; in total, about $1.43 trillion is in circulation. **Old paper notes are turned into compost.**

4 Many countries are switching to polymer banknotes. These **plastic bills are cleaner, longer-lasting, and harder to forge** than paper money. Old notes can be recycled to make other plastic products.

5 **Today, most money doesn't exist as hard cash.** Instead of exchanging coins or banknotes, many people buy things and carry out other financial transactions by entering figures into a computer or using bank debit and credit cards.

6 This Iron Age gold coin from the 1st century BCE, bearing the image of a horse, was found in southern Britain. **Early coins**, which were made from silver and bronze as well as gold, **had real value as precious metals.**

MONEY TALKS

For thousands of years, people have exchanged money for goods and services. Many different forms of cash have been used, from shells and stones to precious metals and plastics. Today, money is often just numbers on a computer screen.

7 The world has 180 currencies. Of these, the US dollar is used more often for trade and in more countries than any other currency. The British pound has been around the longest— since the 8th century.

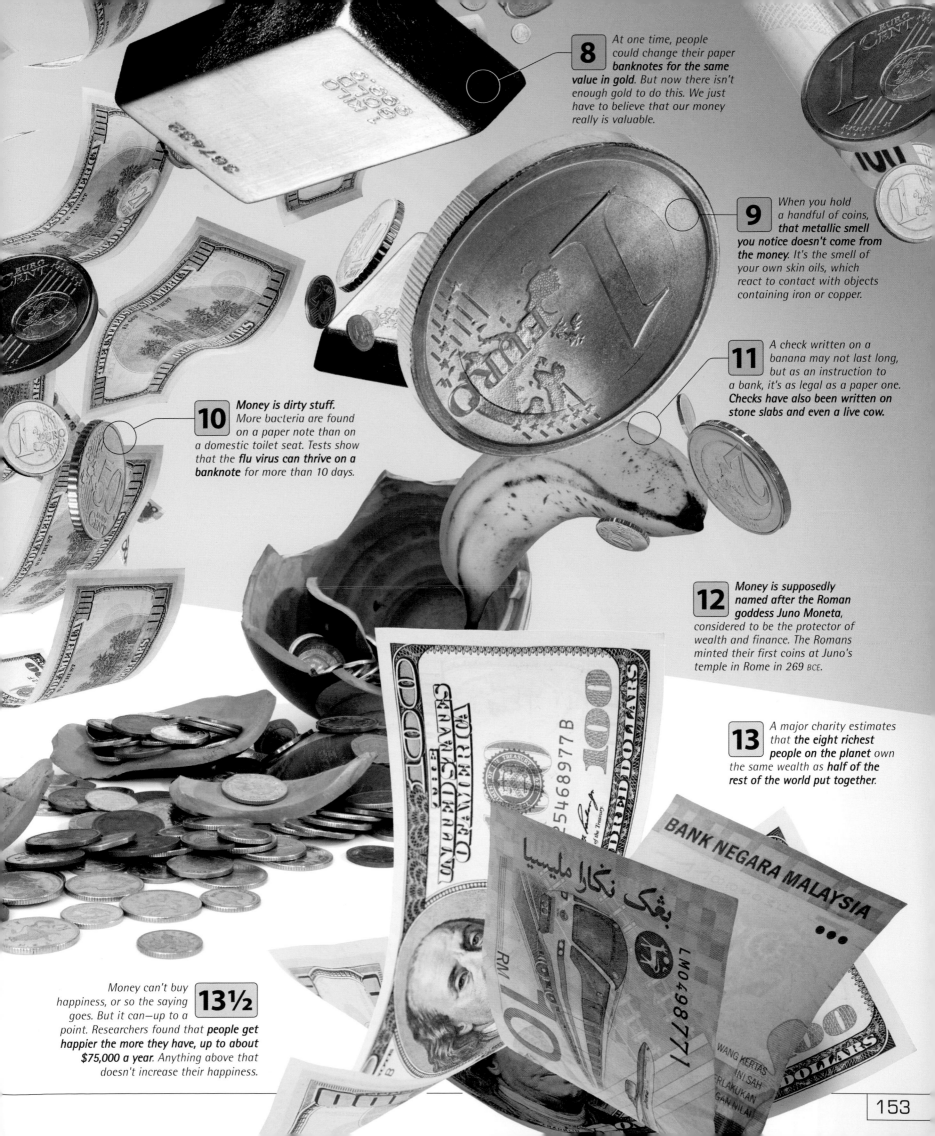

8 At one time, people could change their paper **banknotes for the same value in gold.** But now there isn't enough gold to do this. We just have to believe that our money really is valuable.

9 When you hold a handful of coins, **that metallic smell you notice doesn't come from the money.** It's the smell of your own skin oils, which react to contact with objects containing iron or copper.

11 A check written on a banana may not last long, but as an instruction to a bank, it's as legal as a paper one. **Checks have also been written on stone slabs and even a live cow.**

10 **Money is dirty stuff.** More bacteria are found on a paper note than on a domestic toilet seat. Tests show that the **flu virus can thrive on a banknote** for more than 10 days.

12 **Money is supposedly named after the Roman goddess Juno Moneta,** considered to be the protector of wealth and finance. The Romans minted their first coins at Juno's temple in Rome in 269 BCE.

13 A major charity estimates that **the eight richest people on the planet** own the same wealth as **half of the rest of the world put together.**

13½ Money can't buy happiness, or so the saying goes. But it can—up to a point. Researchers found that **people get happier the more they have, up to about $75,000 a year.** Anything above that doesn't increase their happiness.

1 In 1969 the Internet began as ARPANET, a network of computers, linking just four universities. It took an hour to send a five-letter message. For many years, it would continue to be a mostly text-based system used by universities and scientists.

2 In 1971 the first email was sent between two computers. The sender, programmer Ray Tomlinson, just danced his fingers along the keyboard, so the first message was something like QWERTYUIOP! Today more than three million emails are sent every second.

3 The smiley emoticon :-) was invented in 1982, by US computer scientist Scott Fahlman. He wanted to be sure people knew when he was joking. About 6 billion emoticons (made up of keyboard characters) are used each day, and they have evolved into emojis (pictures).

5 In 1991 in the UK, the first webcam was set up in the computer lab at Cambridge University. It filmed the coffee-maker, so that researchers could see if the pot was empty or not without having to leave their desks. That webcam was not switched off until 2001.

4 Everything changed in 1990–91, when British pioneer Tim Berners-Lee put together the HTML computer language to mark up documents so they could be viewed by anyone over the Internet. He also developed the first browser to view the documents, and the world's first website. The World Wide Web was born!

6 Internet usage has grown at a rapid rate, from 200 users in 1982, heading toward 3.2 billion users today, in more than 200 countries. The busiest country online is China, with 731 million users at the end of 2016. That's over half the population.

7 The Internet is now a huge network of servers linked by more than 550,000 miles (885,000 km) of underwater cables, which would reach to the Moon and back. The cables are vulnerable to damage from ships' anchors, fishing nets, earthquakes, and even shark bites, so wherever possible they are buried out of harm's way.

INTERNET LINKS

The Internet has brought an information revolution. This vast network connects many millions of computers at the same time and people can access and share information over the Internet using a system called the World Wide Web (WWW).

8 Wiki means "quick" in Hawaiian, and is also the name of part of a website that is open for people to contribute to. The most famous wiki is **the online encyclopedia Wikipedia, a collection of wikis in more than 295 languages**. Most contributors work for free, but they don't always agree on the facts. This can lead to edit wars. Most of these are trivial, but sometimes things get nasty!

9 So many new websites are added to the web that it is impossible to confirm its exact size, but the milestone of **1 billion websites was reached in September 2014.**

11 Social networking website **Facebook has more than 1.2 billion daily users**. English Queen Elizabeth II launched her Facebook page in 2010, but it is not possible to send friend requests! The first person to receive 100 million Facebook "likes" was Colombian singer Shakira in 2014.

10 The world's most popular search engine was called BackRub, until, in 1997, it was renamed Google. Today, **Google processes more than 40,000 queries a second**—that's 3.5 billion searches a day and 1.2 trillion searches a year.

12 Internet users share pictures, music, and videos by uploading them to websites. **The most popular video-sharing site is YouTube, which first exceeded 10 billion views in a month in August 2009.** The first film was uploaded in 2005 when Yakov Lapitsky recorded a short clip of his friend, YouTube founder Jawed Karim, just standing by elephants in San Diego Zoo.

13 Spam is electronic junk mail. Spammers send millions of emails, usually trying to sell things. **In a bad month, up to 97 percent of emails sent are spam.** The electricity used to send a year's worth of spam is equivalent to the annual output of four big power stations.

13½ Don't believe everything you read on the Internet! **Anyone can put up a website, and the accuracy of information is often unknown.** It is a good idea to check whether the website address ends in .gov or .edu, meaning it is a government- or education-based site. Reading the author's history also helps determine the reliability of the website.

1 The crunchy brown leaves that litter the ground in fall come from deciduous trees—**trees that shed their leaves during the colder seasons.** Leaves need light to make food, so they fall off in the darker winter months and grow back in the spring.

2 Succulent plants can survive in incredibly dry conditions by storing water in their fleshy leaves. **The biggest desert cacti can suck up 5 bathtubfuls after a rainfall**—enough to sustain them through four months of drought.

3 Used as far back as the time of the ancient Egyptians, the opium poppy has been one of **over 70,000 plant species that we use in medicine.** Today the plant is made into the powerful painkiller morphine.

4 Bamboos are giant grasses that grow into thick forests. **New shoots of giant bamboo grow up to 3 ft (1 m) in 24 hours**—the fastest recorded for any plant.

5 Kissing under the mistletoe may be a friendly Christmas tradition, but the plant itself is a vicious parasite. **Mistletoe steals its nutrients from a host plant, usually a tree.** It wraps around branches and burrows its roots deep into the wood to cling on.

PRECIOUS PLANTS

Plants are livesavers for the human race—emitting breathable oxygen into our atmosphere, providing food for us to eat, and medicine to heal us. At the bottom of most food chains, plants support almost every animal on Earth.

6 There are 25,000 different types of orchids—the largest family of flowering plants. Many use tricks to lure in pollinating insects: the hammer orchid attracts male wasps by looking and smelling just like the body of a female wasp.

7 Climbing plants climb in order to survive—scrambling over others to reach for sunlight and air. *Their thin, touch-sensitive tendrils grow quickly, coiling around any supports they find.*

8 Bonsai are conventional trees that are grown in containers, restricting their root systems and keeping them small. Despite their miniature size, the oldest is thought to be more than 800 years old.

9 Cones store the seeds of many large trees. *Coastal redwoods are the tallest cone-producing trees,* with the record holder reaching 379 ft (115.5 m)—higher than a 30-story building.

10 *Just 1 percent of an average tree is living tissue.* The other 99 percent is made up of dead cells—which form the inside of the tree and provide structure for the living cells on the outside.

11 Mosses are natural sponges that can soak up large amounts of water. *Bog moss was used to make bandage dressings during World War II* because of its absorbant properties.

12 *Ferns are the descendants of some of the first plants on Earth,* dating back nearly 400 million years. These primitive plants are one of many that absorb toxins, helping remove pollutants from air and soil.

13½ *Seaweeds look like plants*, but in fact they belong to a different group of organisms called algae. Single-celled algae are the *ancestors of all today's plants.*

13 The Venus flytrap is the most famous carnivorous plant— a master at trapping unwary insects and digesting their bodies for nutrients. *Its spiky-toothed leaves can snap shut in less than a second.*

GLORIOUS GREEKS

Ancient Greek civilization is seen as a golden era. It reached its peak in the 5th century BCE, producing many great thinkers and leaders, and many grand buildings—including the Parthenon in Athens, which was completed in 432 BCE.

1 Ancient Greece was not one unified country but a collection of many city-states (self-governing cities with their own laws) that shared a common language and religion. Athens was the most powerful city-state and the world's first democracy—governed by the people.

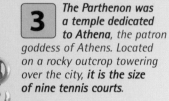

3 The Parthenon was a temple dedicated to Athena, the patron goddess of Athens. Located on a rocky outcrop towering over the city, **it is the size of nine tennis courts.**

2 The ancient Greeks believed that their world was ruled by **many gods**, who they honored, prayed to, and feared. Zeus was king of the Greek gods. His statue appeared on the pediment (the triangular part beneath the roof) at the front of the Parthenon.

Zeus

4 Designed to dazzle, the temple was built using about 24,000 tons of pure white marble. But it was not left gleaming white—**parts were painted in brilliant hues of red, blue, and green.**

5 There are 92 panels, or metopes, all around the temple's outer walls, which were carved on the ground before being lifted into position above the columns. Each side of the building shows a mythological conflict—on this side, gods battled giants.

6 A place of worship has existed on the Parthenon's site for thousands of years. Before the Parthenon, there was another temple dedicated to Athena. The Parthenon was converted to a church in the 6th century CE and a mosque in the 1460s.

7 If the Parthenon's columns were extended into the sky, they would eventually meet. They were built to slant inward, to counteract an optical illusion that makes straight columns appear to slant outward.

8 Philosophy was important to the ancient Greeks, and many of their famous philosophers, such as Plato, are as famous today. Some of the teachings were quite extreme: **Pythagoras told the ancient Greeks that they shouldn't eat beans because they held the souls of the dead.**

9 The first recorded Olympic Games were held in 776 BCE at Olympia. Athletes competed naked and sporting events included chariot racing. Wars between city-states were not allowed in the month before the games, so spectators could get to the events safely.

10 A 525-ft (160-m) long, marble frieze (a strip of decoration that ran around the inner wall) portrays the great procession at the Panathenaic Festival, which celebrated Athena's birthday.

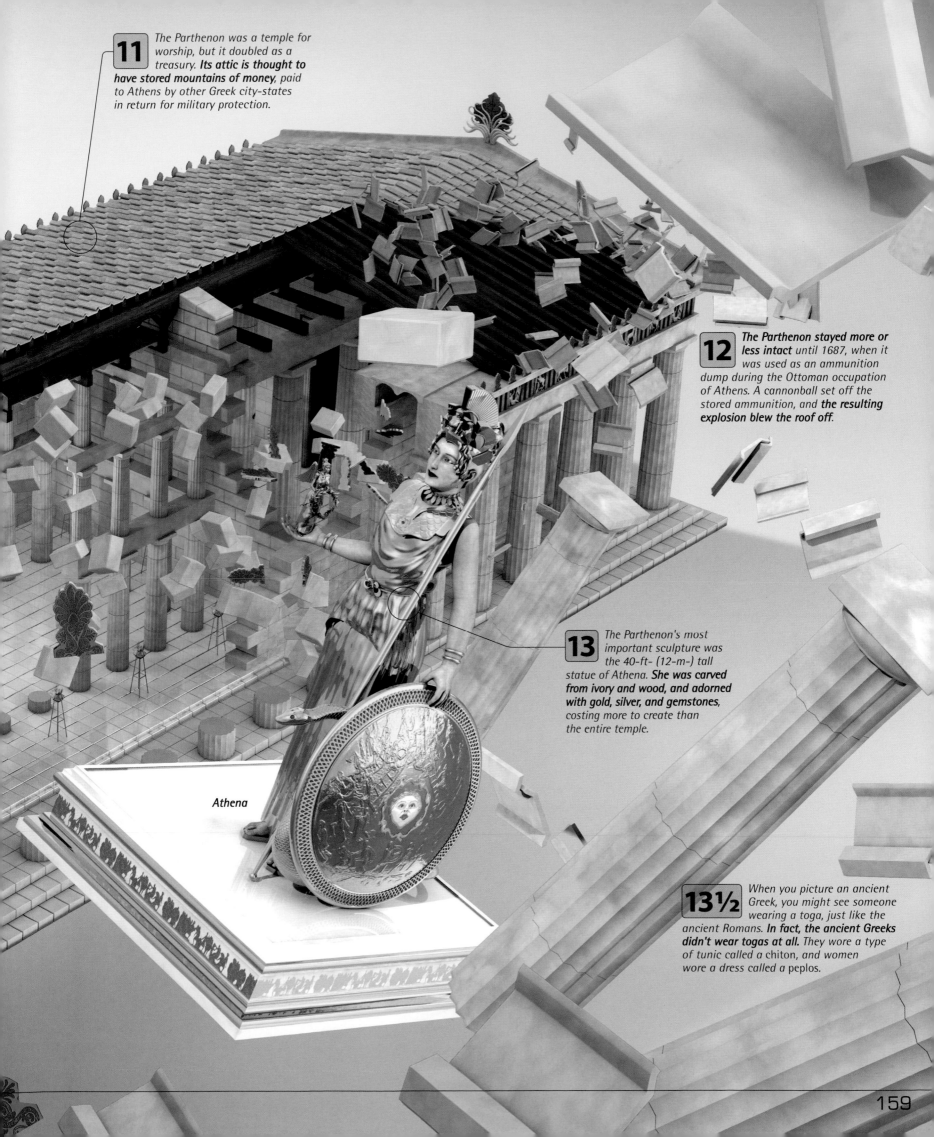

11 The Parthenon was a temple for worship, but it doubled as a treasury. **Its attic is thought to have stored mountains of money,** paid to Athens by other Greek city-states in return for military protection.

12 **The Parthenon stayed more or less intact** until 1687, when it was used as an ammunition dump during the Ottoman occupation of Athens. A cannonball set off the stored ammunition, and **the resulting explosion blew the roof off.**

13 The Parthenon's most important sculpture was the 40-ft- (12-m-) tall statue of Athena. **She was carved from ivory and wood, and adorned with gold, silver, and gemstones,** costing more to create than the entire temple.

Athena

13½ When you picture an ancient Greek, you might see someone wearing a toga, just like the ancient Romans. **In fact, the ancient Greeks didn't wear togas at all.** They wore a type of tunic called a chiton, and women wore a dress called a peplos.

CROCODILE SMILE

Crocodile ancestors first appeared on Earth 240 million years ago and since then they have become increasingly deadly predators. These stealthy hunters are found in many tropical regions, lurking in rivers and lakes ready to launch an attack.

1 *This **American crocodile** is one of **23 different crocodilian species,** an order that includes crocodiles and their close relatives **alligators and gharials.** It is one of several species that is now **vulnerable due to illegal hunting.***

2 *Crocodiles have the **strongest bite ever measured.** Their jaws are so powerful that scientists estimate the **bite of a large crocodile would be second only to that of a T. rex.***

3 *Although **a crocodile's jaws can snap shut with enormous force,** the muscles for opening them are quite weak. You could **keep a crocodile's jaws shut by putting a rubber band around them.***

4 *Positioned on the top of the head, a **crocodile's eyes** allow it to **watch for prey** while the rest of its body remains submerged. The eyes can even **retract into their sockets** if the crocodile is attacked.*

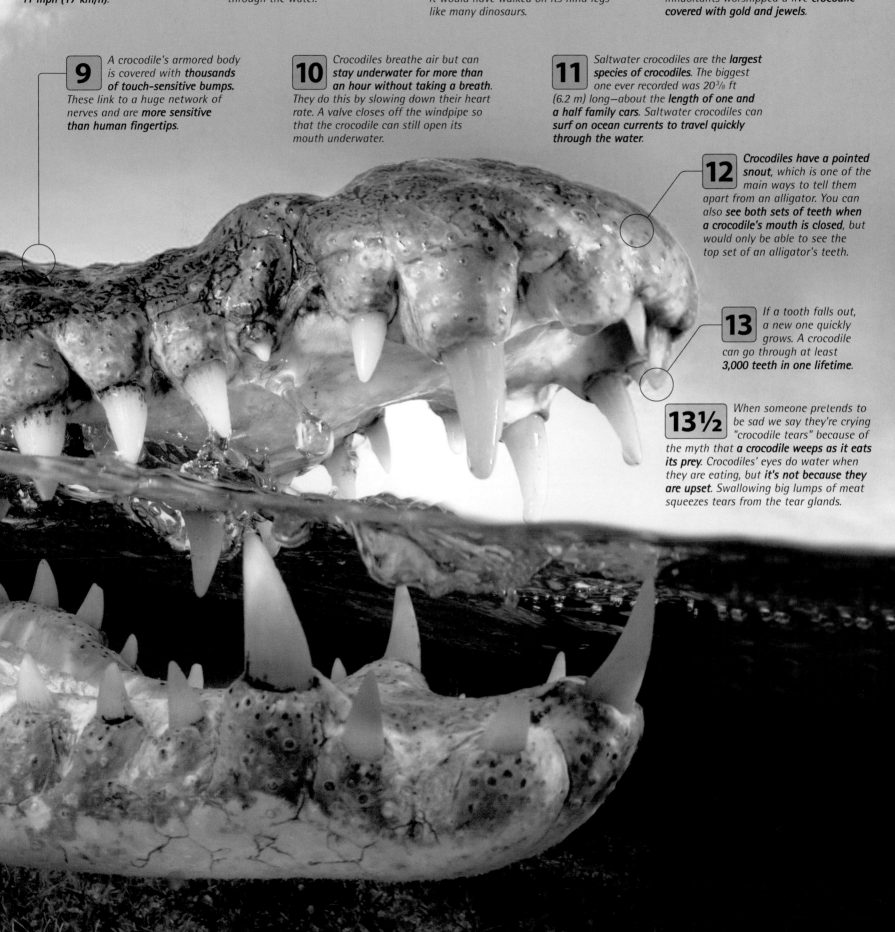

5 The crocodile typically *hunts by ambush*, using its *powerful hind legs and tail* to launch itself out of the water. On land, it can *run at around 11 mph (17 km/h)*.

6 A crocodile can *swim at speeds of up to 20 mph (32 km/h)*. Tucking its legs in, the crocodile uses strokes of its *powerful muscular tail* to propel it through the water.

7 Before the dinosaurs, *giant crocodile ancestors* ruled the Earth. The *9-ft (2.7-m) Carolina Butcher* stalked the land 230 million years ago. Named for its *fearsome bladelike teeth*, it would have walked on its hind legs like many dinosaurs.

8 The *ancient Egyptians often mummified crocodiles* and had a crocodile-headed god called Sobek. One of their cities was known as *"Crocodilopolis,"* because the inhabitants worshipped a live *crocodile covered with gold and jewels*.

9 A crocodile's armored body is covered with *thousands of touch-sensitive bumps*. These link to a huge network of nerves and are *more sensitive than human fingertips*.

10 Crocodiles breathe air but can *stay underwater for more than an hour without taking a breath*. They do this by slowing down their heart rate. A valve closes off the windpipe so that the crocodile can still open its mouth underwater.

11 Saltwater crocodiles are the *largest species of crocodiles*. The biggest one ever recorded was 20³/₈ ft (6.2 m) long—about the *length of one and a half family cars*. Saltwater crocodiles can *surf on ocean currents to travel quickly through the water*.

12 *Crocodiles have a pointed snout*, which is one of the main ways to tell them apart from an alligator. You can also *see both sets of teeth when a crocodile's mouth is closed*, but would only be able to see the top set of an alligator's teeth.

13 If a tooth falls out, a new one quickly grows. A crocodile can go through at least *3,000 teeth in one lifetime*.

13½ When someone pretends to be sad we say they're crying "crocodile tears" because of the myth that *a crocodile weeps as it eats its prey*. Crocodiles' eyes do water when they are eating, but *it's not because they are upset*. Swallowing big lumps of meat squeezes tears from the tear glands.

DOWN TO EARTH

Without the force of gravity there would be no Universe as we know it. Gravity holds stars and planets together, and keeps you and everything else, including air, on Earth. It makes things fall when they drop—or jump, like this diver.

1 There are invisible forces at work in the Universe. You may not be able to see them but they push and pull on matter. *The force of gravity only pulls (attracts); it does not push (repel).*

2 The force of gravity at the very large scales of planets, stars, and galaxies is extremely powerful. On everyday scales, though, it is weak—gravity can be overcome by *the electromagnetic force that makes a magnet cling to the refrigerator.*

3 *Wherever people are on Earth, the force of gravity pulls them toward its center. Gravity makes the diver accelerate toward the water.*

4 *The gravitational influence of the Moon, and to a lesser extent, the Sun, causes the oceans to bulge.* As Earth spins, different parts of the world experience high and low tides under the bulging oceans.

5 *There are regions in space where the force of gravity is so huge that even light is sucked in.* Black holes are pitch black, but they are not really holes—they are *packed with mass, giving them immense gravity.* If you fell toward a black hole, it would stretch your body thin, like pulling an elastic band.

6 *In midair, the only two forces acting on the diver are gravity and air resistance, or drag.* Air resistance increases with speed. It is a tiny force on this diver—but a skydiver can reach such high speeds that air resistance balances out gravity and the skydiver stops accelerating, reaching "terminal velocity."

» Newton's law

The first proper theory about gravity was the work of English scientist Isaac Newton, who published his "Universal Theory of Gravitation" in 1687. Newton worked out that every object attracts every other object, and that the strength of the attractive force depends upon the mass of the two objects and the distance between them.

Two objects of the same mass are attracted to each other by the force of gravity.

Double the mass and the gravitational force is four times as strong.

Double the distance and the gravitational force reduces to one-quarter of its strength.

ACKNOWLEDGMENTS

DK would like to thank:

Ann Baggaley, Jessica Cawthra, Ashwin Khurana, Anna Limerick, and Fleur Star for editorial assistance; Dave Ball, Samantha Richiardi, and Smiljka Surla for design assistance; Hazel Beynon for proofreading; Helen Peters for the index.

Special thanks to Sheila Collins for all her help in the final stages of the project.

The publisher would like to thank the following for their kind permission to reproduce their photographs:

Key:
a-above; b-below/bottom; c-center; f-far; l-left; r-right; t-top

6 **123RF.com:** Soloviova Liudmyla (br). **Dreamstime.com:** Dave Bredeson (tc); Skypixel (cla). **6-7 Dreamstime.com:** Yifang Zhao (b). **7 Dreamstime.com:** Furtseff (ca); Pavel Konovalov (bl); Guido Vrola (br). **10 123RF.com:** Subbotina (clb). **Dreamstime.com:** Shariff Che\' Lah (bl); Nerss (c); Tomboy2290 (bc); Yurakp (cla). **10-11 Stefan Podhorodecki. 11 123RF.com:** Mohammed Anwarul Kabir Choudhury (tc). **Dreamstime.com:** Goncharuk Maksym (cb); Yurakp (crb). **Getty Images:** Amriphoto (ca). **Reddit:** https://www.reddit.com/r/pics/comments/18lxyw/hala_truit (c). **12-13 Turbo Squid:** 3d_molier International / Elements of the image: Generic Sport Roadster. **14 Dreamstime.com:** Hery Siswanto (bl). **14-15 Manpreet Singh. 16-17 Dreamstime.com:** Plazaccameraman (b). **16 Dreamstime.com:** Anna1311 (br, tc); Ruta Saulyte (c). Jim Frink: (cla). **17 Alamy Stock Photo:** David Newton (tc). **Steve Axford:** (cla, tl). **Dreamstime.com:** Anna1311 (tr); Taiftin (crb); Geografika (ca). **20 Dorling Kindersley:** Tim Parmenter / Natural History Museum, London (tl, tr). **Dreamstime.com:** Igor Kaliuzhny (bc). **20-21 Getty Images:** Stockbyte / George Doyle (c). **21 Dorling Kindersley:** Tim Parmenter / Natural History Museum, London (tl, bl). **Rex Shutterstock:** Shutterstock (tr). **22-23 Turbo Squid:** Locomotive_works / Elements of the image: Orleans 1893 Steam Locomotive. **24 Dreamstime.com:** Kurhan (clb). **25 Dreamstime.com:** Juri Samsonov (bc). **28 NASA:** (cla). **30-31 Stephen Frink Collection:** James Watt (Shark). **32-33**

Dreamstime.com: Jacek Kutyba | (b). **32 123RF.com:** Marek Uliasz (bl). **Alamy Stock Photo:** Art Collection 3 (cl). **Dorling Kindersley:** Gary Ombler / Durham University Oriental Museum (ca, c, cb). **Dreamstime.com:** Keith Wheatley (tr). **33 Dorling Kindersley:** Dave King / Durham University Oriental Museum (ca). **Dreamstime.com:** Ammza12 (bc); Bethbee | (tl); Okea (tc); Olga Popova (clb); Robyn Mackenzie (cra); Py2000 (c); Ramvseb1 (cb); Piero Cruciatti (br); Sergey Lavrentev (crb). **38-39 Sash Fitzsimmons. 40 Dreamstime.com:** Skypixel (tl); Magdalena Żurawska (cla). **41 Dreamstime.com:** Les Cunliffe (tc, ftr, fcra); Aldo Di Bari Murga (tl); Sergeyoch (tr); Zagorskid (ca); Alexander Pladdet (cra); Mikhail Kokhanchikov | (clb); Stephen Noakes (br). **42 123RF.com:** Thawat Tanhai (cra). **42-43 123RF.com:** Alexandr Pakhnyushchyy (b). **43 123RF.com:** Werayut Nueathong (cb); Golkin Oleg (clb); Andrey Pavlov (br). **46-47 Dušan Beňo:** (HseFly). **50-51 Stefan Podhorodecki. 53 123RF.com:** Grafner (bl). **Alamy Stock Photo:** Chris Willson (c). **Dorling Kindersley:** Museum of Design in Plastics, Bournemouth Arts University, UK / Gary Ombler (tl). **Dreamstime.com:** Thanarat Boonmee (cl); James Steidl (clb); Vitalyedush (cb); Prykhodov (crb); Razvan Ionut Dragomirescu (br). **54 Dorling Kindersley:** Colin Keates / Natural History Museum, London (cb); Harry Taylor / Sedgwick Museum of Geology, Cambridge (br). **56-57 Turbo Squid:** MilosJakubec / Elements of the image: Watch Movement. **58-59 Dreamstime.com:** Okea (c). **58 Dreamstime.com:** Palex66 | (tc). **60-61 Turbo Squid:** Malevolent_King / Elements of the image: Centurion. **62 123RF.com:** Anuwat Susomwong (clb). **Alamy Stock Photo:** Blickwinkel (bc). **Dreamstime.com:** Dio5050 (bl); Artem Podobedov (cl); Maturos Yaowanawisit (cb); Ewa Walicka (tl); Verdateo (tr). **63 Dreamstime.com:** Cornelius20 (crb); Tamara Kulikova (tr); Sahua (bl); Dmitry Knorre (c); Okea (ca); Justas Jaruševičius (br). **Getty Images:** Photos Lamontagne (tc). **64-65 Dreamstime.com:** Wawritto. **66-67 Alamy Stock Photo:** Reuters / Christopher Pasatieri (US Transport Military Sci Tec). **72-73 Dreamstime.com:** Rainer Junker (DeepOc8). **72 Alamy Stock Photo:** Brandon Cole Marine Photography (br). **FLPA:** Minden Pictures / Norbert Wu (cr). **Dr Alan J. Jamieson, Newcastle University, UK:**

(tr). Fredrik Pleijel: (tl). **Science Photo Library:** Dante Fenolio (ca); Dante Fenolio (cl). **73 Alamy Stock Photo:** AF Archive (fbl). **FLPA:** Minden Pictures / Norbert Wu (ca, tl). **Getty Images:** Visuals Unlimited, Inc. / Michael Ready (tr). **National Geographic Creative:** Emory Krlstof (bl). **Natural Visions:** Peter David (tc). **Science Photo Library:** British Antarctic Survey (bc); Gregory Ochocki (cb/DeepOc7). **SeaPics.com:** D. R. Schrichte (c). **76-77 Getty Images:** Barcroft Media. **78-79 123RF.com:** Igarts. **80-81 Turbo Squid:** DeVisCon / Elements of the image: Ceremonial knight armour. **86-87 NASA:** GSFC / SDO. **88 Dreamstime.com:** Isselee (ca); Tjkphotography (cl). **89 Alamy Stock Photo:** Brandon Cole Marine Photography (tr); Cultura RM 89-80c; **Dorling Kindersley:** Natural History Museum, London (tc). **Dreamstime.com:** W. Scott Mcgill (cra). **FLPA:** Minden Pictures / Norbert Wu (tl). **92-93 Dreamstime.com:** Juri Samsonov (ca). **93 123RF.com:** Jesus David Carballo Prieto (tc). **Photoshot:** Daniel Heuclin (cr). **98-99 123RF.com:** Arsgera (c); Katisa (t). **98 123RF.com:** Reinis Bigacs (clb); Valentyn Volkov (cla); Phloenphoto (ca). **Dreamstime.com:** Tracy Decourcy (br). **99 123RF.com:** Ifong (ca); Olga Popova (clb); Baiba Opule (bl); limpido (cr). **Dreamstime.com:** Jiri Hera (br); Thelightwriter (crb). **Rex Shutterstock:** Shutterstock / Paul Grover (tl). **100 Dreamstime.com. Science Photo Library:** (bc). **100-101 Dreamstime.com:** Dave Bredeson (ca); Guido Vrola. **101 Dreamstime.com:** Zoya Fedorova (cr); Furtseff (ca); James Steidl (c); Ari Sanjaya (tr). **104-105 Getty Images:** Henrik Sorensen. **110-111 Getty Images:** AFP / DPA / Patrick Pleul. **116 Dorling Kindersley:** Bill Schmoker (cl). **117 Dreamstime.com:** Steve Byland | (cra). **118-119 Turbo Squid:** puperpaxa / Elements of the image: Viking Ship Drakkar. **120-121 Stephen Locke. 123 Alamy Stock Photo:** Blickwinkel (tl). **Phuket Scuba Club:** http://www.phuket-scuba-club.com/blog/2012/03/recent-dive-buddies/cuttlefish (cra). **128-129 © Red Bull GmbH:** Red Bull Content Pool / Bavo Swijgers. **130 123RF.com:** Antonel (tl); Sergey Goruppa (cl, br); Number001 (bl). **Dorling Kindersley:** Gary Ombler / Thackeray Medical Museum (c). **Dreamstime.com:** Newbi1 (cb). **130-131 Dreamstime.com:** Russal (bc). **131 123RF.com:** Bombaert (tc); Jakub

Gojda (ca); Leonello Calvetti (clb); Dmitriy Syechin (bc); Robuart (tr). **Dreamstime.com:** Newbi1 (cr). **132-133 Yuri Beletsky. 134 123RF.com:** Subbotina (cr). **Dreamstime.com:** Andrey Armyagov (bl); Anna Kucherova (cra); Okea (cl); Vladyslav Bashutskyy (bc); Paulpaladin (tc). **135 Dreamstime.com:** Jens Stolt (tr); Hannu Viitanen (cl). **Getty Images:** RPM Pictures (clb/Colour1). **142-143 Turbo Squid:** iljujjkin / Elements of the image: Concert Grand Piano Yamaha . **144-145 Matthew Smith:** (PortManWar). **146 Dreamstime.com:** Dvmsimages (c); Okea (tl); Newbi1 (ca); Eric Strand (tc); Postnikov (tr); Alexander Pladdet (ftr); Dmitry Rukhlenko (cb); Zelfit (cl); Elena Schweitzer (bc); Ahmad Firdaus Ismail (crb). **146-147 123RF.com:** Bayberry (cb). **Dreamstime.com:** Vladyslav Bashutskyy (tc). **147 123RF.com. Dreamstime.com. 152 The Trustees of the British Museum:** Chas Howson (l). **Dorling Kindersley:** Canterbury City Council, Museums and Galleries (cl). **Dreamstime.com:** Andres Rodriguez (c); Yulan 52 (ca). **152-152 Dreamstime.com:** Irochka (ca). **152-153 Dreamstime.com:** Gradts (t). **153 Alamy Stock Photo:** Rachel Husband (clb). **Corbis:** Mark Weiss (tl). **Dreamstime.com:** Olesya Tseytlin (br). **156-157 Dreamstime.com:** Cloki. **156 Kay Bradfield / www.beastsandblossoms.com:** (br). Dreamstime.com. **157 Dreamstime.com:** Dibrova (cb); Joystockphoto (l); Yap Kee Chan (c); Juliengrondin (tc); Leigh Prather (ca); Verastuchelova (br); Johannesk | (cr). **160-161 Andy Murch. 162-163 Agustin Muñoz. 164-165 Mauritius Images. 166-167 Solent Picture Desk / Solent News & Photo Agency, Southampton:** Kemal Selimovic

Cover images: *Front*: **123RF.com:** Bayberry ca, Soloviova Liudmyla bl, Rasslava bc, Subbotina cra; **Dreamstime.com:** Jiri Hera tl, Justas Jaruševičius fbl, Okea br, Juri Samsonov cl, Verdateo crb, Hannu Viitanen cla, Guido Vrola ftl; *Back*: **123RF.com:** bl, Subbotina clb; **Dreamstime.com:** Dvmsimages crb, Jlcst b, Elena Schweitzer cb; **Getty Images:** Amriphoto cla; *Spine*: **123RF.com:** Bayberry t

All other images © Dorling Kindersley
For further information see:
www.dkimages.com

8 Today there are about 600 million pet cats in the world. The US is the more than 85 million, followed by China, Russia, Brazil, and France.

9 The long, flexible tail helps the cat balance. Domestic cats keep their tail vertical, but wild cats hold them horizontally or between their legs. Some cat breeds have no tail. The tailless Manx cat, which has long back legs and a round rump, was for a long time wrongly thought to be a "cabbit"—a cross between a cat and a rabbit.

10 The ancient Egyptians considered cats sacred and worshipped them. When a sacred cat died in ancient Egypt, it would be mummified and placed in a tomb, and people would shave off their eyebrows in mourning.

13½ Purring is often assumed to be the sign of a contented cat. In reality, the purr is self-soothing, so cats purr for many different reasons, such as feeling scared, sick, or in pain.

13 Using their strong legs to push off, cats can leap up to six times their own height. They prepare to leap by crouching down like a coiled spring with all four paws placed together. This gives them maximum power when they uncoil and take off.

11 The saying goes that cats have nine lives, because they almost always land on their feet. This is because of the righting reflex—an instinctive ability to twist the body the right way up while falling. A cat is more likely to survive a fall from ten stories than two because a longer fall allows more time for the animal to right itself (don't try this at home!).

12 In Medieval Europe, cats came to be associated with witchcraft. In Ypres, Belgium, cats were thrown from a tall tower each year in a festival called the Kattenstoet. A modern festival still takes place today, but with toy cats rather than real ones.

» Cat claws

The claws of cats are made from keratin, the same protein found in human nails. Cats use their claws to climb, catch prey, tear meat, and protect themselves. Unlike those of most other carnivores, cat claws are fully extendable. To extend and retract the claw, the cat uses two tendons inside the foot, contracting one while relaxing the other. The outside layer of each claw is shed every few months, revealing a new one underneath.

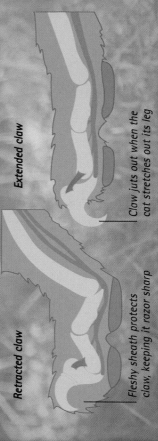

Retracted claw

Extended claw

Claw juts out when the cat stretches out its leg

Fleshy sheath protects claw, keeping it razor sharp

GLOSSARY

air resistance
The force that slows down objects moving through the air, also known as drag.

alloy
A material made from mixing a metal with other metals or elements to give it greater strength. For example, steel is an alloy made of iron and carbon.

altitude
The height of an object or a point above sea level.

amphibian
A cold-blooded vertebrate animal that lives both on land and in water, such as a frog or newt.

antibiotic
A medicine that destroys disease-causing organisms such as bacteria.

arachnid
One of a group of eight-legged invertebrates such as spiders, scorpions, mites, and ticks.

archaeological
Relating to the study of ancient objects or areas to find out about how people lived in earlier times.

Arctic Circle
An imaginary line, at the latitude of 66° 32'N, that encircles the Arctic region surrounding the North Pole.

arthritis
A disease that affects the joints, making them painful, swollen, or stiff.

arthropod
One of a group of invertebrate animals with external skeletons and jointed legs. Arthropods include insects, arachnids, crustaceans, and centipedes.

asteroid
A small body of rocky material that orbits the Sun.

atmosphere
The layer of gases that surrounds Earth and other planets.

atom
The smallest possible part of a chemical element that can exist by itself.

Aztec
People or objects from the Aztec empire, a once-powerful civilization that flourished in Mexico and Central America between the 14th and 16th centuries.

bacteria
A microscopic organism made of one cell. Some bacteria carry disease and are harmful, but many others, such as those used to make yogurt, are not.

battery
A device that produces electricity as a result of chemical reactions.

black hole
An area in space where a large star has burned out and collapsed in on itself. A black hole has a strong gravitational pull that nothing, not even light, can escape.

blubber
The layer of fat under the skin of whales, seals, walruses, and other sea mammals.

buoyancy
The ability of something to float in water.

caecilian
One of a group of wormlike, legless amphibians that live in muddy burrows or in water.

calligraphy
The art of writing in a decorative style, using brushes or broad pens.

carbon
An element that appears in solid form as graphite and diamond.

carbon dioxide
A colorless gas, present in air, that is made from carbon and oxygen atoms. Carbon dioxide is produced when things burn in air and when we breathe out. Plants make use of it to grow.

carbon fiber
A material made from thin threads of strong, heat-resistant carbon.

cardiac
To do with the heart.

carnivore
A meat-eating animal.

cell
The smallest unit of a living organism. Cells are the building blocks from which plants and animals are made.

centurion
In ancient Rome, the army officer in command of 80 soldiers.

cephalopod
One of a group of marine mollusks that includes octopuses, squid, and cuttlefish.

cetacean
A group of marine mammals that includes whales and dolphins.

chlorophyll
The pigment in plants that makes them look green. Chlorophyll absorbs sunlight, which a plant uses to make its food.

circuit
An unbroken path that allows electricity to flow around it.

city-state
A city that has its own independent system of government. City-states first appeared in ancient Greece, where the city of Sparta was ruled by its own king, and Athens was ruled by a politician.

comet
A body of rock and ice that orbits the Sun. The long "tails" of a comet are formed from dust and gas.

composite
A material made from two or more different materials. A composite is often stronger than the individual materials from which it is made.

compound eye
An eye that is made up of many small units each with its own tiny lens. Found in animals such as flies and spiders.

conductor
In physics, a material through which heat and electricity flow easily.

contaminant
A harmful substance that pollutes water, soil, or air.

continent
A very large landmass. Earth has seven continents: Africa, Europe, Asia, North America, South America, Australia, and Antarctica.

crustacean
An animal with a hard external skeleton and paired, jointed legs, such as a lobster.

crystal
A naturally occurring solid material with atoms that are arranged in a regular 3D pattern.

cuneiform
An ancient system of writing developed in Mesopotamia (now Iraq). Cuneiform consisted of wedge-shaped characters made on clay or stone.

deity
A being that people worship, such as a god or goddess.

democracy
A political system in which the people can choose the leader or political party they wish to run their country. The word comes from the ancient Greek for "rule by the people."

density
A measure of how concentrated the matter of an object is—so, for example, a brick is more dense than a feather. Density is calculated by dividing an object's mass by its volume.

digit
A finger or a toe. Can also refer to the numbers 0 to 9.

digital
A way of representing information in binary form (with only the numbers zero and one). Computers and electronic gadgets like cell phones store, process, and transmit information in digital form.

DNA
The abbreviation for deoxyribonucleic acid, the chemical found inside each cell of all living things. DNA carries information telling the cell what to do to grow and function.

drag
Another name for air resistance.

ecosystem
A community of living things (such as plants and animals) and nonliving things (such as soil and water) in a particular area, which all depend on each other.

electric current
The movement of electrically charged particles, usually electrons, which can move freely in metal wires.

electrode
An electrical contact, made from a conductor, that connects the energy from a circuit to something nonmetallic outside it.

electromagnetic spectrum
The whole range of electromagnetic radiation, which is energy in the form of waves, and includes visible light, infrared, ultraviolet, radio waves, and X-rays.

electron
A tiny negatively charged particle. Electrons are found in every atom, but they can often move between atoms.

element
A substance consisting of only one type of atom, and which cannot be broken down into simpler substances.

embryo
An unborn animal or human in the earliest stages of development.

energy
The ability of something to do work, such as moving or giving out light and heat.

Enlightenment, the
The period of European history in the 18th century when people tried to reason for themselves and gain a new understanding of the world.

Equator
An imaginary line, at the latitude of 0°, that encircles Earth halfway between the north and south poles, and divides it into the Northern and Southern Hemispheres.

erosion
The wearing away of surfaces such as soil or rock by the action of wind, water, and sometimes glaciers.

ethane
A flammable gas that can be used as fuel.

exoskeleton
The hard, outer skeleton of crustaceans and insects that protects the soft body inside.

feminism
The belief that men and women should have the same rights and opportunities.

fiber
A thin, threadlike piece of material. Natural fibers are made from plants such as cotton, but artificial (synthetic) fibers are made by a chemical process.

filament
A flexible thread, such as the thin coil of wire in an incandescent light bulb that glows as electricity flows through it.

force
A push or pull that changes an object's speed, direction of movement, or shape.

fossil
The remains or impression of a prehistoric plant or animal preserved in rock.

fossil fuel
Any fuel, including coal, oil, and natural gas, formed naturally from the decayed remains of long-dead plants or animals.

French Revolution
The period of violent upheaval between 1789 and 1799, when the French people rose in revolt against their country's monarchy and political system, and established France as a republic.

frequency
The number of times something happens within a specific time. A high-pitched sound is described as high-frequency because it is produced by an object that vibrates many times every second.

friction
A force between two things that are in contact, which tends to stop them from sliding past each other. It slows things down and also produces heat.

fungi
A group of organisms, including mushrooms and toadstools, that feed on the living or decaying matter in which they grow, and reproduce using spores.

galaxy
A vast collection of stars, dust, and gas held together by gravity. Our Solar System lies in a galaxy called the Milky Way.

gas
A state of matter in which the particles (atoms or molecules) are not attached to each other and move freely.

germinate
In botany, what a seed does when it begins to grow and put out shoots.

g-force
A measure of how much heavier or lighter you feel when your body is rapidly accelerated (its motion is changed), such as on a roller coaster.

glacier
A large, very slow-moving river of ice, formed over a long time. Glaciers occur in the cold areas surrounding Earth's poles, and in high mountain ranges such as the Alps and the Himalayas.

gladiator
In Roman times, a person who fought other people, or animals, in big arenas as entertainment for the people. Most gladiators were slaves or prisoners.

glucose
A type of sugar that can be converted to energy once it has been absorbed. Plants, animals, and humans all need it—and plants produce it in their leaves.

graphite
A soft form of natural carbon. It has many uses, for example, in pencils.

gravity
The force of attraction (pull) between any two masses in the Universe. On Earth, gravity pulls things down toward the planet's surface.

harpsichord
A keyboard instrument popular in the 16th to 18th centuries, before the piano was invented.

helium
A nonflammable gas—often used in party balloons.

hemisphere
One half of a sphere—often refers to one half of Earth (the Northern and the Southern), or one half of the brain.

herbivore
An animal that eats only plants.

hieroglyphs
A writing system, invented by the ancient Egyptians, that used picture signs to represent words, sounds, and ideas.

hydrogen
A very light, flammable gas. Together with oxygen, it makes up water.

icecap
An area of permanent ice covering a large area, especially near the poles.

Industrial Revolution
The development of new technologies during the late 18th and early 19th centuries, leading to the rapid growth of mechanization and to social change.

insulator
A material that prevents energy, such as electricity or heat, from passing through it easily.

insulin
A substance produced naturally in the body that regulates sugar levels in the blood.

Internet
A network through which computers around the world can exchange information.

invertebrate
One of a group of animals without a backbone. Invertebrates include insects and crustaceans.

Iron Age
The period of history lasting from about 1300 BCE to 700 CE, during which people learned to work iron and to use it to make weapons and tools.

ivory
The hard material that forms the tusks of animals such as elephants and walruses.

jet engine
A type of engine that burns fuel continuously in a huge cylinder. It produces a fast-moving, backward jet of hot gas that pushes an aircraft forward.

karaoke
Entertainment in which people sing over prerecorded tunes played by a machine.

keratin
The substance that makes up nails, claws, reptile scales, and hair.

larva
The young form of an insect, such as a caterpillar, that has hatched from an egg but has not yet fully developed.

laser
A device that produces a concentrated beam of light, produced by energizing atoms inside a tube.

laser sensor
A device used to measure exact distances, or decide exact positions of objects, with the help of a laser beam.

lava
The hot molten rock thrown out by an erupting volcano.

LED
The abbreviation for light-emitting diode, a device that produces light when an electric current passes through it.

legionary
In ancient Rome, a soldier serving in a legion, which was an army division of several thousand men.

lens
A curved piece of glass or plastic that bends light rays. Used, for example, in a telescope to make distant objects look clearer or bigger. Also, the clear part of the eye that focuses light to form images.

light-year
The distance light travels in one year—about 6 trillion miles (9.5 trillion km).

liquid
A state of matter in which atoms or molecules are loosely linked but not joined rigidly together.

locomotive
A self-propelled engine that is powered by steam, electricity, or diesel to pull a train.

magma
Molten rock in Earth's hot interior, which may emerge as lava through cracks in Earth's crust or during a volcanic eruption.

magnetic field
The area around a magnet in which magnetic forces act.

magnetic poles
The two ends of a magnet, where the magnetic field is strongest. Also refers to the points on Earth's surface where the planet's magnetism is strongest, near the north and south poles.

mammal
A warm-blooded animal with a backbone that feeds its young with milk from its own body. Most mammals give birth to live young, except a few egg-laying species, such as the platypus.

mandible
In many animals, the lower jaw bone. In insects and arthropods, mandibles are paired mouthparts used for grasping or as weapons.

mass
In physics, the amount of matter an object is made of.

Maya
Refers to the Maya civilization in Central America, which was at its peak from around 250–900 CE.

medieval period
Also known as the Middle Ages, the period of history between the 5th and 15th centuries CE.

metamorphosis
A process of body changes that some animals pass through to become adults; for example, the transformation of caterpillars into butterflies.

meteorite
A chunk of space rock that passes through Earth's atmosphere and lands on the planet's surface.

methane
A flammable gas that can be used as fuel.

microbe
Another word for microorganism.

microorganism
A tiny single-celled creature seen only with a microscope. Microorganisms include bacteria and viruses.

microscope
An instrument used for magnifying objects too small to be seen with the naked eye.

mineral
A solid material that occurs naturally and has specific characteristics, such as a particular chemical composition and crystal shape.

molecule
A group of two or more atoms chemically joined together.

mollusk
A soft-bodied invertebrate, often protected by a hard shell. Snails, slugs, mussels, and octopuses are mollusks.

Morse code
An electronic system for sending messages in which letters and numbers are represented by dots and dashes.

nanoparticle
A very tiny particle, with a diameter of around 0.00000004 in (0.0000001 cm).

Neanderthals
An early species of humans that appeared in Europe and the Middle East around 200,000 years ago and became extinct 40,000 years ago.

neon
A rare, colorless gas that glows red when electrified in a vacuum (space without air). It is used in neon signs.

neuron
A nerve cell that is part of the body's nervous system.

neutron
An uncharged particle in the nucleus of an atom.

nitrogen
A transparent gas that makes up a large part of Earth's atmosphere.

nocturnal
Describes an animal that is active during the night.

nucleus
The central part of an atom, consisting of protons and neutrons.

nutrient
Anything eaten or absorbed by a living thing in order for that organism to live and grow.

nutritious
Describes food that contains vitamins, minerals, and other substances that humans, animals, and plants need in order to grow and stay healthy.

nylon
A strong, lightweight, synthetic material made by a chemical process.

omnivore
An animal that eats both other animals and plants.

optical illusion
Something that appears to be different from what it really is, because the eye and brain are tricked by color, light, and patterns.

orbit
In astronomy, the course of one object around another, such as the path of a moon around a planet.

orchestra
A large group of musicians who play music together on various instruments, including strings, brass, woodwind, and percussion.

ore
A rock or mineral from which an element, such as a metal, can be extracted.

organ
In biology, a part of a human, animal, or plant that is specialized to do certain things, such as the brain of an animal.

organism
A living thing, made up of one or more cells.

oxygen
A gas that makes up one-fifth of Earth's atmosphere and is essential for breathing.

particle
A tiny object, such as a smoke particle. A subatomic particle is a particle smaller than an atom, such as an electron.

Persian
The language also known as Farsi, mainly spoken in Iran, but also in Afghanistan and Tajikistan.

petrochemicals
Chemicals produced from crude oil (petroleum) that can be used to make plastics, medicines, cleaning products, and many other things.

philosophy
The study of ideas about issues such as knowledge, truth, reality, and the meaning of life.

photosynthesis
The set of chemical reactions by which plants make their food. They use energy from sunlight to convert water and carbon dioxide into sugar (glucose) and oxygen.

pigment
A natural substance in cells of all living things that gives them color, such as chlorophyll, which makes plants green. Also a substance that is mixed with oil or other bases to produce colored paints.

pitch
The description of how high or low a particular note is on a musical scale.

polyglot
A person who can speak many different languages.

polymer
A molecule made up of identical smaller molecules, called monomers, joined together. Plastics are examples of polymers.

predator
An animal that hunts other animals for food.

prehistoric
Describes the time before written history.

pressure
A measure of how hard a force pushes on a surface. Pressure depends on the strength of the force and the area of the surface.

proboscis
A long, bendy snout of an animal, such as an elephant's trunk, or a mouthpart such as the sucking tube of some insects.

proton
A positively charged particle found in the nucleus of an atom.

pupa
The inactive, nonfeeding stage of an insect's development, between living as a larva and becoming fully adult.

radioactivity
The processes by which the nucleus of an unstable atom disintegrates, giving off particles of energy known as radiation.

radio wave
A type of invisible electromagnetic wave that travels at the speed of light and can be used to carry sounds, TV pictures, or other information.

refraction
The bending of light as it passes from one material to another material of different density.

Renaissance
Meaning "rebirth," a period in Europe from the late 14th century to the 16th century when there was a new interest in the arts, philosophy, and science.

retina
The light-detecting layer at the back of the eye.

robot
A machine, often computer controlled, designed to carry out a series of actions automatically.

rocket
A cylinder-shaped object that moves at high speeds, powered by burning fuel.

sarcophagus
Used in ancient times, a large coffinlike container, usually made of stone, in which a dead person was placed.

satellite
An object that orbits a planet. An artificial satellite is a spacecraft that orbits Earth. The Moon is a natural satellite of Earth.

scavenger
An animal, such as a vulture, that feeds on the remains of dead animals.

sodium
A soft white metal.

Solar System
Our part of the Universe, made up of the Sun and the eight planets, including Earth, that orbit around it, together with other objects such as moons, asteroids, and comets.

solid
A state of matter in which atoms or molecules are rigidly joined together.

spam
Electronic junk mail.

spores
Tiny cells, produced by a fungus or plant, that can grow into a new fungus or plant without being fertilized.

steel
An alloy (mixture), made mostly of iron and carbon, that is stronger and more versatile than iron alone.

subspecies
A subdivision of animals or plants within a species.

succulent plant
A plant such as a cactus that has thick, juicy leaves (or stems) for storing water.

supersonic
A speed faster than that of sound—which is around 760 mph (1,230 km/h).

synthetic
Made from artificial substances. Materials such as nylon and plastic packaging are synthetic.

tectonic plates
The large, constantly moving pieces that make up Earth's crust (outer layer).

telescope
An instrument for looking at distant objects. Optical telescopes gather light using mirrors and lenses, while radio telescopes detect objects in space by picking up the radio waves they emit.

toxic
Another word for poisonous.

translucent
Of a substance, allowing light to pass through but not enabling images on the other side to be seen clearly.

tsunami
An enormous ocean wave, usually caused by an underwater earthquake or volcanic eruption.

ultraviolet
A type of electromagnetic radiation that is similar to light, but invisible to humans. Ultraviolet (UV) light has a higher frequency than visible light as well as a shorter wavelength.

venomous
Describes an animal that injects poison into its prey or attacker.

vertebra
One of the bones that make up the backbone (spine) of an animal.

vertebrate
An animal with a backbone.

virus
A microscopic particle that invades living cells and causes diseases.

wave
A back-and-forth or up-and-down motion that travels through or over a material and carries energy.

wavelength
The length of a wave, measured from the peak of one wave to the peak of the next.

webcam
A video camera that can send live pictures to a computer.

weight
The strength of the force of gravity on an object. The more mass an object has, the greater its weight.

World Wide Web (WWW)
A global information system consisting of linked websites that can be accessed through the Internet.

X-ray
High-energy electromagnetic radiation that travels at the speed of light. Used in medicine to take pictures of solid internal body parts.

INDEX

Bold page numbers refer to main entries

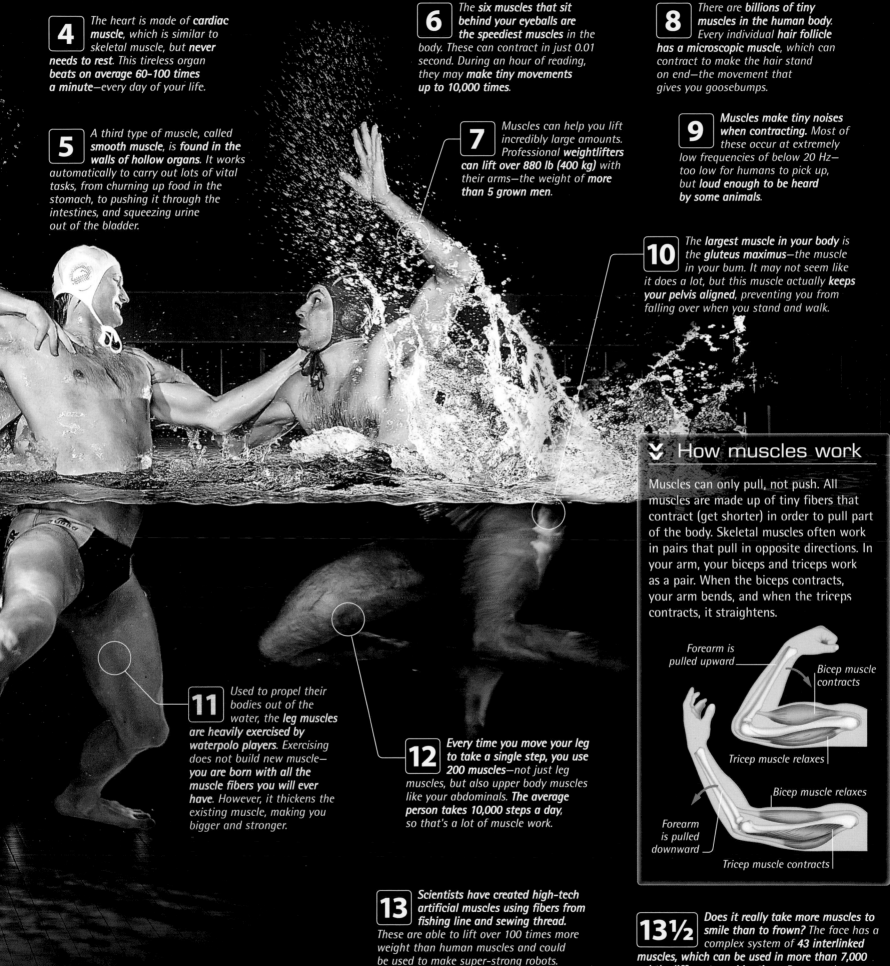

4 The heart is made of **cardiac muscle**, which is similar to skeletal muscle, but **never needs to rest**. This tireless organ **beats on average 60-100 times a minute**—every day of your life.

5 A third type of muscle, called **smooth muscle, is found in the walls of hollow organs**. It works automatically to carry out lots of vital tasks, from churning up food in the stomach, to pushing it through the intestines, and squeezing urine out of the bladder.

6 The **six muscles that sit behind your eyeballs are the speediest muscles in the** body. These can contract in just 0.01 second. During an hour of reading, they may **make tiny movements up to 10,000 times**.

7 Muscles can help you lift incredibly large amounts. Professional **weightlifters can lift over 880 lb (400 kg)** with their arms—the weight of **more than 5 grown men**.

8 There are **billions of tiny muscles in the human body.** Every individual **hair follicle has a microscopic muscle**, which can contract to make the hair stand on end—the movement that gives you goosebumps.

9 **Muscles make tiny noises when contracting.** Most of these occur at extremely low frequencies of below 20 Hz— too low for humans to pick up, but **loud enough to be heard by some animals**.

10 The **largest muscle in your body** is the **gluteus maximus**—the muscle in your bum. It may not seem like it does a lot, but this muscle actually **keeps your pelvis aligned**, preventing you from falling over when you stand and walk.

11 Used to propel their bodies out of the water, the **leg muscles are heavily exercised by waterpolo players.** Exercising does not build new muscle— **you are born with all the muscle fibers you will ever have**. However, it thickens the existing muscle, making you bigger and stronger.

12 **Every time you move your leg to take a single step, you use 200 muscles**—not just leg muscles, but also upper body muscles like your abdominals. **The average person takes 10,000 steps a day,** so that's a lot of muscle work.

13 Scientists have created high-tech **artificial muscles using fibers from fishing line and sewing thread.** These are able to lift over 100 times more weight than human muscles and could be used to make super-strong robots.

⌄ How muscles work

Muscles can only pull, not push. All muscles are made up of tiny fibers that contract (get shorter) in order to pull part of the body. Skeletal muscles often work in pairs that pull in opposite directions. In your arm, your biceps and triceps work as a pair. When the biceps contracts, your arm bends, and when the triceps contracts, it straightens.

Forearm is pulled upward

Bicep muscle contracts

Tricep muscle relaxes

Bicep muscle relaxes

Forearm is pulled downward

Tricep muscle contracts

13½ **Does it really take more muscles to smile than to frown?** The face has a complex system of **43 interlinked muscles, which can be used in more than 7,000 subtly different combinations**. Because there are so many different types of smile or frown, **it is impossible to say which uses the most muscles**.

CURIOUS CATS

From a roaring lion to a purring pussycat, all felines belong to the same family. Almost all wild cats live and hunt alone, but domestic cats are very playful and affectionate, making them one of the world's most popular pets.

1 *The domestic cat is descended from the African wildcat.* They are almost identical in appearance, and both use their sharp vision to hunt at dawn and dusk. However, *the African wildcat is larger and more aggressive,* and does not interact with humans.

2 *Cats have been living alongside humans for thousands of years.* The earliest evidence of domestication is a cat skeleton found in a human grave in Cyprus, dating back 9,500 years. Cats originally started living alongside humans to catch rats and mice feeding on grain stores.

3 *This cat is a British Shorthair—one of the most ancient cat breeds.* It is large and muscular with a round face, fine fur, and short legs. Breeds are different types of the same species of domestic animal. *There are roughly 50 different breeds of cat.*

4 *Cats' big ears draw sound waves into the inner ear,* so the cat can detect the direction of a noise. *A cat can turn each ear independently* through several degrees to pick up specific sounds.

5 *This fluttering butterfly has captured the cat's attention.* In the wild, cats hunt, trap, and kill *creatures such as mice and birds.* These hunting instincts are evident when pet cats play, focusing on a moving target and trying to catch it with their paws. Unlike dogs, *cats can twist their wrists and elbows,* so they can grab their prey in a "hug" and deliver a killer bite to the neck.

6 *The cat's whiskers are stiff hairs with super-sensitive nerve endings at the roots.* They are used to judge distance so a cat is sure it can fit through a gap—if there is room for the spread of the whiskers, then there is room for the width of the body.

7 *A cat's shoulders are incredibly flexible.* As in humans, the collar bone connects the shoulder blade to the breast bone, but in cats the collar bone is tiny. This frees up the shoulder, making it much more mobile, meaning that *a cat can squeeze its shoulders* though any space big enough for its head.

MUSCLE POWER

Despite being made of the tiniest fibers, muscles are incredibly powerful—lifting our limbs, powering our organs, and shunting blood around our body. Tough and strong, these soft tissues make up 40 percent of our body weight.

1 *Skeletal muscles pull on the bones to make them move. There are around 650 in your body, arranged on top of the skeleton in overlapping layers, and **they are the only muscles you can move voluntarily.***

3 *There are no muscles in your **fingers**, only tendons moved by the skeletal muscles in your hands. **Tendons are tough, cordlike bands of tissue** that connect muscles to the bones they move.*

2 *Water polo is **one of the most physically demanding sports in the world**. Players must pass and tackle without touching the bottom of the pool. **Moving around in water is much harder than on land** because your muscles have to work against water resistance.*

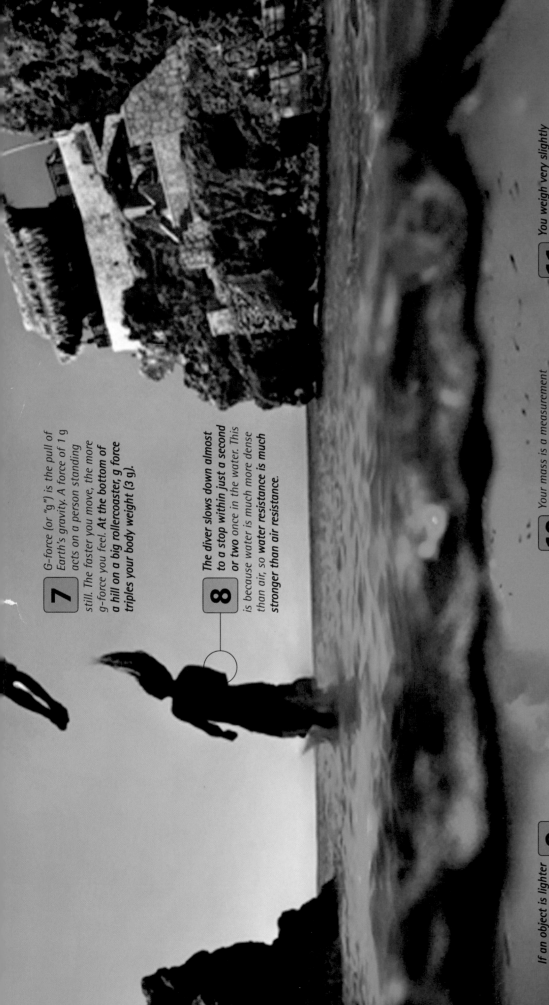

7 G-force (or "g") is the pull of Earth's gravity. A force of 1 g acts on a person standing still. The faster you move, the more g-force you feel. At the bottom of a hill on a big rollercoaster, g force triples your body weight (3 g).

8 The diver slows down almost to a stop within just a second or two once in the water. This is because water is much more dense than air, so water resistance is much stronger than air resistance.

If an object is lighter than water, buoyancy outweighs gravity and the object floats. Gravity pulls the diver down, but water pressure pushes him upward, making him buoyant, so he floats to the surface. **9**

10 Your mass is a measurement of how much matter you are made of. Your weight measures how much gravity pulls on your mass. Earth has six times more gravity than the Moon, so an astronaut standing on the Moon weighs one-sixth of his weight on Earth. However, his mass remains the same.

11 You weigh very slightly less when the Moon is directly overhead— for example, at midnight on the night of a full moon. The gentle tug of the Moon's gravity works against the pull of Earth's gravity, reducing your weight.

12 Gravity grows stronger nearer the center of the planet. This means the gravitational pull on the diver in the sea is very slightly higher than when he was on top of the cliff.

13 In the deep sea, it is hard to tell which way is up because the view is the same in all directions. Some fish sense Earth's pull with "earstones"— floating deposits in their heads that are drawn down by gravity.

13½ You may think that astronauts in the International Space Station float because there is no gravity in space. In fact, there is gravity, holding the craft in orbit. The astronauts are experiencing weightlessness because in orbit they and their craft are technically in a state of free fall.